'ATH
The Odyssey

by Anthony H Lewis

ATHENE BOOKS

About The Author.

I was born, in a miner's terraced house, in a small Warwickshire mining village in 1937. A disastrous first marriage ended leaving me broke and depressed. My meeting with, and subsequent marriage to Jean, was a turning point in my life and saved my sanity.

Choosing to live on a narrowboat and to be continually cruising was, in the main, her idea. It was a move we have never regretted and continue to get extreme pleasure from.

I had been variously employed as a Motor engineer, a Draughtsman, a Social Worker with R.N.M.D.S.F, a Youth Worker and finally a Senior Youth and Community Education Officer.

I have two daughters from my first marriage and two step-sons from my wedding to Jean in 1990.

I took early retirement in 1991 and Athene was launched in the same year. I hope you enjoy sharing our life through the medium of print.

Anthony H Lewis

"ATHENE": The Odyssey Continues

ATHENE BOOKS

"ATHENE" : The Odyssey Continues

ATHENE BOOKS

ISBN. 0 9532033 2 8

PUBLISHING HISTORY
Athene Edition published 1999.

Copyright © 1999 Anthony H. Lewis. 1999.
The right of Anthony H. Lewis to be identified as the author of this work has been asserted in accordance with the Copyright, Designs and Patents Act 1988.

Conditions of Sale.
This book is sold subject to the condition that it shall not, by way of trade or otherwise, be lent, re-sold, hired out or otherwise circulated without the publisher's prior consent in any form of binding or cover other than that in which it is published and without a similar condition including this condition being imposed on the subsequent purchaser.

Typeset in 9.5/11 pt. Bookman
by N.B. Services.
Graphics by N.B. Services

Printed in Great Britain by
Print Express Services Ltd.
Frodsham, Cheshire

The cover photo appears with the kind permission of "TheWolverhamptonExpress and Star".

Cruises of "Pallas Athene" 1994~1995

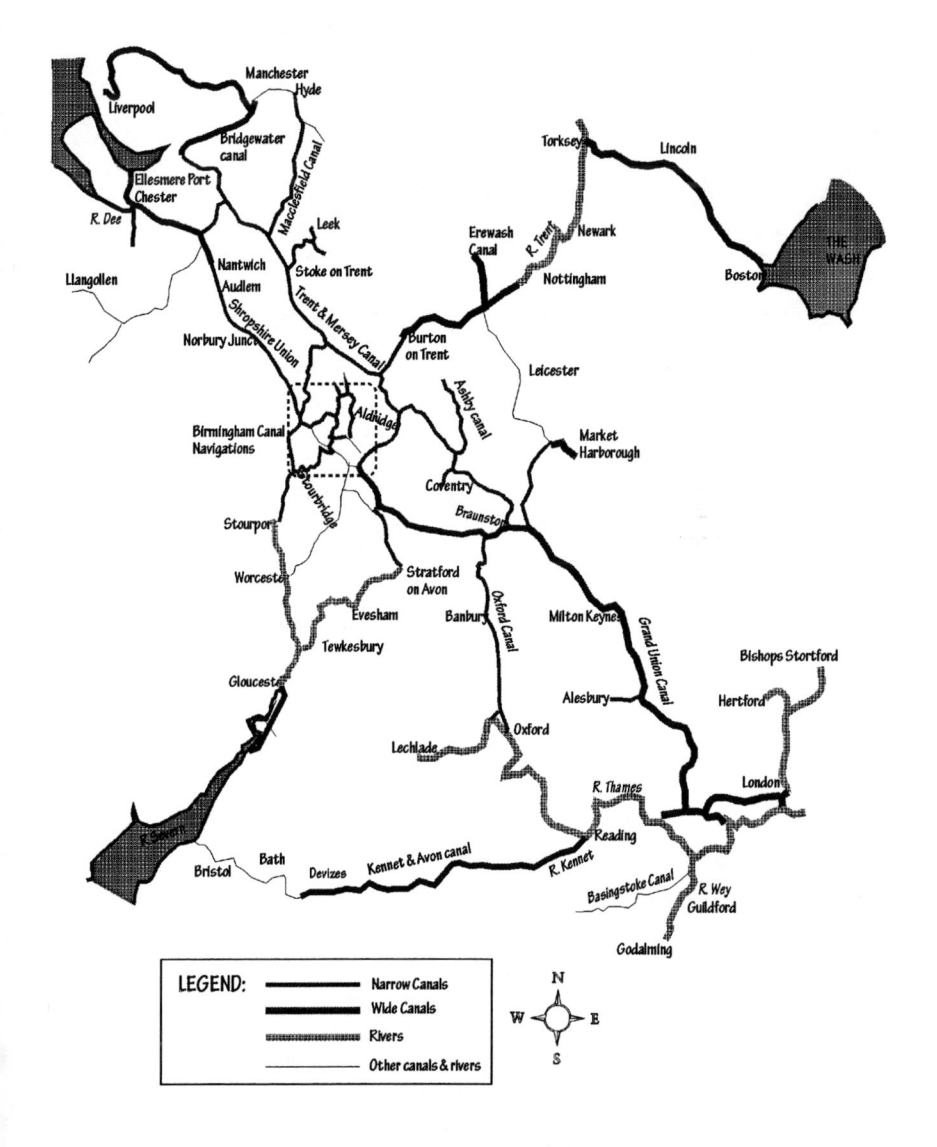

By the same Author.

Athene; Anatomy of a Dream.　　　　Auto-biographical.
The Idylls of an Un-repentant Romantic.　Poetry Anthology.

Poetry Today (Penhaligan Page)
have also included the following poems in Anthologies:

To a Hunting Barn Owl	in	"Nothing Left Unsaid"
Contentment or Life Afloat	in	"Poets in Harmony"
To a Narrow Boat Cat	in	"Life!"
Mallards	in	"Windows of the Soul"
Pollution	in	"A World for Tomorrow"
To My Love	in	"The Poetry Today Book of Sonnets"
Love Changes Everything	in	"A Special Place"
An Early Start	in	"Poetic Soul"
Dawn on the Canal	in	"Timeless Rhymes"
Journey into Spring	in	"One Day at a Time"

CONTENTS

Poem.	An Early Start
Prologue	
Chapter 1.	Hiatus.
Chapter 2.	An Arresting Experience!
Chapter 3.	Locks and yet more Locks!
Chapter 4.	Towards the "Dreaming Spires."
Chapter 5.	Old Father Thames.
Chapter 6.	Locks Bridges and Reed Beds!
Chapter 7.	Devizes to Thames.
Chapter 8.	On the River Thames again.
Chapter 9.	What a Wey to go!
Chapter 10.	London Layover.
Chapter 11.	On the Grand Union.
Chapter 12.	"The Harboro' Stripper."
Chapter 13	Seen that! Got the Tee Shirt.
Chapter 14	In the Steps of the Legions.
Chapter 15	Rally Round-up
Chapter 16	Sharpness, Here we come!
Chapter 17	Bank Holiday Sojourn.
Chapter 18	Puppets & Circuses.
Chapter 19	Aqueducts and Locks.
Chapter 20	On Home Ground.
Chapter 21	Pleasure & Pain.
Chapter 22	Christmas Cruising.
Chapter 23	Winter Layover.
Chapter 24	Animal Anecdotes.
Afterwards	
Glossary	

INTRODUCTION

In my first book; '"Athene" Anatomy of a Dream'. I sought to add interest, to what could have amounted to little more than a personal log, by recording the events as I remembered them rather than from a written record. This way I felt that the reader would gain something of the flavour of the impression made on me by events rather than a politically correct rehearsal of cold facts

Using my Log book as an "Aide Memoir", I was able to recall events and experiences, although, occasionally, time had smoothed the edges and/or enhanced the narrative with memories of similar experience that were outside the purely chronological time scale.

"Odyssey" is based firmly on our experiences during our cruises so I have employed similar techniques in an attempt to write a more readable and enjoyable book, without deviating from the basic veracity of the events described.

To take an example!

Jean and I moor up at the end of a long, tiring day. Water conditions have been poor, many locks unbalanced and difficult. Now, the day is over, fenders are down, mooring lines secured, we can relax and treat ourselves to a drink. Whiskey and Dry Ginger for Jean, Vodka and Lime, for me. Long, cool drinks, not trebles with a splash!

The brunt of locking has been taken by Jean, (she is steadfast in her refusal to steer the boat.) and so I prepare an evening meal. For me this is also a pleasure, not a chore.

I love cooking!

After we have eaten, we relax and talk over the events of the day.

Now the elements of hard work and difficulty fade as we recall the beauty of the scenery, an amusing conversation with a group of Gongoozlers or the antics of the wildlife. Into the discussion are added memories of similar days and events. When recalling that conversation maybe three years later, what I remember is the over-riding sense of pleasure, fulfilment and joy that we felt, even though that may be enhanced by events that themselves were not integral with the day.

Details are accurate, if selective, and where the chronology is not perfect I hope the remembered impression makes a more powerful and emotive impact than a mere factual diary entry.

Similarly, when we have had, a "bad hair day", other events may be recalled and computed, while the more pleasurable elements of the day are suppressed. That period may well impinge on my long-term recall as a sharp reverse spike on our graph of life, rather than a peak.

It is impossible to spend one's life cruising the waterways as we do, without feeling constrained to comment on a wide variety of subjects that have left a lasting effect on our way of life.

I always seek to ensure that my remarks cannot be misconstrued or regarded as being put forward as universally valid comments on particular aspects of life.

They are, my thoughts and feelings, tempered by experience, which is often the best yardstick to measure life against.

Faced with serious, antisocial behaviour, I have often chosen to pass comment, usually in such a way that, only the perpetrators of the offence are liable to recognise themselves, if indeed they are capable of judging their activities by the yardstick of other people's perceptions.

Early sales figures and feed-back from "Anatomy" have prompted me to write a sequel. I hope "Odyssey" will prove to be a worthy successor and that it will find it's niche with those folks who enjoy boats and boating and are open-minded enough to share, another boater's concepts of "life afloat".

If you are a boater, "Good Cruising", if you are dipping into this book out of curiosity or because you've nothing else to read, I hope your appetite will be whetted to find out more.

Anthony. H. Lewis
Somewhere in England

Dedication.

To my wife Jean, who turned my life around, I dedicate this volume in the sure knowledge that this and any other works I may produce rely on her support and love, to keep my motivation active.
Jean I Love You!!

Acknowledgements.

My thanks to Steve Chuter of N.B.Services, not only did he do the typesetting and graphics, he provided an invaluable service by proof-reading and helping me to clarify some of my more obscure paragraphs.
This book is better because of his efforts.

To Terry Pratchett & Colin Smythe, his agent.
Thanks Terry for showing your generous nature in taking time to talk with and encourage another author, albeit a very small fish in a large pond!
Colin, your encouragement & advice were much appreciated as were your kind words!

An Early Start.

Four-thirty, the world holds it's breath;
Outside, the silence is hung with a pearly sheen,
While overhead, the skies lighten perceptibly.
On the bows, I fill my lungs with freshness,
Air like champagne, expands my senses.
I am conscious of the flutter and hiss of my breath,
The swish of blood through my arteries.
Around the boat, the water is like a pewter mirror;
Everywhere I look, an inverted world interfaces with reality.
Our doppelgänger, wears a reversed name
Adding a touch of the exotic to the mundane.
My trainers squeak on the gunwales,
Then, crunch on the gravel of the towing path.
With painful suddenness, the silence is shattered.
The sound of steel ringing on steel,
A sucking noise as the for'ard mooring stake is pulled.
The rustle of coiling ropes, then a fender drips,
Lifted from the water, to lie, inboard.
Ripples, circling from this movement, break the illusion.
At the stern, I slide back the engine room hatch,
The deck hatch, clangs against the swans-neck;
Two turns on the shaft greaser, check the bilges.
The hatch, closes with a bang. Pumps whine,
Water gushes out, more ripples distort the vision.
The key clicks, the ignition warning sounds it's raucous note.
With a roar, the diesel engine, turns, and fires;
Grey smoke stains the fading mist.
The other mooring ropes are cast off, the pins retrieved.
The clutch is engaged, power feeds to the propeller,
Sixty-five feet of steel, stirs, then slowly, comes to life.
The still waters part, our boat's bows, thrust forward,
Another day's cruising has begun.
Nothing marks our sojourn but a smoky haze,
We depart, and peace descends once more.

Antony H. Lewis.
September 1996

"ATHENE" the Odyssey Continues.

PROLOGUE

Our final evening on the public moorings at Weybridge, saw the return of my familiar butterflies.

At various times during our cruising, we had been confronted by situations which created some unrest in my mind.

Long, narrow tunnels, tall aqueducts, striding high over valleys, supported on slender legs. Now, I, who had a penchant for getting sea-sick on wet grass, was about to tackle, the tidal section of England's largest river, the Thames.

In the event, we would be leaving the tidal waters at Brentford and not at Limehouse, nevertheless, this unknown quantity still held the power to make my nerve ends twitch.

Okay! So we had traversed the river from Oxford to the head of navigation at Lechlade!

Right! We had completed the return passage, through Oxford, Reading, Henley and we had arrived at Weybridge.

Now two more locks would bring me to Teddington, the final lock before the tidal section.

According to my map, our passage to Teddington Lock would be interesting, taking us past a number of notable landmarks.

Desborough Cut was closed, this meant that we would be required to navigate the old course of the river. Our guidebook talked of nasty shallows and shoals. Passage through this section, would take us past the outskirts of Shepperton, home of the famous Film Studios.

Of course, Weybridge itself hosts the remnants of the Brooklands banked Oval, beloved of motor racing enthusiasts everywhere, and now the site of an aircraft factory.

Chief among the distractions en route, would be the Hampton Court Palace and Gardens.

This wonderful example of Tudor architecture, would serve to distract my attention from the impending threat, which loomed so large in my mind.

Our timing would be critical for this passage. Thames Lock on the Brentford Cut was only open at certain stages of the tide. At Richmond, the Half Tide Lock, provided an alternative route, should the tide weirs still be closed.

The list of warnings in our book, were quite sobering.

1. *High tide at Teddington and Brentford, is one hour later than at London Bridge.*
2. *Spring tides are best avoided, choose neap tides.*
3. *Choose a calm, clear day.*
4. *Make sure your boat has, an anchor and warp, a reliable engine; adequate fuel and fuel reserves.*
5. *Know the sound signals and, keep to the right.*
6 *Wear life-jackets.*
7. *Study the Tide tables.*

Our Thames licence expired the following day, so much for a choice of calm, clear days with a neap tide.

"Athene" had a powerful engine, it was reliable and we had the requisite anchor and warp, plus ample supplies of fuel.

We did not have, life-jackets or tide tables, although we had consulted with the lock-keepers and had received up to the minute timings of expected lock openings, tide heights and information that prevailing winds could throw these timings out by an estimated twenty minutes.

These anomalies, served to cloud my mind with paranoia, I could visualise "Athene", racing out into the North Sea on a strong ebb, while I fought, to restart the engine and our anchor and warp, dragged happily behind us.

Never underestimate the power of the mind, to present you with illogical, irrational thoughts, when you are doubtful about an outcome.

Common sense said, Leave on slack water at high tide, take advantage of the ebb to make a clean, fast run.

My mind said, If you leave it that late, something will go wrong, you will arrive after the tide-lock has closed and spend the next eight hours stranded on mud banks. The next tide is at three in the morning no staff will be on duty, so you will spend another twelve hours, sitting on a mud bank.

We set off to reach Teddington, two hours before high tide.

Negotiating the boom by the dredger, we entered the old river. With our engine throttled back in deference to the numerous moored cruisers, a weather eye open for shoals and our course executing some rather tight turns, the passage kept us on our toes for its duration.

Once back on the main river, we were able to take up a station a little to the right of midstream, increasing revs to move along at a respectable pace.

Here, the river was wide and deep, our passage left little trace in the way of wash.

The approaches to the locks, were marked by signs warning of weirs and the currents they created.

Forget keeping to the right, weirs were given a wide berth, whichever side it meant steering on.

Unlike on the majority of canals, water flow dictated that extra care needed to be taken while waiting for permission to enter the lock.

Once in the chamber, the engine had to be switched off and the boat held bow and stern by the mooring lines to prevent movement during the lock operation.

After negotiating the first two locks, the glories of Hampton Court Palace, spread out before us. As we passed the water gate, it was easy to envisage the Royal Barges, decked out in cloth of gold, landing the Royal entourage at the Palace, to spend yet more time, feasting and carousing with their Monarch.

All too soon, the buildings and gardens disappeared astern, reality reasserted itself.

Arriving at Teddington with time in hand, we elected to press on. This meant, that we would be pushing "Athene" against a strong tidal flow, not exactly how it should have worked. In fact we found the river flow unchanged for reasons we had yet to discover.

Emerging from under the railway bridge at Richmond, we lined our bows up on the navigation arch of the Twickenham Road Bridge.

As we did, it was disconcerting to find that the arches of the bridge at the Half-Tide Lock, were still blanked off by the steel shutters of the tide barrier.

We throttled back to tick-over and as our speed bled away, it became obvious that the shutters were gradually rising. The action was a concertina fold into holding cavities built into the arches. Like a safety curtain at a theatre, the shutters rose and opened our path into the true tidal stream.

The lights changed from Red to Green, We were free to proceed, and for the first time I felt the full press of the tide flow.

In spite of this "Athene" behaved like the lady she was and without any hassle, set out to show us her mettle. We pushed smartly along, water piling up under her bow and swirling past the stern, which was buried low into the stream.

Blasé now, we pressed gamely on, to arrive at Brentford with the tide, still rising.

The exit into the Grand Union Canal was on the left and involved a one hundred and twenty degree turn across the current into a relatively narrow channel, lined on the left hand side by rather solid looking stone walls.

Midstream, the tide flow was at its strongest, tidal water, riding over the weight of the normal downstream flow. The result was a stretch of broken water with currents, eddies and rips, running in all directions, directly across our path into the haven of the canal.

No sweat! Fifty yards past the entrance, bags of left-hand down a bit, hit the power, Nothing to it!

As "Athene" careered upstream, broadside on to the flow, past the entrance to the canal and with our propeller cavitating as we bounced in the turbulence, I finally managed to clear the wall with our bows and continue upstream to execute a leisurely one hundred and eighty degree turn, to put us back on course for our second attempt.

This time I angled our approach, emerged from the tide race on the left hand side of the river with room to make the turn into the cut in the relatively slack water closer to the bank.

It had been a hairy few minutes, my heart still had teeth marks on it but we had mastered another boating skill.

Yeah! Life on the river was great too!

1.
Hiatus.

Our first full season of cruising ended as we tied up on the long term moorings at Streethay Wharf. Although officially engaged in "continual cruising", the first week in November saw the start of B.W.'s winter programme of stoppages, for repair and maintenance, of large sections of the canal system, this severely restricted our options.

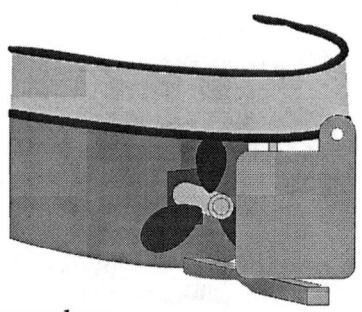

We had two projects in mind for ourselves.

Firstly, we had decided to have one final stab at getting our electrics sorted out. Our list did not stop there, we intended to have "Athene" taken out of the water, in order that we could re-black her bottom, check the anodes and examine the condition of the stern gear, rudder and propeller, all of which were subject to considerable wear in the shallow waters in which we had been operating for much of the period since her launch.

Secondly, we had booked a six week package holiday with "Airtours", to the George Cross Island of Malta; we were scheduled to fly out on January 4th. 1994.

Dave Reynolds, a marine electrician who we knew and trusted, had agreed to sort out our electrics and to that end had checked them over thoroughly and had outlined the programme of work which was required.

Due to the disruption this would create, we deferred the start until the boat was on the hard standing and we had left for Malta.

Although she would be out of the water during our stay in Malta, we had reserved the right to scrape and repaint her bottom on our return. The other items of work were detailed, in writing, and left for the yard to complete while she was high and dry.

During November and December, we finalised arrangements for our holiday, finished off a number of small projects in the boat, which we had not been able to tackle while we were cruising and, enjoyed a number of social events in the City of Lichfield.

Although without a cinema, the Cathedral, the Town Hall and several other venues, offered a varied programme of events from light Opera through to Jazz.

The Cathedral was hosting a Jazz concert by Johnny Dankworth and Cleo Lane, for us this would be a rare treat.

For the concert, the Cathedral was packed and an appreciative audience were treated to a masterful repertoire of Jazz classics, sympathetically performed, with great polish and expertise. As if overawed by the surroundings, the pieces, unfortunately, seemed to lack some of the sparkle and spontaneity which is the hallmark of the best Jazz.

However, towards the end of the evening, the floodgates opened, Johnny and the Band, ditched the "polished performance" mode, a spark ignited. Trumpet, trombone, saxophone, clarinet, bass fiddle and drums, tossed notes from instrument to instrument with wild abandon. Over all this frenetic pulse, Cleo filled the air with "Scat", her voice racing through chords and stanzas with a power and clarity that stood the hair up on the back of your neck. Suddenly the audience was on it's feet, stamping and applauding, gone the previous reserve, this was sublime.

The Bible, talks of praising God, on the harp, lute, cymbal and psaltery, in it's own way, that concert became a celebration of all that was good about shared musical experiences, it became an act of worship, worthy of the building in which it was taking place.

The carved figures of Kings, Saints, Apostles and Martyrs that decorated the towering walls, were almost persuaded to leave their niches and celebrate with us.

In December, we found ourselves, in the Cathedral for another celebration. A local Choral Society were performing, Handel's "Messiah". This Oratorio, seems to have the power to lift any performance. We were thrilled as the sacred music, filled our hearts and lifted our souls in praise of God.

Sacred and Secular, both at home in that wonderful setting and both inspirational.

On Bonfire Night, we attended a performance in the Town Hall, of Gilbert and Sullivan's Operetta, "The Mikado". A glorious evening, Lichfield Amateur Operatic and Dramatic Society gave a clever interpretation of the score and the choreography of the piece. To our amusement, the average age of the "Three little maids from School", was 55+, but the whole programme and the performances, were excellent.

Our catholic taste in entertainment, furthered two more visits to the Town Hall. One to see Mel Gibson's "Hamlet", the second to be amused by "Giggerty", a black Country Group who performed, folk songs and monologues with a distinctly local flavour and more to the point, not a little reference to the area's canal heritage.

Still not weaned off my need for a daily "fix", in the way of a newspaper, I found myself faced with a two mile walk in each direction to achieve this. Still, the exercise would keep me fit.

The railway station was within walking distance, this would enable us to pay visits to Mum and my sister Joan, on occasions.

Heather, my elder daughter, lived in Alrewas, four miles away. This involved walking along the A.38(T), not a healthy occupation and the bus service was erratic. In the event, we made a habit of meeting her for coffee in Lichfield on Fridays or Saturdays. When possible she would bring our Grandchildren.

It was really strange, after a prolonged period of cruising, to find ourselves with a base and the need to follow a more or less regular pattern of life. Mains electricity on tap, fresh water, just a hosepipe's length away and pump-out facilities, if required. The Bowen's had installed a small launderette, so even our laundry needs were catered for. Coal and smokeless fuel was available, ground clearance had left the area littered with branches which just needed sawing to length to become useful additions to the fuel pile.

The television and video, were tuned in and we settled down to a life of something approaching decadence and inactivity. Bored, we quickly identified work still needing to be done on the boat, areas of the fit-out that had been skimped were reassessed and completed!

Christmas was approaching, we were anticipating visits from all three of our children who were living out of the area. They each had partners, which meant a possible six extra bodies on the boat. Since four was the maximum number we could sleep on the lounge floor, we needed additional accommodation. Ray had a small day-boat fitted with a diesel fired heater, which we were able to hire for the holiday period, and which would serve as a dormitory for the overflow.

True to form we had quickly identified the best of the local Car Boot Sales and discovered the regular stock clearance sales held from time to time, at the Lichfield Guildhall.

Our hoard of Christmas gifts was greatly enhanced as a result of our visits to these sales. Buying gifts at competitive prices was a real plus. We were however, careful not to fall into the trap of buying 'cos the price is right. If you don't need something its not a bargain, whatever the price.

Jo, Ian's partner, insisted that as Jean was so intense in her passion for bargains, that she would have *"I bought it in a Sale!"* stencilled on her shroud. Still, these particular sales, eked out our restricted budget. We were not able to overspend, with six weeks self-catering in Malta to pay for immediately following the festive season.

Our Christmas decorations went up on the first Sunday in Advent, as was our tradition. This year they could not stay up till Twelfth Night, we would be in Malta by then.

The local taxi-cab hire company, with whom we had established a good rapport, regularly drove fares to Birmingham International Airport. However, Ray had offered to take us to the airport for our outward journey. We would still need a taxi for the return trip at 0130 hrs.

During the Autumn, we had been involved in one of those amazing co-incidences that occur from time to time.

Moored up for a few days at Middlewich, we had taken a bus into Northwich, in search of an Abbey National Building Society office.

In the shopping precinct we overheard a conversation A couple were talking about a package holiday to Malta that they intended taking early the following year.

With our usual cheek we had commented on the co-incidence and inquired whether they had visited Malta before, as we were totally at a loss to know what it was like as a holiday venue.

It proved to be their first time, but amazingly they were booked, with the same company, to the same destination, on the same flight, for the same period of time.

Some co-incidence!!

The Christmas arrangements worked well. Our guests came and went, enjoyed the festivities, caught up with the news, and, last but not least, shared the giving and receiving of gifts with us.

An "Icicle" cruise was held on Boxing Day, in company with the boats of the Tamworth Cruising Club followed by a Social evening held in the room over the chandlery. Food and drink, fun and entertainment, were shared and a good time was had by all.

New Year passed quietly. We completed our preparations for our flight to Malta.

The couple from Northwich proved to be Sue and Godfrey, we later discovered that, they too had a narrowboat, a small one called, "Penguin", which was moored at Rugley.

We thoroughly enjoyed our stay in Malta. Walking was one of our passions and we managed to cover around two thirds of the Maltese coast-line on our wanderings. During stops on our rambles, we spoke to local fishermen and admired their beautifully painted fishing boats whose lines were so graceful. We had a number of photographs of "Athene" with us and took great pleasure in showing them round and enjoying the comments. Our new-found friends seemed fascinated by our stories of life on board.

One afternoon, we had dropped into a small bar in Marsaxlokk, one of the main fishing villages. Our hosts were perturbed to find that we did not have the Eyes of Osiris, on the bows of our boat. This meant we had no Goddess to guide our path and to protect us during storms and fog. Worse, it left us vulnerable to anyone who wished to put the "evil eye" on the boat, we did not have the talisman to deflect these powers.

Our return was requested, for the same time the following week. It meant a special trip, but not wishing to offend, we did this with good grace and were greeted by them, buzzing with excitement. True to their word our friends met us in the bar. They had a presentation to make. A beautiful pair of carved wooden "eyes", exquisitely painted. They extracted from us a promise, that we would install the eyes in our bows at our earliest convenience.

As we parted from them, they made a promise, "Sail your boat into Grand Harbour in Valetta and you will never have to buy a drink on the island".

It will be a cold day in Hell before we keep our half of the bargain, although we did our best to convince them of our difficulties in this matter!

From our Hotel balcony, our room looked along a promontory, reaching out into the bay. At the far end stood the chateau that had been converted into a Gambling Casino. Although neither of us were inveterate gamblers, the flashing signs over the building, exerted a fascination over us.

We had to give it a try!

Assembling a small amount of stake money and, with a strict injunction to ourselves to stay within our limits, we set off towards the object of our temptation.

Jean had decided to leave the actual gambling to me, she would just soak up the ambience and perhaps a couple of whiskey and dry gingers.

Clad in evening dress (Jean) and dinner jacket, black bow-tie and a cummerbund, to hold in my paunch, we walked down the long drive towards the imposing building.

As it was only nine thirty in the evening, the building was almost empty. Leaving Jean in the lounge, I headed for the Slot-machine Hall; better start gently!

After about half an hour, a few small jackpot wins and few losses, I had amassed a sizeable pile of tokens.

Now for the Big Time!!

Changing the tokens for gambling chips, I discovered that the minimum stake was £1.M. or £1.74 Sterling. I didn't collect any of the larger denominations. Modest pile of chips in hand, I approached the tables.

The only game I was confident that I could understand, was Pontoon. Translated to the French, the language of gambling, that was Vingt-et-Un, here it was on offer as Blackjack.

No problem about getting into a game, three punters and a croupier made up the total complement on the table I chose. From the large piles of multi-coloured chips at one station, it was occupied by a high roller.

The games followed a pattern I was familiar with, again I enjoyed a run of useful if unspectacular wins and only minor losses. Eventually my confidence got the better of me. I split a pair of aces and chanced my arm!

I lost!

Not disastrously but heavily enough for common-sense to re-assert itself, I left the tables.

When I cashed in my stock of chips and removed our original stake from the total, I was left with a profit for the evening of £11.M. or about £18. Sterling.

We called it a night and swaggered back to the Hotel feeling, wicked, decadent and exultant, all at the same time.

All too soon the six weeks of our holiday were over, we flew back to Birmingham, refreshed and ready to begin work on "Athene's" hull.

Typically, the weather on our return was bitter with severe overnight frosts. This made it difficult for us to complete our tasks.

Dave had been busy and revamped the whole electrical system. He expressed amazement at the condition in which he found the wiring. All the ancillary instruments had been removed and much of the over heavy relay system.

The generator had been repositioned, our battery bank increased from 3 to 4 and moved to the opposite side to reduce cable lengths. The Heart Interface had been re-sited nearer to the batteries to reduce the voltage drop across the connections. Everything looked good!

Much of the work had been completed but the rudder and stern gear were still awaiting attention.

The hull had been power washed and we were able to scrape the steelwork down during the afternoons when the temperature was slightly higher.

One of our priority tasks was to prepare sections on both sides of the bow, paint them sky-blue and mount our gift from the Maltese fishermen. We became, what must have been almost unique on the British Waterways, a narrowboat, with genuine, Mediterranean Basin, "Eyes of Osiris", mounted on our bows.

The anodes were good for another three years, and the tank black over B.W. Primer, combination had proved most effective, little extra work was required. We painted the hull with two coats of "Comastic."

She looked great!

With the repositioning of items in the engine room complete, Ray was able to weld in the frame to carry the sliding panels of $^3/_4$" Marine-Ply which would serve to case the engine and footwells. The main benefit of this would be felt in the reduced noise levels experienced by the steerer during cruising.

The weather stayed inclement and with the rudder only partially modified, the day arrived when "Athene" was due to be craned back into her natural element.

Nothing had been removed from the boat, hundreds of pounds worth of Bone China and Crystal were in place on the Welsh Dresser and in the cupboards.

To see her lifted into the air in a pair of chain slings was heart-stopping. There she hung, swinging gently, until at last, the chains clanked and "Athene" was lowered into the water, parallel to the dock.

She was safe, back in her element again!

According to the official stoppages list, B.W. would be working on sections of the canal that covered all our routes out of Streethay, until at least the end of March. With this extra time available to us, we decided to repaint the upper part of the hull, above the rubbing strakes.

Firstly, we fitted in a short shake down cruise to test out the electrics, under cruising conditions. We sailed to Fradley Junction and back. The electrics behaved impeccably.

Heather and Nick, my daughter and her husband, brought our two grandchildren to Fradley and we were able to dine at the "Swan", a well-known local, canal-side hostelry.

While we had the opportunity, we checked out the Canal magazines and booked "Athene" into a number of shows and rallies. This gave us the basis for the years cruising itinerary.

As usual, our first port of call would be Polesworth, on the Coventry Canal, here we would be able to spend a short time with Mum, before we disappeared into the maze of waterways once more. It would be our final opportunity to collect mail from my sister, who acted as our collect address.

After that our first visit would be to the Ashby Canal and the Bi-centenary Rally being held at Cheney Wharf.

From there we intended to head for the Stratford Canal and a visit to Stratford upon Avon. Returning to Napton Junction and then turning onto the Oxford Canal for the trip to Isis Lock to transfer to the River Thames.

The purchase of a fifteen day Thames License, would cover a cruise to Lechlade at the head of navigation, and our return via Oxford to Reading.

Here we would turn onto the Kennet and Avon Navigation, hoping to make the trip to Bath and Bristol. To add extra interest we had booked a berth at Bishops Canning Swing Bridge, the site of the 4th. Annual Devizes Boat Rally or Canalfest 94.

On our return to Reading we would need to purchase a second fifteen day Thames Licence, to take us to Weybridge, the River Wey and the Basingstoke Canal. Both these waterways were in the hands of Trusts and required additional permits before we could cruise them. A Boat Rally was due to be held at Mychett Wharf on the Basingstoke, so we had booked into that as well.

We could then complete the Thames cruise with a trip to Brentford, then to Paddington and Little Venice, via, the Grand Union, Bulls Bridge and the Paddington Arm into the centre of London.

The Lee and Stort River Navigations offered a route to Hertford and Bishops Stortford, the return would lead us down to the Limehouse Basin.

From there, we could enter the Thames Tideway and travel, via the Boat-Race course, to Brentford where we could re-enter B.W. waters in the form of the Grand Union Canal. A nice steady cruise through the Heart of England and we would be back in the Midlands in time to decide upon our plans for the winter. That would depend on how the season had gone and if any particular items of work needed sorting out.

We felt rather pleased with our plans and could hardly wait to get moving.

Problems with water levels delayed our start until the second week in April.

Then, it was all systems GO!!

2.
An Arresting Experience!

At last the day of our departure dawned. Everything was stowed on board, the fenders lifted out, the mooring lines loosed and coiled securely inboard. The fuel tank and the fresh water tank had both been topped up. The gas locker held two full bottles in addition to the one already on line.

We were ready for the off!

A blast on our twin klaxons, a quick wave to our friends and we glided gently past the lines of moored boats, our engine just ticking over.

Clear of the moorings, we increased our revs, and began the relatively short first leg of our cruise, along the Coventry Canal to Fazeley Junction, then up the two Glascote Locks and on to moor up at Polesworth.

We had allowed extra time as the water levels were still seriously depleted and as this canal had never been known for having a deep navigation channel, we needed to proceed with extreme caution, to avoid fouling the propeller with weeds and rubbish.

We collected our mail, enjoyed a couple of days with Mum and, duty done, we set off to cover our planned itinerary.

The Ashby Canal is entered at Marston Junction, where there used to be a stop-lock which also acted as a Toll collection point. Without this lock, the waters of the Ashby and Coventry Canals are mutually affected by water levels. As the Ashby is even more notorious for its shallow navigation channel, this problem was exacerbated.

With time in hand before the Bi-Centennial Rally, we decided to travel to the canal's terminus at Snarestone Basin. A bridge repair had closed the navigation for eighteen months. This had now been completed and for the first time we would be able to reach the terminus.

We could add the crooked, 250 yd. long, Snarestone Tunnel to our list of completed tunnel navigations.

Twenty-two miles of lock free water make this a popular canal, its major drawback was the almost total lack of accessible shopping areas.

I was gradually being weaned off my daily fix.

Stopping at Hinkley Wharf, we made the long trek into town. Fenda Products was located here and we were able to purchase a number of additional items of brassware that we still needed. It was Market Day and we were also able to re-stock our vegetable store and purchase meat and fish for the freezer compartment.

Next day, moored on the Shenton Wharf, we paid our second visit to the site of Richard III's defeat at Ambion Hill. We then made the long walk into Market Bosworth, using field paths.

History held an endless fascination for us both and we never tired of exploring areas with a noteworthy past, either in terms of historical interest or in terms of its Industrial past.

Market Bosworth had made the most of its historic links with the famous battle that had immortalised the town's name. A quick glance along the shop fronts in the High Street confirmed this fact.

We pressed on to Shackerstone, where we again broke our cruise, this time to visit the Railway Museum. Enthusiastic restoration groups have recovered a number of types of engine, mainly Steam, which had been transported to the extensive sidings, often by road. Here an active project was underway, repairing and refurbishing the engines with a view to eventually using them on the Battle Line, the length of restored line which supported a service between Shackerstone and Shenton for the benefit of the tourists.

When we left the wharf for the last leg of the cruise to the terminus, we were to receive full vindication of our long held opinions about the essential role played by regular dredging and maintenance in keeping the waterways open to navigation and aerating the water for the health and well-being of the fish stocks.

Fisherman after fisherman, hailed us from the banks saying,

"Thank God the boats are back, another winter without you and this length of water, would have become a muddy ditch full of dead fish!"

Sorry conservationists! Please listen to the voices of reason!

If the rest of the canal was short of water, that final stretch was diabolical. At least, some maintenance had been commenced and the boat movements were breaking down the drifts of dead leaves, rotting on the bottom, and silting the channel. And, incidentally bringing back oxygen into the stagnating water.

From the terminus, the route of the disused section could be clearly seen, stretching to Measham and through to Moira. There, a large kiln formed a focal point for the attention of visitors.

Mining subsidence closed the canal, created by the very operations that had prompted its building. It was intended that the canal should eventually link up with the Trent and Mersey Canal at Burton on Trent.

Now mining had ceased, the cause of the problems had disappeared. With modern technology able to overcome the difficulties created by the coal mining, it may be possible to restore the canal to its original terminus, or even to complete the final link up with Burton.

Apart from the sanitary station and the water point, there is little at the basin to attract boats, unless you crave real peace and tranquillity, there are no shops within easy walking distance.

We overnighted here, topped up our fresh water tank, and set off towards the rally site, in good time to be allocated our mooring.

As our entry had been comparatively late we found ourselves on good firm moorings but situated some little distance from the Rally site. These were Boat Club moorings and many of the members had moved their boats into the basin at the centre of the Rally area.

We had no problem with this, our only difficulty was the movement imparted to our boat by any craft passing at more than a slow tick-over. This was basically due to the shallowness of the water.

Our offer to help with the erection of the Marquees was accepted with alacrity. We soon found ourselves included as part of the working group.

The Rally itself, was great fun. We enjoyed making new friends and were invited on board a number of boats. A courtesy that we were happy to reciprocate.

Dressed in Victorian boat peoples costume as had become our practice at rallies, we found ourselves as usual, the focus of attention for many of the visitors. We showed a considerable number round our boat and offered them hospitality.

There was a large presence from the Market Harborough Police, who were busy recruiting participants into the Boat-Watch Scheme. Local Television was also there and on Saturday afternoon we found ourselves, on board "Athene", entertaining a group of Policemen and women, plus the T.V. Camera crews. One of the local P.C.'s was a ruddy faced, dumpling of a man with twinkling blue eyes and a white beard..

The group were relaxing on our boat, drinking coffee and tucking into large slabs of home-made cake. Our P.C. friend, lying back in his chair, feet up on a stool, pointed out that really he should not be seen to be associating with vagrants of No Fixed Abode! Jean invited him to try taking an anchor for a swimming lesson. The laughter that greeted this remark, was a measure of the rapport we had established with this group.

The moorings were beautifully kept and a number of boaters, had taken extra care with their small patches. Some had created small gardens complete with garden ornaments. We discovered one such ornament, discretely hidden by foliage, this discovery we could make use of.

Next time we received a visit from our friends from the Force, we made an excuse to accompany them down the moorings towards the exit, when they left. Reaching the plot in question, we drew their attention to the sculpture.

There, beautifully painted, was a piece depicting, two Gnomes in a somewhat compromising position. Supine, the figure of a rosy-cheeked, well upholstered Gnome with bright blue eyes and a white beard. He was clad in nothing but a policeman's helmet and a broad smile.

Kneeling astride the junction of his thighs, a female Gnome, well built with an excellent pair of lungs, a police woman's hat and cravat, a contented smile and nothing else. Amid roars of laughter all round, we enquired how long he had been spending his off duty hours, posing for garden ornaments.

Next day the celebrations continued. The organisers had thoughtfully made arrangements for, milk, bread and newspapers to be delivered to the site.

I was a happy man!

Still in costume, we were wandering among the stands, when I was accosted by a group of the Boys in Blue. In front of an audience of highly amused visitors, I was "arrested", and immobilised for a photo-call. Hand-cuffs are not the most comfortable accessories I have worn with costume.

All too soon another enjoyable interlude was over, we bade our new friends "Goodbye", and set off to make our way, sedately back to Marston Junction.

From there it is one and a half miles, in the direction of Coventry, to Bedworth. Here I had a cousin, Sid, who had been born and raised on the working boats plying out of Sutton Stop. His family moved "onto the bank" while he was still a youngster.

Later, he retained his connection with the canals, by taking up employment with one of the local firms, which still made use of canal transport in its business.

Sid and his wife, Dot, had arranged to meet us at bridge 13, then they could come aboard and see what a modern boat had to offer.

It was a happy visit. Sid was impressed by our fit-out as, like my father, his experience of boats was restricted to his knowledge of the old working boats and their extremely restricted accommodation. We showed them round our boat and they admired our handiwork. When we showed them photographs of the start of our fit-out when the boat was in a mess, their sympathies were all with Jean for the upheaval and untidiness that she had endured.

The following day, Sid and Dot paid us a second visit, this time bringing with them their daughter, so that she could also see the work that we had done in the boat. We felt that this was quite a compliment from an old style boatman.

As the town of Bedworth was so close we did a large shopping trip which would stock our larder for a number of days

Although we were within five miles of the City of Coventry, we decided not to make the trip into the terminal basin on this occasion. On our previous visit, water conditions were poor and levels low. Our confidence that things might have changed was not great and since the basin was due to be refurbished and improved, we decided to time our next visit when these alterations were complete.

We left the Coventry canal via the stop lock at Hawkesbury junction (Sutton Stop to the boaters of old) where it joins the North Oxford Canal. Hopefully water levels would be better along that section of our cruise.

Our first experience of the North Oxford had been in the March of the previous year when conditions had been wet and cold with overnight icing. Now its was May, the trees and hedgerows were in leaf and the blossom made a brave show. The waterfowl had all been busy and broods of hatchlings from the very young to teenagers filled the air with shrill squeaks.

One characteristic of the North Oxford when it was first built by Brindley, was its extremely twisting course as it contours its way through the countryside. Years later the course was redesigned, bypassing many of the larger loops by using cuttings and embankments to carry the channel. The original 36 miles of canal was reduced by almost 14 miles.

Many of the loops can still be identified by the beautiful cast iron bridges, made at Horseley Iron Works, Wolverhampton, which still span the truncated channels.

It is a truly rural canal, with open vistas across farmland, and sheltered, tree lined stretches. A balm to the soul!

Water conditions had improved and we made good time to our next stop at Rugby.

Since we had begun our life on the canals, one thing has been high on the list of priorities and that was recording the locations of good shopping areas, This one was high on our list. Good moorings with very little interference from local young people looking for mischief and with a large Supermarket and a number of other large stores within three or four minutes walk of the canal.

The town of Rugby itself was a long way from the water but the walk was attractive, mainly along footpaths as opposed to pavements and roads.

As a town it has little to differentiate it from any number of similar sized shopping centres. However it has a few other claims to fame, particularly literary ones.

The children's story, "Tom Brown's Schooldays." is set in Rugby's large Public School. The more recent series of novels, cataloguing the life and times of Tom's arch enemy, the bully Flashman have immortalised the town. One of our National sports. "The game played by men with oblong balls." took its name from this same school, upon whose playing fields the deviations from the rules of soccer were first enacted.

Our store cupboard was fairly well stocked so we had little need to use these excellent facilities.

Another plus in favour of the large canalside supermarkets was that they offered a bank of cash dispensing machines, which meant that normally it was unnecessary to visit a bank. Unfortunately the dispenser dedicated to dispensing cash for the group of banks entrusted with my cash, was out of order, I had to make a trek into town anyway.

Next day we pulled stakes and set off. We were soon at the three locks of the Hillmorton Flight.

After the previous years difficulties at this flight, encountering a large submerged object in a lock entrance, I was extra careful with my approach. There was no problem, we entered and left the lock in good order.

At Braunston Turn I swung right under the double arched bridge onto the waters of the five mile pound that leads to Napton Junction. Along this stretch, the waters of the Grand Union and the South Oxford Canals combine, sharing a straightened channel made when the GU was built. On reaching Napton we intended to follow the course of the G.U. towards Birmingham and the junction with the Stratford Canal. We would be returning to cruise the South Oxford later that year.

Once past the Braunston Turn we entered new waters, for us, and a wide range of new vistas was laid out ready for our exploration.

3.
Locks and yet more Locks!

Leaving the long pound at Napton, we were soon faced with the first of the 46 locks on the twenty-two mile stretch of canal ending at the Kingswood Junction. Up to that point, all the locks were broad, a fact which meant that our passage time would be substantially increased and we would be required, wherever possible, to share locks in order to conserve water supplies. During the late morning and afternoon periods, this was not a problem as there were sufficient boat movements to make the practice viable. However our habit of making early starts to avoid travelling in the heat of the day, made lock sharing slightly problematic, as few boaters seemed to follow our lead.

During that first afternoon, we negotiated the three Calcutt locks and the ten in the Stockton and Long Itchington flights.

The "up-side" of lock sharing meant that Jean had assistance in the operation of the heavy mechanisms.

That afternoon, we did not find anyone going the whole of the distance but a number of smaller boats did accompany us through some of the locks in the flight.

On a flight of broad locks it is possible, with boats of a similar length, to breast up and link the two craft with ropes, then, using only one engine it is simple for one person to guide the pair through the locks while the remaining crew members lock wheel and prepare, open, and close the locks.

On that particular day, all the boats were considerably shorter than "Athene".

Later that afternoon, we moored up at the "Two Boats Inn". Here we enjoyed an excellent bar meal before turning in for a restful night.

A short cruise in the early morning mist, took us to the Bascote flight, two of which form a staircase. Between there and Radford

Semele, the locks loomed up at approximately half mile intervals. The scenery was truly rural with the locks making regular intrusions into an otherwise gentle, slow cruise. Wildlife abounded. Rabbits, particularly had become well established along many towing paths and the sight of whole families, sitting beside the water, watching curiously as we cruised by, was enchanting.

By midday we had arrived at Royal Leamington Spa, intending to spend at least a couple of days exploring this quintessential Victorian Spa town.

The moorings were less than salubrious, being lined on one side by waste ground and on the other by Industrial development.

A coterie of drunken derelicts, congregated on a wooden bench just forward of our bows, Jean was more than a little perturbed,

I went on to the bows and engaged them in conversation. This lead me to conclude that they were essentially harmless and, if we did nothing to disturb or antagonise them, neither we, nor our boat, were in any danger from the group. In fact, being treated as human beings for a change, appeared to bring out the best in their nature and for the whole of the period we were moored there, they appeared to take it upon themselves to ensure that our boat was not approached during our numerous absences.

We had been warned by locals that, leaving a boat unattended, even during daylight hours, was an invitation to vandalism or worse. In spite of our absences, our boat was unmolested for our entire stay.

We explored the town, enjoyed our visit and since then, have never passed the Spa without spending at least a couple of days enjoying the friendliness and hospitality of its inhabitants. Even the incidence of vandalism has been reduced as the moorings and their environs have been gradually improved.

Another short cruise took us into the vicinity of Warwick. The canal carefully skirts the town but, from bridge 49, home of "Kate Boats", a one-mile walk along heavily trafficked roads, led us into the town centre.

Before we had married, we had made a number of trips to the Midlands and visited, among other places, the castles at Warwick and Kenilworth. We had not really explored either town, now we could remedy at least 50% of that lack.

Warwick has one of the finest castles in the country and it is a major tourist attraction.

The remainder of the town is equally interesting with large numbers of well preserved or restored buildings housing a wide variety of museums and the like.

One of our major interests was the exploration of historic buildings. We were in our element!

Previously we had only be able to indulge ourselves during specially planned excursions or while on holiday. Now, since we had taken up residence on a continually cruising narrow-boat, our horizons had broadened immeasurably and we had almost unlimited opportunity for exploration, at least along the line of our travel.

After two enjoyable days in Warwick, we braced ourselves for the final leg of our cruise to Kingswood Junction.

A major obstacle lay in our path, the twenty-one locks of the Hatton flight. From bridge 53 or Middle Lock Bridge, the next seven locks form a tight, steep, straight flight, known locally at the "Stairway to Heaven." The lock gear is distinctive and its white painted, inclined cylinders, containing the mechanism, line the vista of gates, tapering off into the distance.

After negotiating the two Cape Locks, we arrived at the foot of the Hatton flight while it was still relatively early. We waited for the customary 30 minutes for another boat to appear. None arrived, and, as the locks were fairly well in our favour, we set off up the flight.

Progressing slowly, we had reached the third lock in the first group, when we became aware of movement off our stern. A sixty foot hire boat had started the climb and was gradually overhauling us. We waited in the lock chamber where, after a short time, we were joined by the second craft.

As this boat was a reasonable length I offered them the opportunity of breasting up with us and finishing the flight as a pair. They agreed at once and in no time we had the boats secured abreast and their engine was turned off. I was left to manoeuvre the boats while the rest of the crew began the cycle of opening and closing the gates, operating the paddles while others went ahead to prepare the next lock. (Lock Wheeling.)

Our progress up the flight speeded up immeasurably!

Going ahead with the lock wheelers, Jean saw another breasted pair descending. It was a restored Motor and Butty which had been fitted out as a mobile classroom and living quarters for small groups of school children, youth groups and social services parties.

It was difficult to identify the type of group on board, but as the boat began its descent into the lock chamber, the young people were swarming all over the two boats. Walking along the roofs, jumping from one roof to the other as well as passing and re-passing each other on the very narrow gunwales.

The sterns of both boats held groups of long haired somewhat scruffy adults, evidently "in charge" but taking no notice of the mayhem going on around them. Jean carefully pointed out the inherent dangers in the allowance of this behaviour and was taken aback to be told, "F— off and mind your own business you F—-ing nosey old cow! Weren't you ever young, they're just having a bit of fun!"

We have amassed a catalogue of incidents, accidents and the odd fatality since then, Watching the behaviour condoned by so-called "responsible adults", the length of the list comes as no surprise to us.

Further up the flight, we were approached by a second breasted pair. These were similarly fitted out and this time contained staff and pupils of a girls school. This group were proud to be identifiable.

Their behaviour was exemplary. Groups of girls were being detailed for tasks, these were carried out under supervision and instructions on safety and method were being offered. In conversation with a number of the groups, Jean was impressed by the enjoyment they were obtaining from a job well done and the knowledge and understanding of a bygone way of life that this pointed up.

Jean's rather battered belief in the general good in people was somewhat restored!

Looking down the flight from the top of the "Stairway to Heaven", it was amazing how accurately the flight was aligned with the spires of Warwick Cathedral. It was almost as if the surveyor, laying out the route to be taken, had used the spires as a prominent reference point!

At the summit, we separated the boats, thanked our locking partners and set off once more towards our projected evening mooring.

Between us and Kingswood Junction lay the short Shrewley Tunnel but fortunately, no more locks!

A small arm links the Grand Union and Stratford Canals at Kingswood, via one lock which lifts the channel into a lagoon that helps to maintain water levels on the lower end of the Lapworth Locks.

We entered the southern section of the Stratford at lock 21 and were immediately faced with the first of the 35 narrow locks on the thirteen mile cruise to Stratford upon Avon.

After our exhausting climb up the Hatton locks, we moored for the night in a beautiful, rural stretch of water in the long pound between locks 24 and 25.

Pressing on down the locks next morning, we experienced one of those mishaps that bring the most blasé of us back to earth with a bang and remind us of the importance of vigilance and concentration, when involved in a regular, repetitive operation.

Well into the flight and moving like clockwork, we were overtaken by a large party of ramblers. Fascinated by Jean's labours, they chatted to her about such things as locking and her life on the canal.

Having seen the boat safely into a lock, Jean closed the top gate and proceeded towards the bottom gates surrounded by ramblers. Reaching the gates, she wound open the paddles. Concentrating on steadying the boat with the engine, I was looking towards the gates so that I could check our forward movement in time.

Unbeknown to either of us, the top gate had taken a unilateral decision to swing open. With the paddles up and little else happening, it occurred to us that something was amiss. Glancing sternward, I saw the problem and shouted to Jean to close the sluices. Simultaneously, one of the hikers decided to help and shoved hard on the balance beam, as the gate moved, the water flow caught it and dragged it shut with a shattering crash.

The water level in the chamber dropped instantly, "Athene" seemed to go into free fall. I was driven, hard down onto my heels as the plunge ended and a normal descent was achieved.

Jean made light of the situation, jokingly asking about spotting, "the deliberate mistake!" But we both felt severely chastened and resolved never to get sidetracked from the essentials of safety in an inherently dangerous situation. Locking is only as safe as you make it!

It was a lesson to take to heart!

Pausing to get back our composure, we proceeded to descend the flight in a much more circumspect frame of mind. However we soon got back into our stride and began to maintain our usual confident progress.

Incidents like that served to ensure that we never became over confident in our approach to the way of life we had chosen.

A feature of this canal were it's aqueducts. Designed by Benjamin Bevan, they are of a very distinctive style. Unlike most, the towing path is built into the structure at the base of the channel so that the whole of the narrow, cast iron trough, is exposed above it. To pedestrians, boats cross the aqueduct at eye-level.

The Wooton Wawen and Yarningdale crossings are relatively short but the Edstone Aqueduct at almost six-hundred feet in length, carrying the boats high over a deep valley containing a road and railway, was for me, almost as daunting as the Pontcysyllte aqueduct in Wales.

It's approach from Odd Lock, is straight and clear, the full extent of the crossing becoming clearer as it is neared.

The statutory cross wind was blowing and although I would be on the towing path side of the boat, the fact that it clung to the channel some five or six feet below me, did nothing to ease my sense of vertigo.

Although I had negotiated the "Pont" twice, that experience had done little to inure me to the feeling of foreboding that overcame me as I bumped my way along the channel, pinned by the wind to the non-towing path edge. The height above the valley floor was no more than 70ft, not nearly as high as the "Pont", but still enough to make the passage a personal challenge. As usual I fell back on to my old argument, "If you can't face up to the challenges, don't stick with the life-style." I had no wish to change my mind so, the challenges must be met and overcome! End of story!

Once clear of the aqueduct we were less than six miles from Stratford but with a further sixteen locks to negotiate.

Although a beautiful, rural canal, the Stratford owed its very existence to the effort that the Local Canal Society put into restoration work. They had done a fantastic job in getting the route re-opened but the chronic lack of finance created immense problems. The canal was full to the level of the run-offs but lack of regular dredging had resulted in long stretches where deep draught crafts like ours had considerable difficulty making passage.

Another problem was the condition of the lock gates and chambers. With no money available for replacement gates etc., much effort had been expended in the refurbishment of the original structures. In spite of this work many of the gates and chambers were showing their age. Water loss via leaking gates and culverts was high and many of the gates were so out of balance that they were very difficult to open and close.

At Wilmcote we entered a flight of eleven locks in groups of three, five and three, very closely set.

After this flight the next lock stands in splendid isolation.

At bridge sixty-four the whole aspect of the canal changed dramatically. The approach to Stratford was a bewildering assortment of industrial sites, engineering works, gas works and power lines. One could be excused for thinking that this was a section of the B.C.N. rather than the run-in to one of England's most famous tourist locations. The canal is left severely alone and little of the beauty of the town is evident along this section.

Descending the final four locks as they meandered through this industrial wilderness, we arrived at the bottom to see the canal disappear into a dismal, rectangular opening beneath what was evidently a major road. Groping our way beneath this low "bridge", made lower and narrower by the construction work taking place, we suddenly popped out into a broad basin, lined with boats of all sizes and everywhere on the surrounding quays, hordes of tourists.

Completing a circuit of the basin, we discovered that the one remaining mooring space was a little too short for "Athene". Fortunately the boats on either side were manned and the crews re-moored, extending the space until we could fit our sixty-five feet alongside the quay.

We thanked them profusely and thought back to our visit to Llangollen and our reception by the owner of a G.R.P. cruiser, who was convinced that he had an inalienable right to a mooring space three times the length of his boat.

The feeling of being part of the scene was overwhelming but was slightly tempered by concerns about the proximity of large numbers of tourists many of whom seemed to have little or no sense of respect for private property.

Towards evening we felt the boat rocking. Coming out onto the bows we found that a group of young French nationals were playing tag around our stern, running along her gunwales and jumping on and off the rear deck. Jean remonstrated with them in what she could remember of her classroom French, but to no avail. Co-incidentally, I decided that we had picked up some rubbish on our prop, during the last stages of the descent, so I needed to get onto the stern to check the weed-hatch. Strapping my diver's knife around my waist, I walked through the boat and opened the doors leading to the deck. As I emerged the group melted magically away.

I wonder why?

We remained moored in the basin for four days and were delighted to find that the vast majority of tourists were fascinated by the boats and were anxious to ask us questions for as long as were prepared to make ourselves available to them,

One abiding memory is of two young Japanese girls, who, in spite of their small grasp of English and our total lack of Japanese, nevertheless were able to convey to us their desire to photograph us with "Athene". We posed, then offered to photograph them with the boat. Eventually we communicated our offer to them, of a visit "behind the scenes".

They were enchanted and enchanting. With wide eyes, girlish giggles and much clapping of hands, they expressed both their admiration for the boat and its appointments and the sense of honour that they felt in being allowed to share with us our home and our hospitality. They left declaring in wonderful fractured English, that the visit would remain the highlight of their stay in our country.

That type of experience always left us feeling that so much could be done to further International relationships if the leaders and politicians could share the same experiences as ordinary people when they were prepared to reach out the hand of friendship towards each other.

Among the specialist shops in Stratford is one dedicated to the promotion of "Rosie and Jim", a young children's Television programme about two puppets who live on a small narrowboat called "Ragdoll", and the marketing of merchandise relating to the series. Jean and I had caught a couple of episodes and although not overlie impressed by the role models presented to the young viewers, the programmes had raised awareness about the existence of the canal system and the people using it, as well as awakening interest among adults about the possibilities of holidays etc. on canal boats.

As "Ragdoll's" livery was predominantly green and red and similar to ours, we were always hearing young children outside the boat, demanding of their parents the whereabouts of "Rosie and Jim", our boat having been identified as, "a Rosie and Jim Boat."

Having decided to spend a few days at Braunston and to take in the Boat Show, we reluctantly turned our backs on the town and set off to climb the daunting collection of locks up to the Junction.

The weather had remained fine and water conditions for the return had not improved.

With the general run of traffic away from Stratford we were faced with lock after lock against us. Having little option but to press on, we were thrilled when eventually we neared a lock, just as another boat was exiting the chamber.

At last our luck had changed!

This lock was located beside a Pub and had a bridge just below it. As "Athene" rose in the chamber we saw a group of young people at a table in the pub garden, bang down their half full glasses, race out of the garden and over the bridge. They ran along the lock-side and disappeared up the towing path. As we neared the moored boats between the two locks, a hire boat, mooring lines trailing, was pushed into our line of travel. I throttled back to avoid a collision and saw the group of young people from the pub, coil the ropes and start the boat's engine. As they moved towards the lock they were obviously cock-a-hoop at having stolen a march on a couple of old codgers in a big, private boat.

We, like Queen Victoria, "were not amused!"

They remained in front of us, all the way to the junction, fooling around, making heavy weather of lock operations, taking their time and then leaving Jean to lower the paddles and close the gates while they went on their merry way.

If "Canal Rage" had been invented at that time, I could well have found myself, overcome!

Just before the junction, frustrated beyond measure, we stopped to re-fill our fresh water tank, and allow our tormentors to get clear.

As we left the lock and pulled over towards the moorings, another boat entered the lock, bound for Stratford. A second boat was waiting to descend having just taken on water. It was a small hire boat with an equally diminutive crew. They were knee high to sparrows and getting on in years.

"Capt. Bligh", at the tiller, shouted to his tiny wife, "You've seen how it's done, now get on with it." She obeyed!

Painfully she wound up the paddles and watched the lock fill. Then she closed the paddles and attempted to open the gate.

In spite of the roars of "encouragement" from her martinet of a skipper, the poor old lady was getting nowhere. Taking pity on her, we went over to lend a hand. The water level inside the lock was six inches down.

Sampson could not have opened the gate!

We re-opened the paddles and explained the necessity of opening the gates before closing the paddles. Even water leakage can create enough pressure to keep the gates from opening.

She was pathetically grateful and queried how far they needed to travel to find moorings alongside a pub. (It was nearly five-thirty by this time.) Our information, approx. two miles and eight locks was not met with rejoicing.

We wished them good "cruising!"

It seemed totally inadequate!

Round the corner, in the short arm leading to the Grand Union, we moored up for the night against the old off-loading wharfs.

Faced with the return trip down the Hatton locks, and the nightmare possibility of the boaters from Hell creating havoc on the flight, we holed up for a couple of days and explored the area.

Leaving early after our short break, we arrived at the top of the Hatton locks just as other boaters were beginning to stir. A sixty-two foot boat was about the cast off and we offered to breast up with them for the descent. They agreed to meet us at the top lock and we continued towards the first set of gates ready to get preparations underway. No other craft were ready to move, the locks were in our favour, so we opened the gates and entered the first chamber to await our new partners.

After a short time, their boat appeared and entered the lock to lie alongside "Athene". The introductions made we found that the boat that we had joined, was skippered by an ex-Police Surgeon. He was acquainted with Jean's brother, who was a Circuit Judge.

The family were experienced boaters and in no time our craft were securely breasted and ready for operations to commence. I remained at the tiller of "Athene" while the other group took turns in stationing someone on the stern of their boat, in case any problems arose.

As usual, Jean seemed to enjoy the exercise, not least because it gave ample opportunities to chat and exchange gossip with a group of interesting people who were also knowledgeable about the canal scene.

Jean assured me that, during a conversation with the ex Police Surgeon about finding odd things floating in the canal, e.g. dead bodies, his advice, delivered I'm sure, firmly tongue-in-cheek, was, that anybody finding a body in the canal, should put a respectable distance between them and it, before making an anonymous phone call reporting a suspicious object!

In the event, I am not exactly sure what my reaction might be. Creator be praised!, we have not yet been put to the test, although we are very careful not to explore suspicious looking, plastic wrapped bundles, either on the bank or floating in the water. (Unless of course it is moving or making a noise!)

With the whole of the flight in our favour, progress was rapid. The final lock, was apparently some two to three feet down. The lock-wheelers topped it up, despite the protests from a chap in a thirty-five foot hybrid G.R.P. Cruiser/Narrowboat, who insisted that it was in his favour and that he was ready to begin his ascent. No other craft was in sight!

Imagine our amusement when our breasted pair exited this lock, to be met by a tirade of abuse and invective. On seeing that our boats were actually breasted, the man went ballistic! He informed us that we were breaking every law in the book, including the Ten Commandments and that our actions would be reported to B.W. To add insult to injury, we had stolen his lock!

Seeing no reason to be overlie concerned, we wished him, "Good Locking" and moored up to disengage our boats.

A small black cloud, shot through with bolts of lightning, could be seen making its way up the flight, hovering above a small, white boat!

As it was now time for elevenses, our new found friends invited us on board for some light refreshments. Typically, we were offered the conducted tour of their boat and reciprocated by inviting them aboard "Athene", so that they could explore our home.

Very proud of what we had achieved, we were always pleased to share our experiences with other boaters, to pick each others brains for new ideas and improvements which, at a later date, could be incorporated into "Athene's" fit-out, in order to make our home even more comfortable and welcoming.

Below Cape Locks, we passed the entrance to the Saltisford Arm and noted that it offered full Boatyard services plus 48 hr. visitor moorings, much closer into the centre of Warwick than those at bridge 49. We made a note to explore this arm at a later date and then continued our cruise to Royal Leamington Spa, where we stopped for the night and enjoyed a quiet, relaxing evening.

We were now a little pressed for time but I was conscious that Jean was still feeling the effects of the previous twenty-four hours. In view of this we made a short leg as far as Longhole Bridge, just below Lock 19 and found a secluded mooring where we could rest and recover our depleted energies.

Restored, we reached the Napton Visitor moorings the following evening and, as we now had a little time to spare, we devoted the next two days to exploring the area.

The walk up to the village for a newspaper, was strenuous but it did enable us to fit in visits to the rather attractive 13C. Church and the well known Napton Windmill. It was a disappointment to find that we could not actually enter the mill.

Napton on the Hill is a sprawling village, spread thinly across the hillside, the view from the top made the climb worthwhile to those intrepid souls who undertook it.

The local hostelries were situated rather a long distance from the moorings, the walk alone would be sufficient to deter all but the most ardent drinkers from imbibing too deeply and then having to face the long trek back to the boat.

The short distance to Braunston was easy and lock-free and we arrived at the junction in time to secure a mooring and pay B.W.B for the extra days. We had not booked as official visitors to the show so had to make our own mooring arrangement.

We found a snug, secure mooring, close to the Braunston Turn Bridges.

The next leg of our cruise would take us to the City of Oxford, gateway to The River Thames from the Oxford Canal. The Thames, a large river navigation, had its own rules and regulations and required a license fee for permission to cruise the waters.

We had received an information pack from the N.R.A. and had been able to study it carefully. It was obvious that, we would need to make some additions to our inventory of safety equipment before we could comply with their requirements. Mainly this would involve re-lettering our name, it was too small, and carrying an anchor, chain and warp, appropriate to the size and weight of the boat.

Visiting the Chandlery, we found that the cost of anchors etc., was very high and we looked round for a cheaper alternative. It was suggested to me by a friend who owned a working boat, that the cheapest way of buying was to go straight to the manufacturer and he gave me the address of a firm in the Black Country, which was prepared to sell small orders to individuals. I remembered seeing his stand at a number of rallies in the Midlands.

A request for a catalogue was phoned through and later that week it was delivered to the B.W.B. office at Braunston by the Royal Mail.

The prices were much more in line with the depths of our pockets and we were able to decide on a suitable package of equipment, delivery of which we could arrange at some convenient point on our trip along the South Oxford Canal.

Braunston Boat show was very popular and gradually, large numbers of boats arrived for the event. One of the advertised highlights was a parade of working boats and many of the working pairs on the system had responded to the invitation.

With so many boats in attendance, it would be unfair to seek to name them, as a sure way of delivering a mortal insult would be to miss out, however inadvertently, any of the many old craft taking part. Suffice to say that, the collection was impressive and represented a number of the Canal Carrying Companies, whose names had once been, and in many instances, still were, synonymous with people's memories of the working heydays of the canals and their decline towards a virtual demise in the 1950's.

The restoration and resurgence of these names was heartwarming.

As a Boat Show, rather than a Rally, the ethos at Braunston was very different from that of many of the smaller ones we had attended, in various parts of the country. However the sheer weight of numbers of boats and people in attendance made it interesting and colourful.

When it ended, we remained on our moorings until the number of boat departures slowed down, then next day we set off on our cruise towards Oxford and a new canal to investigate.

4.
Towards the "Dreaming Spires"

We had decided to make our first overnight stop at Fenny Compton Wharf, so that it would be possible to take delivery of the anchor. This decision meant that our day's travel would be fifteen miles and nine locks. An early start would be needed if we were to reach our destination in time for the order to be phoned through and dispatch arranged.

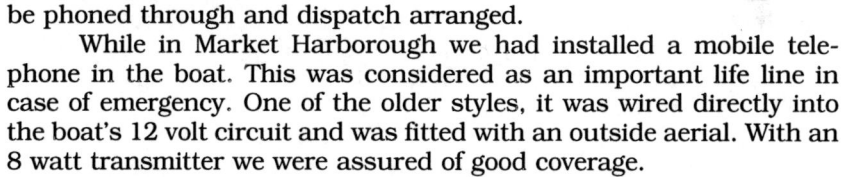

While in Market Harborough we had installed a mobile telephone in the boat. This was considered as an important life line in case of emergency. One of the older styles, it was wired directly into the boat's 12 volt circuit and was fitted with an outside aerial. With an 8 watt transmitter we were assured of good coverage.

Because we lived on the boat and were continually cruising our children had expressed concern over our well being in case of emergencies. This addition to our equipment list has erased their concerns.

At least when we arrived the order could be placed immediately.

The first five miles to Napton Junction, were fraught!

A pair of hire boats left their mooring just as we approached them, then spent their time exploring both banks of the canal as they steered an eccentric course towards their day's destination. I would imagine their difficulties were exacerbated by the fact that the cruiser sterns were being utilised as dog grooming parlours. The steerers were constantly being distracted by the movement going on around their feet.

Every few minutes, large mats of dog's hair would float past our boat, discarded into the wakes of the preceding boats.

This erratic progress made overtaking problematic as the banks were in poor condition and the canal in serious need of dredging and weed clearance.

We fumed "gently", and stayed clear!

Much to our relief both boats turned towards Warwick at the junction.

In common with the Stratford Canal, the locks on the Oxford were narrow but, in spite of it being rated as a Cruiseway, we found many of the lock gates, heavy, unbalanced and difficult to operate.

The six Napton locks lifted the canal almost fifty feet so averaged about eight foot three inches in depth.

Once past Green Lock, a singleton beyond the flight, we saw the odd sight of boats, apparently moored in a field. From that angle we could see the lie of the Old Engine House Arm, now severely truncated, but not the water. This arm is now home to a collection of permanently moored craft.

The Marston Doles pair were the final locks before Fenny Compton and in spite of the earlier delays, we had made good time. By mid-afternoon we were moored up at the Wharf.

A quick phone call to our supplier confirmed that the anchor was ready for delivery and that the boss himself was going to bring it down to Fenny Compton that evening. We arranged to meet him in the "George and Dragon" car park at 8.30 pm., with the cash ready to complete the transaction. In order to identify the location a little more closely, I mentioned the name of a well known local Marina.

After a meal, we went round to the "George" for a quick half.

Eight-thirty came, and went, nine-thirty, ten o'clock, and still no sign of our anchor.

Ten-thirty, we rang the home number we had been given. A female voice answered, confirmed that her husband had left hours ago to make delivery and that she had been anticipating his imminent return.

There was little either party could do except, listen out for the phone and promise that any news would be passed on A.S.A.P.

Eleven-thirty, our telephone rang. The car and the anchor were waiting in the car park of the "George and Dragon" pub, in Tring where the hell were we?

Two marina's were owned by one company, one in Tring on the Grand Union Canal the other at Fenny Compton on the Oxford in Warwickshire.

Our supplier had remembered the name of the pub and my mention of the Marina, he had misplaced the note of the address.

Finding the address in Waterway's World, he had copied down the details, not noticing that there were two sets of information. The first one listed was Tring. This was the location to which he had driven.

The misunderstanding was sorted, we phoned his wife to put her mind at rest and waited.

One-thirty found us, warmly wrapped against the night chills, waiting on the main road, where it crossed over the canal, hopefully waving a torch at any car that might have been looking for a missing boat.

At last, the longed for car appeared and was directed onto the car park. We had prepared a flask of hot tea for the weary traveller but were surprised to find that he had a passenger, an elderly gentleman, who turned out to be his father and who was suffering from emphysema. The hot drink proved to be a Godsend.

After the pair had been warmed through, we off-loaded our purchases. The anchor weighed in at 45kg's and the chain a similar amount, quite a load to carry the four hundred yards to "Athene".

Arriving at the boat, we stowed the gear on the bows and invited our visitors inside for a warm and a bite to eat while we sorted out the cash.

The bill was as small as we had hoped and the cost of delivery had been waived. To me, this seemed unfair so I added £20 to the total and insisted that he took it.

Another phone call to his wife, to reassure her that all was well, then, somewhat recovered from the exertions of their extended trip, they set out once more, this time for home and a warm bed.

All in all, it had been quite an experience. Now we had our anchor and chain, all we needed was a length of suitable rope for the warp.

Between Marston Doles and Fenny Compton, the canal demonstrated very clearly, why contouring led to long canals. It meandered, seemingly aimlessly across the countryside. In practice it was tracing a course around such obstacles as small hills and valleys.

The next section to Cropredy was much straighter but did include two small groups of locks.

Typically, on this canal, flights of locks like those at Claydon, were subject to delays due to traffic build-ups and, of course, falling water levels created by lock operations (in both directions) draining water from the pounds when water supplies were excessively low.

Cropredy was a small, sprawling village, centred mainly around the canal. It's main claim to fame is, that it was here in 1644 that the Royalists achieved a victory over Cromwell's troops under the leadership of General Buller at Cropredy Bridge during the English Civil War.

A number of good pubs, shops and a small boat-yard made it a useful, overnight stop.

The next day saw us complete another easy stage of the five miles and three locks, which took us to the visitor moorings in Banbury.

With such a lot of interesting visits to be made in the area, we had agreed to stay for a few days. Local intelligence advised against mooring below the locks as a gang of young people with walkie-talkies, were watching out for crews leaving boats unattended, then, while one member of the gang monitored the crew's movements and reported back via the radio link, the others could move in and plunder the boat with impunity.

It was possible to lose most of your valued possessions through this type of planned burglary.

We moored above the lock, in company with a number of other boats.

No trouble was experienced!

Our refrigerator had been purchased from Batt's Marine, who were based in Banbury. As the shelf stops had cracked and needed replacing, we rang them up to order new ones. A young man delivered them to the boat, personally, to save us a long walk out to the Trading Estate where they were based.

This was one more good experience to add to our rapidly growing store!

We tend to think of vandalism as a new phenomena, in spite of the derivation of the word itself, now we were becoming more and more aware of the vandalism that had been wreaked by people over the centuries.

Ancient Churches that had been, "Victorianised", were a point in question. We saw many examples of recently restored, unique murals etc., that had been plastered over in the 19C. to sanitise the areas and make them more manageable.

In Banbury itself, destruction of local landmarks went back many centuries. The castle had been removed by Cromwell during the English Civil War, and the famous "Banbury Cross", of nursery rhyme fame, but which was in fact an "Eleanor Cross", one of 12 erected to mark the resting places of Queen Eleanor's coffin on its journey from Grantham to Westminster in 1290, was taken down and smashed, as were many of the others, in 1602, during the reign of Queen Elizabeth I. A replica was raised in the 19C.

In the recent past, the canal basin and wharfs were mainly built over and are now marked by the town's Bus Depot. In 1968, the original bakehouse famed for producing the local, spiced confectionary known as Banbury Cakes, was torn down.

Unable to travel outside the town due to our lack of personal transport, we missed a number of visits to local historical buildings but found that the town itself had retained sufficient character and old buildings to make our stay interesting and enjoyable.

There was still a lot of boat activity in the area, including a hire-boat firm. Tooley's Boat Building Yard was one of the oldest working yards still in existence. It was in this area that we saw the first namesake of our boat, a rather sad looking working boat with her name faded and peeling.

Here, moored against a good, firm bank, I was able to paint "Athene's" name on the bows and at the stern, in letters large enough to satisfy the N.R.A.'s requirements for boats navigating the River Thames.

Slowly our boat was being readied for it's first major river cruise. All that was left to do was to purchase the rope for the anchor warp at the first opportunity.

Leaving Banbury, we set off for our next destination, Aynho wharf.

The lift bridge below Banbury Lock was of a somewhat unusual design, having a heavy balance beam that was counterbalanced and pulled down by means of a short length of chain. When down the operator rested his/her weight on the beam to keep the bridge raised. This one was badly balanced and Jean found difficulty in holding the beam down until a young man gave her a hand. Once the bridge was under control, I slid "Athene" quickly under the upraised roadway.

Reaching the first fixed road bridge, we noted with pleasure that, one of the buildings right next to the bridge, housed a launderette.

This valuable information was entered into our Nicholson's Guide!

Lift and swing bridges were Jean's "Bete Noir" and we were entering an area that bristled with them! Imagine her relief when she discovered that the majority of them were permanently fixed open.

As we passed bridge after bridge held open by its chain, we realised that, what we had thought of as an unusual bridge was, in fact, the standard design for the bulk of the lift bridges on this canal.

During our cruise to Aynho, we found ourselves roughly paralleling the course of the River Cherwell, a very convoluted route through lush water meadows. Lined with trees and deficient of crossing points, it created a formidable obstacle to any desire to explore towns and villages built to the east of it. King's Sutton was one village we had to give a miss.

Before reaching Aynho the canal was bisected by the river, the change of level being accommodated by the one foot deep, Aynho Weir Lock.

We found the visitor moorings excellent, but the long, hot walk up to the village, along a main road, mostly without walkways, was not one to be recommended.

Although the hire boat company based here had a variety of facilities, including a small chandlery, it did not stock the goods we required so our quest for rope continued.

We spent two nights here then set off for Thrupp. Now the attraction was the promise of exploring a deserted village, Hampton Gay.

Still shadowing the river, the canal continued on it's southward meander. The Heyfords seemed set to offer a measure of excitement in the form of low-flying F.1-11 fighter/bombers from the large, local U.S.A.F. base, but we were disappointed. Maybe it had closed down like so many U.S. bases all across the country.

With fourteen miles and eight locks to negotiate, we did not take time out to find out about such details.

At Pigeon's Lock we found a working boat from where were being sold, fenders, ropes, shackles etc., here at last we were able to complete our purchase.

Rope, chain, anchor, swivels and shackles, all were now fitted. "Athene" complied with N.R.A. regulations.

River Thames, here we come!

We arrived in Thrupp, with plenty of time to spare for exploring. After taking on fresh water at the wharf, Jean opened the lift bridge and we moved down towards the advertised visitor moorings. Unfortunately these appeared mainly to have been re-designated as Club moorings leaving only a tiny length of visitor moorings which was already crowded. Managing to tie up some distance from a badly maintained bank, in a questionable (from a legal standpoint) area, we agreed that an overnight stay was all we could reasonably make.

Approaching Thrupp, we had passed by Shipton on Cherwell, which our guide book informed us, had been the scene of a major railway disaster in 1875. On Christmas Eve, nine carriages were derailed and fell onto the frozen canal beneath the railway bridge.

34 people were killed!

This put me in mind of a similar happening during my childhood, when a train on the old L.M.S. line between Euston and Glasgow, was derailed, on an embankment, between Grendon and Polesworth. The long, hot summer had expanded the rails until the expansion gaps had closed up and the track had buckled. The engine and a number of carriages left the rails and plunged down the embankment, into the Coventry Canal, some 20-30 feet below.

This happened in the 1940's and I can still remember, the feeling of shock and horror that swept through our village, even though I cannot recall details like the number of casualties etc.

The proximity of canal and railway in many parts of this country is responsible for the number of incidents of this nature that litter local history.

A deserted village was shown on our map and we decided to pay it a visit. Walking back to bridge 220, as per instructions in the guide book, we left the canal and set off across the fields. After crossing the railway lines (on a pedestrian crossing), we found the church, in splendid isolation. Another couple had collected the key and the church was open; a bonus for us.

The building was very simple and plain with a number of memorial plaques on the walls. It was still consecrated and worship took place on the odd occasions. It's isolation served to make it very peaceful and the nearness of the railway line was not as intrusive as we had thought might be the case. I think the amount of traffic on that line must be quite small.

The Manor House was in ruins and showed signs of having been used locally as a quarry, providing stone blocks for a number of buildings, including the adjoining farmhouse.

Little was left of the village and almost no local information was available.

Such a pity!

As we neared Oxford on the final day's cruising, we passed more and more of the boats that we had begun to refer to as, "hippy hutches." We have no basic objection to people living the life style that suits them, with the rider, that, by doing it, they do not interfere with other folks enjoyment and choice.

Unfortunately, dirty, badly maintained, unsafe craft, moored in, or being lived on, in areas that have a high profile or public visibility, tend to create an antipathy towards the boating fraternity. People like ourselves, on a small fixed income who still manage to squeeze the pensions enough to keep the boats, clean, safe and legal are under severe pressure from the governing bodies, who appear to be set on maximising income and minimising expenditure. The existence of a strong cadre of boaters, prepared to live below what can be considered as minimum standards of safety and hygiene, mitigates against live on board status being seen as viable and socially acceptable.

Shopping in the city a few days later, we were to have an experience that graphically underlined this point.

As was our normal practice when shopping in town, (and most other times when we are not working on the boat.) We were clean, well-groomed and neatly dressed. Faced with the need to place an order for some goods that we were purchasing, I was explaining our position to the assistant. As we were due to move onto the River Thames in a few days I pointed out that living aboard a boat did make it difficult to be in an area for an extended period of time.

Jean was standing alongside me, involved in the conversation. Her normal speaking voice is pleasant and well modulated. As the shop was busy the customers were close together. On overhearing my conversation, the lady standing next to Jean, turned with a disdainful expression and sneered, "Oh dear! You are boat-people!" and, drawing her skirts tightly around her, she stepped carefully back to avoid being contaminated.

Jean was taken aback by this rudeness and responded angrily, allowing her voice to coarsen from its usual tones, she growled the immortal word

"*Yers Missus! water gypsies, that's us. An' prahd uv it.*"

It was not a sensible response and only served to confirm the stereotype! It was however, a natural reaction.

The customer was discomforted, the assistant and other customers who had heard Jean's normal speech laughed and the incident was passed off.

That event, in our minds, still rankles and was, in no small measure, part of the catalyst that hardened our views on the problems that can be created by scruffy boats.

Through the final section into the city, we ran the gauntlet of swing-bridges. As luck would have it, a number were open.

Duke's Cut, offered an alternative route down to the river, As we intended to stay for seven days we carried on towards the promised visitor moorings at the end of the arm beyond Isis Lock.

There did not appear to be a great deal of space available so I pulled into the bank by the lock. Jean walked down the private moorings to check on the situation in the cul-de-sac, which was where the visitor moorings were located. Returning with good news, she reboarded the boat, we moved down and moored up. The stern of our boat was just inside the limit marker, on the legal side.

Towards evening a pair of unkempt, badly cared for working boats arrived. We were informed in no uncertain manner that they were residents and we were occupying their mooring. I pointed out that this was unlikely to be the case and told them I would check with B.W.B. After being threatened with an aggressively wielded mooring stake and warned that my mooring lines would be cut during the night, I took my leave, returned to the boat, and phoned B.W.B. They confirmed my right to the mooring and promised to send the lengthsman down to sort matters out. He arrived at 10.30 pm., reassured us and went off to talk to the other boaters who were now moored, three abreast and directing poisonous glances in my direction. I could not hear what transpired but we had no more problems for the whole of the seven days we had arranged with B.W. that we could stay.

From the foregoing comments, readers could be excused for believing that Oxford was, the "City from Hell", for visiting boaters. That was certainly not the case, but the sheer numbers of residential boats of all shapes, sizes and conditions coupled with a serious lack of space, could and did create the occasional difficulty.

We stayed the full seven days and thoroughly enjoyed ourselves.

Jean had long fancied herself stepping into the role of Steven Speilberg, filming our progress and entertaining friends, relatives and unsuspecting guests, with showings of her epics on cold, winter nights.

Window shopping, we saw a top of the range Panasonic Videocamera for sale in a shop window. An ex-demo model, it was reduced by £400.

She bought it!

Using full sized tapes, this model required the support of the operators shoulder during filming. With it balanced precariously on her shoulder, peering through the view-finder, Jean looked every inch a member of a BBC. Foreign correspondent's film crew.

In common with most newcomers to the art of video-taping, Jean's early efforts had all the thrill and riveting excitement of being hand-cuffed to a fence, watching paint drying. It was missing the tight editing, stimulating commentary and background soundtrack that brought most travelogues to life. Our adventures did not translate into gripping cinema.

Still, as a record of our visits and a reminder of some of the places of interest we found, it was enjoyable.

Woodstock was only a short bus ride away and so we paid a visit to Blenheim Palace.

With the weather staying fine and dry, we made a full day of it. After walking for miles around the grounds and the ornamental lakes, we took the conducted tour around the building itself.

The architecture and decor was stunning, the paintings, silver, porcelain, crystal and furniture fascinating, but perversely, our abiding memory of that day has nothing to do with Blenheim.

Walking back through the village to catch the bus, we stuck up a conversation with a middle-aged lady. She lived in Oxford and was also about to catch a bus back to the city.

In passing she mentioned that her husband was a warder in the prison that overlooked the canal basin in Oxford. It turned out that she was a close relative of Albert Pierpoint the Hangman. An interesting if gruesome conversation ensued, perhaps it says something for our sense of occasion that this was what we remembered most of a very interesting day.

With so many educational establishments in the city, in addition to the University, the streets teemed with young and not so young people, in the uniform beloved of students, baggy tops, distressed jeans and Jesus sandals. It was a hotch-potch of nationalities creating a truly cosmopolitan atmosphere.

There were also a great number of ethnic restaurants and we discovered a Cellar Bar that served authentic Tunisian food. Here we were able to dine on Cous-Cous and Brik, washed down with rough red wine,

Heaven!

For a time, Ian, Jean's youngest son, had worked in a bookshop in Oxford. Exploring the town, we found it. Jean made herself known to the manageress who, to her great delight, remembered Ian with evident pleasure. They shared a few minutes, discussing his current progress and dissecting his character.

Typical of Mothers!

Bookshops are a magnet to me. I can spend many an hour quietly amusing myself, given access to a few shelves of books.

In spite of being surrounded by wonderful architecture representing most periods from Tudor to present day, we found it difficult to experience the same sense of history that we had in other places.

Everywhere was hustle and bustle; the veneer of the 20C. was laid heavily over the scene. Glimpses of beauty, oases of calm, the hush of history and an ambience of venerability, were all there, in small measure, to be claimed on rare occasions but the overwhelming sense was one of the frenetic activity of modern life.

The galleries, museums and even some of the churches, seemed to have misplaced their air of calm and serenity. This was what we sought and often, failed to find.

Perhaps we searched in the wrong places at the wrong times but, instead of our enjoyable times in the City, translating into golden memories, we were left, with a kind of hollowness, that gave a slight negative twist to our many recollections of Oxford.

Walking up and down the residential mooring along the arm towards Isis lock, we passed a fascinating mix of craft. Down at heel, tatty, tarpaulin covered working boats, often with a quota of snarling lurchers, grubby snivelling children and dirty, unkempt adults shared the banks with clean, well cared for craft, usually bright with flowers and with the surrounding bank and towing path, neat, tidy and pleasant. It was good to see so many boats striving to lift the atmosphere of the area and create a feeling of order. Many long term moorings and residential sites are dragged into disrepute by the preponderance of boats, obviously in need of large helpings of T.L.C.

We have not returned to Oxford since then, so my remarks relate to the situation I found in 1994, I am in no position to offer any comments on the way things may have changed in the interim.

It is a matter of record that, years later, a young woman was informed that her boat was unsafe and it was recommended that she moved into a flat in the town while repairs were made. Her demands were excessive and because they could not be met, she continued to live on board with two very young children. A gas cylinder exploded, killing all three.

That happened in Oxford and is the type of incident that adds fuel to arguments from the general public that boats should be kept in a safe and presentable condition.

However ineptly they were presented and implemented, the current Safety Certificate requirements, represent a major step forward in the efforts to ensure that boating is a safe pastime. Not only do they seek to ensure the safety of those boaters who live aboard or spend the summer months cruising, they also protect members of the public, who enjoy strolling along the canal and river banks, admiring boats. Crews of ambulances, fire-engines and other emergency services, who are drawn into incidents, are also protected.

The final piece of excitement was presented by the quarter mile plus trip, back to Isis Lock. There we would be lowered to the river level prior to joining the Thames for our cruise to the head of navigation, at Lechlade.

Sixty-five feet in length, "Athene" was too long to wind in the remains of the canal basin. I would have to go astern for the whole distance.

Our design had given the boat a reasonable ability to move astern, in a relatively straight line, my experience as a skipper had honed that technique. Nevertheless, it was a long distance.

One side of the channel was lined with boats, some, two or three abreast; the offside was lined with overhanging foliage and shallow water.

The manoeuvre proved to be trickier than many of my previous attempts at reversing along moorings, but in spite of the numerous pairs of critical eyes watching us from the boats, we completed the move without a hitch.

A slight delay was experienced while we waited for another boat to complete her descent and clear the lock, then we were free to join the river and begin our cruise.

Our first sight of the Thames was reassuring. Water levels were adequate and the flow was not excessive. With only the lightest of breezes there was none of the choppy water we had encountered on the Trent.

Breasting the current, we took up our station towards the right of centre on the river, then, we set our course for Lechlade.

5.
Old Father Thames

For Jean, the next two weeks were set to be a holiday from her usual chore of operating the locks. During certain hours, all Thames Locks were operated by keepers and we had resolved to ensure that our travels took place within these time parameters.

Arriving at Godstow, the first lock upstream, we were required to complete the paperwork for the issue of our first fifteen day licence. From our observations of the boats sharing that first lock with us, it was evident that, the various regulations that had caused us so much heart-searching, were not as rigorously enforced as we had been led to expect.

After paying our dues, we displayed our license stickers and set off once more.

An early conclusion was, that in common with most river navigations we had travelled, moorings for long, relatively deep-draughted, square-bottomed boats like ours, were few and far between.

Here a majority of craft seemed to be of G.R.P. construction, fairly lightweight and with "vee" bottoms. They could moor practically anywhere.

We certainly couldn't!

The channel was much narrower than I had anticipated and its route was tortuous. We found navigating it more of a problem than we had expected.

Broad bows thrusting against a steady current and many of the bends, tighter and narrower than we would usually negotiate, steering proved to be hard work. At least until I got more of a hang of the new techniques.

Passing through Pinkhill Lock, we saw the embankments of the massive, Farmoor Reservoir looming up over our bows. Here, there was a substantial length of free visitor mooring, still vacant. We took advantage of them and moored up for the night.

The booklets passed on to us by the Godstow Lock-keeper, were full of information outlining the differences we could expect to find during a river cruise. For instance, "right of way" was dictated by ones direction of travel. Boats travelling with the current had priority, they would find slowing down or stopping, considerably more difficult. As flowing water creates sand bars and shallows and large sunken objects cause obstructions, it was important to keep a sharp look-out for marker buoys and to know from their shape and colour, what messages they are meant to convey.

We hammered our mooring pins into the bank and tied off our ropes. It was strange to be required to leave our lines slack, something we would never do on a canal. On a river lifting the paddles on a weir to control the flow, can cause water levels to fluctuate very quickly. The depth of water beneath the hull was important for the same reason.

Schooled into the discipline of watching out for breaking washes that could disturb moored craft, it was an odd feeling to watch cruisers passing at speeds which were sufficient to lift the boat onto its planing hull. The wash may not have been actually breaking, but an eight to ten inch swell running along the river bank was enough to make even a large boat like ours, bounce around when the mooring lines are slack.

These were all strange, new experiences!

The two days it took us to reach Lechlade from Farmoor Reservoir, were filled with interest even though, on these reaches, the river appears to be deserted. The villages and hamlets stand well back, concealed by folds in rolling countryside. The impression was of unspoiled landscapes, only the marching rows of electricity pylons, spreading across the fields reminded us of the nearness of civilisation.

Quaintly named, Tadpole Bridge, with its adjacent riverside Pub, seemed to offer a reasonable chance of finding visitor moorings. We were disappointed, the area was crowded with hire-cruisers from the many yards vying for trade along the banks. Finally, we moored in splendid isolation near to Rushey Lock.

Weirs and lock-cuts, that eased the river's course around narrows and stretches of broken water, as well as catering for the steady rise of the river towards its headwaters, made an unusual change for us and created a large measure of interest.

Next day was spent meandering through water-meadows as we completed our cruise into Lechlade.

A point of interest at the locks was looking out for the markers on the lock buildings which indicated the high point reached by flood water during really bad winters. Complete with details of months and years they were a sobering reminder of just how powerful the forces of nature can be.

Approaching Lechlade, we entered St.John's Lock, the highest on the river. It was here that the statue of "Old Father Thames" had taken up residence after years of mounting guard over the river's source, at Thames Head, near Kemble in Gloucestershire. The meadows between the lock and Halfpenny Bridge offered good mooring against a steep, high bank.

The actual head of navigation was some half a mile upstream near the Roundhouse at the confluence of the Thames, the Coln and the Thames and Severn Canal. (Now derelict.) We decided to leave that section of the cruise until the morning of our departure in seven days time.

Lechlade was heavily orientated towards tourists, with its cafes, restaurants, gift shops, galleries and antique shops. However it held our interest and we enjoyed exploring the area.

Inglesham, a tiny village just beyond the head of navigation, had a dual claim to fame. It was the site of a Mediéval Village which had merged into the background and among the well maintained dwellings. It had a lovely, 13C. church, quite small and plain, which had been rescued from the attentions of the Victorian Church Vandals by none other than William Morris, who loved the village and vowed to protect it.

The peace and calm of these areas attracted visits from a number of poets and writers. It is easy to see why they enjoyed their time here.

On the upper reaches of the Thames we found the cost of "red" diesel, prohibitive. We were assured that once we were past Windsor heading for London, prices would become much more reasonable. Fortunately we had begun our cruise from Oxford with a full fuel tank.

This area was popular and the traffic on the river, heavy. With the need to moor on slack lines still in operation, day-times were not a little uncomfortable.

At least the countryside was reasonably flat and we spent our days exploring the area. Walking was a pleasure and a number of architectural gems were waiting to be visited.

All too soon our time here was over and we had to make use of the remaining days of our license by cruising down to Reading and the beginning of the Kennet and Avon Canal.

Timing our trip so that we arrived at St.John's Lock in time for the first keeper operated passage of the day, we set off towards the Round House and the exercise of winding the boat. The warning of sand bars created by the water flow of the two rivers, had left us feeling distinctly apprehensive.

As was her wont, "Athene" behaved impeccably and we completed the manoeuvre without the slightest difficult, then headed for the lock.

With the current hastening our passage and the "right of way" with us, we made good progress on our return trip to Oxford.

Downstream from our point of entry, we found that the river was hemmed in by housing and industrial development, until we reached Salter's Boatyard at the start of the Christ Church Meadows. The extremely low bridge at Osney marked the highest point that could be navigated by large cruisers with flying bridges. From here onwards they would become a regular part of the scenery.

The river banks at Christ Church were lined with boat-houses and further progress was hampered by the need to keep a sharp lookout for rowing boats. Not the usual tourist hire boats but skiffs, singles, doubles, fours and racing eights, all so busy concentrating on their own progress that they seemed to be unaware of the approach of seventeen and a half tonnes of rather solid steel. In situations like this power should give way to rowed craft but a sixty-five foot narrowboat is not exactly nimble when it comes to rapid changes of course.

The names over the club-houses read like a Who's who of the sport and Jean's video was busily whirring away recording the various sightings.

Almost immediately after the club houses ceased to line the banks, we came upon a truly depressing sight, the remains of wooden working boats and the occasional house boat, burnt out or sunk littered the inshore shallows. Possibly this was a legacy of the demise of water borne transport of goods around the country.

As the sprawling conurbation of Oxford was left behind, the river reached Sandford Lock, the deepest one on the upper reaches with a fall of nearly nine feet. After this we entered a wide, five mile long reach, with views ranging from the beautifully manicured grounds of Nuneham Park, to the wooded hillside of Lock Wood. Civilisation seems to have taken a step back away from the river banks and left the open fields to be colonised by the ubiquitous electricity pylons.

In need of fresh water and with our toilet waste holding tank in serious need of pumping out, we moored above the lock at Abingdon. Here we were not only able to complete both tasks but a word with the N.R.A. staff elicited permission to moor up on the 24 hour visitor moorings for an extended stay.

Our timing was good as we had, quite unknowingly, arrived on the day prior to the Ock Street Mayor Making, an old custom that had been extended into a National Morris Dance event, with teams from all over the country here to perform their dances in the streets for the benefit of the crowds.

Here was an event worthy of the attentions of Jean's video recorder!

Walking into the town centre, we crossed the weir and followed the bank of a muddy stream that entered the river by the lock. In this channel we saw a reminder of the anomalies created by doting parents pandering to the demands of their children during the Mutant Hero Turtle craze. Red eared terrapins bought as pets proved to be, not particularly active, smelly and a little vicious. They were dumped in their hundreds and now have become established in the most unlikely areas. On a log, basking in the sunlight and ignoring everything, was a large terrapin. In what should be a hostile environment they appeared to be thriving. Capable of inflicting a nasty nip with their beaks, the creatures are better viewed than approached.

After a brief stroll around the town to acclimatise ourselves with its layout, we returned to the boat for a quiet evening. Next day we returned to the town-centre, this time Jean had her Video recorder fired up and ready!

It was indicative of the way our culture had learned to defer to the media, that, contrary to the normal situation she expected to find with adults vying for the best viewing positions, here Jean found herself ushered forward and offered her choice of viewing points, and this with the connivance of the spectators.

She had no sound crew etc. yet the sight of a large, shoulder held camera among all the "palmcorders" to hand seemed to trigger an instinctive reaction that this was "Media". It was all part of the "wave at the camera" and "Hello Mum!" syndrome.

At Eynsham Lock we had met a couple from the Wirral, who were cruising on their imaginatively named boat, "Hull 25". At Abingdon, our paths had crossed again. Chance acquaintances occasionally develop into long distance friendships carried on through correspondence. We travelled together for a while before separating after exchanging addresses. We were destined not to meet again for over four years, yet when we did, the years fell away and we picked up where we left off, so to speak!

The architecture of Abingdon was well worth the few days we spent there. We visited some splendid almshouses which were in the process of being rewired and spoke to the man in charge of the work. His account of their history was enthralling but even more so, his tales of working on the restoration of Windsor Castle after the disastrous fire.

While they were tracing burnt out wiring etc., the workmen had discovered a variety of tiny rooms and passages which had been created over the years. Alcoves had been blocked off, passageways truncated and sealed, in some instances sealed areas still had windows to the outside walls, and all this laid down over the centuries. No skeletons were unearthed belonging to long forgotten "dissidents" but the idea of lost, secret chambers appeals to "children" of all ages. He may well have been romancing a pair of gullible tourists or have been related to Billy Liar, but we enjoyed his stories.

Our time was running out but we still had enough for two more overnight stops. We negotiated our way through Abingdon Lock and set our course for the Roman Town of Dorchester.

Cruising along the waterfront we passed the entrance to the River Ock, which was also the start of the Wilts. and Berks. Canal, sadly now added to the long list of defunct waterways.

It was distressing to be reminded like this of how much of our Waterway's Heritage had been lost, but heartening to hear from time to time of the progress made by local restoration groups as they sought to return these forgotten waterways to their former prosperity.

Sutton Courtenay beckoned and we would have loved to have paid our respects at the grave of Eric Blair (George Orwell.) who did so much to put Wigan on the map. He was buried in the churchyard there and the village abounded with other historical buildings begging to be visited, but we took "a rain check" on that stopover.

Maybe next time!

Slowly, the river was becoming more substantial and the weirs increasingly impressive.

Small lengths of free, short-term moorings were available courtesy of N.R.A. but usually, mooring rights were owned by individual entrepreneurs who then collected mooring fees from boats every evening. At this time the going rate appeared to be around £2.00 to £2.50. I would imagine that this has increased substantially since 1994.

Round the bend below Day's Lock, we moored up against the banks of the meadow, near to the entrance to the River Thame (without an "s".) a tributary upon whose banks Dorchester was built.

Once the Cathedral City of Wessex, the town's Abbey Church is an impressive building founded in the 7th.C. Many Roman finds were made in the area but most of them are housed in the Ashmolean in Oxford rather than in the small local museum.

Walking into town along the course of the Thame, took us through earthworks and buried ruins with the church bulking large in front of us. This was another area of galleries, craft shops and antique sellers but it was interwoven with a wonderful mosaic of superb historical buildings.

The church contained a stone framed "Jesse" window, one of the most important examples of this type of work. Here the skills of mason and stained glass artist had been merged to produce poetry in solid form.

Humbling in its beauty!

Our appetites were well and truly whetted but we were rapidly running out of time.

Surrounded by history, with new prospects on offer in almost every town and village that we cruised past, we had entered into cultural overload. One day we would return and spend time just drifting from mooring to mooring while we explored our surroundings.

With two more nights at our disposal we agreed to overnight at Goring and Reading. This would give us two easy days cruising of approximately eleven miles per day. With these distances and assisted passage through the locks, Jean was getting her holiday break in a big way.

On the run into Goring the river followed a broad, easy path, but now, towns and villages were gradually creeping closer to her banks. Spires and Church towers showed among woodland, indicating the presence of villages and at Wallingford, an ancient Royal Borough, with its slim, open-work spire, evidence of occupation dating back to Saxon times was to be seen.

Our experiences on the canals, had shown us that the windows of opportunity for mooring long craft, only opened at particular times on the busy sites. These times usually occurred between ten-thirty am. and one pm. with a second one between three and five pm. The first when late risers cleared the moorings, the latter reflected, the after lunch cruise time.

On the river, lock manning took place after nine am. and as many people took advantage of this, there was a tendency to leave overnight moorings earlier and so lengthen the morning window as they sought to get in a reasonable period of cruising before lunch.

Jean and I tended to dine on the move and seek moorings during the afternoon window.

It usually worked well!

That morning we moored up during the early window. We arrived at Goring Lock around eleven-forty-five and found the mooring, virtually empty. We had covered six miles between Benson and Cleve locks and then the half mile reach to Goring. The shortest pound on the river.

It offered a good overnight stopping point with a wide variety of cafes, restaurants and pubs the old adage "Goring is boring" seemed to hold true but that is probably a wicked calumny.

Studying our guide books, we had reached the conclusion that, the Kennet and Avon was not overlie blessed with convenient stopping places where it would be possible to complete major grocery shopping sprees. Reading, boasted a large riverside Supermarket complete with mooring. We resolved to make our final stop there in order to stock up on provisions.

When we finally arrived we found the moorings shallow, crowded and much shorter than we had hoped for but we managed to squeeze into a space and indulge in a hectic couple of hours shopping.

The cruise from Goring had been uneventful. The river was broad and placid, while the scenery stayed varied and interesting. Many of the beautiful riverside properties had small boat-houses, a legacy of the days when it was "de rigueur" to own and run a boat if you lived by the river. Today most of the boat-houses were sad, neglected and silted up.

One thing missing from the narrative to date, is a detailed account of the passage through a Thames Lock. This is different in so many important aspects to the procedure of locking on canals.

With most Thames locks, the first indication of its proximity is the appearance of a "Danger Weir. Keep Left or Right!" notice. This can be anything up to half a mile from the lock, depending on how many channels the river has laid down over the years.

On a canal, the lock completely spans the channel, river locks however are often tucked coyly away in a large expanse of watercourses, weirs, guard-rails and markers.

The lock at Mapledurham was built around 1777 and the main weir sometime in the 13th C. It was the first Thames lock to be fully mechanised, back in 1956.

Approaching from upstream, the boater is faced with a large expanse of water, bristling with warning signs and pilings, with an arrow pointing towards an insignificant group of buildings, tucked away in the right hand corner of the reach.

With heavy traffic in both directions, congestion and delays could reasonable be expected. This is alleviated by the fact that the lock chambers are so large that they can accommodate up to a dozen or more boats of varying sizes at each cycle of operation.

Queuing for entry into the lock involves, mooring against the weir piling, which doubles as a mooring bay for waiting boats or keeping station on the river if the holding bay is full.

The lock-keeper calls the boats forward, his word is Law! If he wishes to change the order in which the boats enter the chamber, to achieve a safer mix, then he will do so. To this end large steel boats are often given priority, in order that they can be close to the bottom gates and against the lock wall.

A measure of antipathy is known to exist between steel, G.R.P. and wooden boat owners. With a modicum of common sense, compliance with instructions and patience, the advent of accidents could be pretty well eradicated.

On entering the chamber at the lock-keepers directions, boats must be secured bow and stern and the engine, switched off!

This leaves control of the boat, entirely in the hands of the rope handlers.

With the sluices open and the boat descending, it has a tendency to move forward. The rope handlers must allow for the change in level while ensuring the lines are tight enough to prevent the boat hitting the gates or, even worse, another boat.

With the water levels equalised, the lock gates are opened, the engines are started and the boats leave the lock, in strict order. Once clear, the jockeying for position begins as the faster, lighter cruisers, seek to get clear of their feared rivals, the heavier, slower, steel boats.

Watching a £300,000, flying-bridge, ocean going craft tiptoe out of the lock with one of its triple outboards burbling away on tick over, is a strange sight. Moments later, its stern is wreathed in white, exhaust smoke as three massive outboards, delivering heaven knows how many H.P., kick in, and she lifts onto the planing hull and you are left watching a rapidly diminishing white dot transfixed on the broad arrow of waves marking its progress.

So much for speed limits!

Later we had an experience that helped us counter the reserve that seemed to exist between the "Gods" who owned these large craft and we mere mortals.

Moored overnight near to Windsor, we found ourselves in company with a beautiful, white ocean-going cruiser. The owners were friendly and we enjoyed some interesting conversations. At one point they were joking about the need to protect their boat from too close contact with "pig troughs". We informed them, that we were not looking to get our beautiful paintwork marred by contact with a "Chambourcy Pot" (an up-market "Yoghurt Pot".)

Next day, when we entered the lock, the banter about "pig troughs" and "Chambourcy Pots" continued as we laughed and joked before tying up, alongside each other. The lock-keeper was "gobsmacked" to use a rather crude modern phrase, he was unused to such camaraderie between owners of steel and G.R.P.

Our final sighting of the boat was a rapidly diminishing, white dot, transfixed etc.,etc.!

The entry into Reading was marked by an increasing encroachment of housing and industry, coupled with a proliferation of boat yards. These no doubt accounting for the large increase in the numbers of moored craft lining the banks.

After passing through Caversham Lock and before we reached the Supermarket moorings, we saw a boatyard offering diesel at much more reasonable rates. With our concerns about the availability of supplies on the K&A, we stopped to fill our tank and take on fresh water.

In common with many yards on the river, the fuelling wharf was only long enough to accommodate the 30/40 foot craft that formed their usual cliental. We did manage to squeeze in and were able to fill our tanks.

From our viewpoint on the yard we were able to see, not only the moorings at the Supermarket but also the gasometers that flanked the entrance to the River Kennet and the K&A Canal.

After shopping for groceries and other essentials, we moved down to the turn off. Once into the canalised river we became aware not only of the adverse current but also the shallowness of the water.

Passing through Blake's Lock, we then turned into the basin and moored by the Museum. This was one of the few areas within the City limits that it was safe to moor.

Next day we would gird our loins and head for Bristol.

Water levels permitting!!

6.
Locks, Bridges and Reed-beds!

Between Reading and Bristol, the canal boasted 105 locks and countless swing and lift bridges, spread over a distance of 93 miles. These were broad locks and as the Kennet and Avon was still designated as, "a remainder canal", we were not too hopeful of their condition, based on our previous experiences, in spite of the reassurances that we had been offered.

Booked into the 4th. Devizes Boat Rally or "Canalfest 1994." to be held at Bishops Canning, we had a fixed date to build our schedule around.

The lack of back-pumping facilities on the Caen Hill Flight of locks at Devizes, was creating problems. Passages needed to be booked in advance, and only two days per week were open for transit.

If the weather remained as hot and dry as at present, even that small concession could find itself under the threat of withdrawal.

Cruising through the centre of Reading was odd. Most towns with a large expanse of waterfront, albeit canalised river, would have seen the tourist attraction in the picturesque quality of the boats, particularly narrowboats. In common with what we were to experience in most towns along our route, boats, especially long ones, were considered a necessary evil and certainly not to be pandered to, by the provision of well dredged, adequate moorings.

Beyond the narrows, which were controlled by boater operated traffic signals, we arrived at County Lock. With only a small drop, it should have been simple, in spite of it's accompanying weir. In fact it proved to be one of the most awkward, difficult locks to negotiate, more so when approached from upstream.

After the lock, we passed beneath the ring road and approached Bear Free Wharf, which we checked out as possible future moorings. The area had an unsavoury air, it did not give a feeling of security, particularly in view of the litter of beer and lager cans among the wine and spirit bottles strewn over the ground.

As a canalised river it had obviously been used for trade during the heyday of horse-drawn barges. Looking at the stands of crack willow and enormous reed beds encroaching onto the water course, the fallen trees and branches all but blocking the navigation, it was almost impossible to imagine a time when such traffic moved freely on these waters.

Once Fobney Mill Lock and the pumping station were passed, Reading blended into the horizon behind us and passage became much more pleasant and open.

With progress to date, slow and difficult, we began to look for a quiet, restful mooring. We recognised an unpalatable truth; along this canal, large expanses of good mooring, to which we were accustomed, became as scarce as hen's teeth!

Eventually after an increasingly frustrating cruise, we negotiated Burghfield Lock, then broke the cardinal rule of boating. For the first time, we tied up for the night on the tail of the lock moorings.

The end of day one. Jean was "knackered."

Somewhat refreshed but conscious of the warnings in our guide book relating to Theale Swing Bridge, we made what we considered to be an early enough start to reach the lock before the morning rush hour.

The two locks prior to the bridge sank our efforts. By the time we had arrived, traffic was moving steadily over the bridge.

I put Jean ashore, she approached the bridge and studied the operating instructions. After waiting for a break in the traffic, she closed the barriers and began to operate the mechanism. Within seconds she was engulfed in a deluge of car horns and foul language as she struggled to open the bridge. As the barrage grew in intensity, one driver left his vehicle, pushed up the barriers and in spite of the fact that the hydraulic clamps were now dis-engaged drove over the bridge upon which the other vehicles followed suit. The noise of the unlocked bridge crashing down on the clamps, brought out the woman who lived in the bridge cottage. Instead of solidarity and concern, she rounded on Jean and began to berate her. Burning with humiliation and distress rather than anger, Jean flung the windlass down and ran off.

I moored the boat and went up to sort matters out, I had reset the barriers and was struggling with the bridge when Jean came back. Together we completed the operation and I returned to "Athene" to take her through. After re-mooring I went back to the bridge to assist in the closure. From my appearance on the scene, the brave souls in their cars maintained a discrete silence.

That episode, almost totally destroyed Jean's already damaged confidence in her ability to operate swing bridges efficiently.

Were it not for the fact that we were booked into the Rally and our dues had been paid, "Athene" would have reached the next winding hole, and there we would have written the K&A experience off totally.

With Jean now paranoid about their operation, we approached the next two swing bridges with trepidation. Fortunately they offered no problem. Sulhampton was hand operated but carried no road traffic, while Tyle Mill was motorised.

Our troubles returned at Ufton. Hand operated, with windlass controlled hydraulic clamps, it proved impossible for one person to work. The controls required 40 plus turns of the windlass to operate the hydraulics, as soon as the winding stopped, the catches would re-engage; its hydraulics were leaking. A second person was needed to open the bridge while the first controlled the windlass. Once more the road carried traffic.

Not a good omen!

I collected "Athene" cleared the bridge and moored to await Jean. Meanwhile she had closed the bridge and was resetting the hydraulics. A motorist, apparently incensed at the delay, left his car to deliver a lecture on sex, travel and the affinity of the weaker sex to those bovine examples that graced our meadows. He was informed, in no uncertain terms, that he would be better advised to expend a little of his excess energy on assistance rather than advice, if he wished to speed up his progress.

I think, by now, my readers are aware that if I were to prepare a list of my favourite cruising canals, the K&A would be unlikely to be credited with any kind of entry.

On reaching Woolhampton, we negotiated one final motorised swing bridge, then tied up for the night on the pub moorings below the lock.

Neither of us were in the mood for cooking so we decided to settle for a bar meal. The publican amused us by seeking to buy my "Safari" hat as he was going on holiday to Kenya and wanted to look like a seasoned traveller. My hat had been purchased at the hatter's seconds shop at Atherstone. It was well worn and I was proud of its unique shape. The product of much use and not a little abuse.

It was not for sale!

The next leg from Woolhampton to Newbury was only seven miles and nine locks, it took six hours, a measure of the continuing problems we were facing with swing bridges and poorly maintained locks. Good moorings remained scarce and most locks had inadequate hardstanding.

Most of the countryside was attractive and varied, the canal could have given its users a great deal of pleasure. A whole range of relatively minor inadequacies had accumulated to create a deep negative feeling. Even the Turf-sided locks with their historical connotations, which almost anywhere else would have sent our minds racing back into the past as we imagined bygone days, failed to impress. Our minds were much more aware of the general air of neglect and decay which permeated the scene to register the positive aspects. As boaters, lack of water, neglect of hardware, the encroachment of reedbeds and a chronic lack of mooring, were points of maximum importance and damned our vision of the canal in general terms.

In the past I had been involved in a very minor way, in the Devizes to Westminster Canoe race, I was aware of the massive amount of work put in by local people in restoring the canal and re-opening the navigation. Twenty years work had culminated in the early 1990's when the route had re-opened. Perhaps the failure to be granted "Cruiseway" status had dogged progress, but it was hard to reconcile what we were finding now, with the glowing reports that had been made about the K&A's future, when it was reopened.

Past Greenham Lock and entering Newbury, we began to see, almost for the first time since we had entered the canal, flocks of water fowl around the boat. The more usual Mallard crosses were evident but also large numbers of hybrids based on exotic and fancy breeds that had escaped from captivity.

As we came alongside the wharf to take on water, I took the way off the boat, switched off the engine and stepped ashore with the stern rope. Jean was ashore with the bow line. We had lowered the fenders ready to tie up, when a brood of ducklings, Mallard/Muscovy crosses, darted between the boat and the wharf. Not wishing to finish up with pressed duckling, we fended "Athene" away from the coping. Mama came up to point out to us the difficulties that her brood was in, and fussed round our feet as we sought to shoo the hatchlings out of danger. The main problem was that they were half way along the boat and unwilling to pass either of us to clear the danger zone. Eventually, I held the stern close to the bank, while Jean, released the bow rope and circled behind the tiny balls of fluff and was at last able to direct them towards open water. Mama stayed at her feet until the little ones were safe, gave her a few well chosen words then swam off to check on how her little ones had fared.

Mission accomplished!

Initially we tied up on the public moorings near to the park opposite the large car and motor-coach park, that had once been covered by the warehousing and wharfage of a canal in the vintage years when water transport ruled. One small building remained, housing a local Waterways Museum run by the Kennet and Avon Trust.

Later we crossed over the canal and paid a visit to the site, to see what information was available relating to the operation of canal trade in the Newbury area.

A couple of locals asked us where we had moored our boat, when we pointed it out to them, on the far side, we were advised that groups of young people roamed the park after dark and one of their less endearing habits was, cutting or loosening the mooring lines on boats tied up there. Not only would this be irritating, it could also prove to be dangerous as some 150 yards downstream, was the first weir for the Greenham Lock.

They recommended that we negotiate the next lock and swing bridge, then find a mooring along the area knows as West Mill. Here, it seemed, boats were relatively secure.

We had soon obeyed these suggestions and were safely tied up on the moorings at West Mill.

The town offered a full range of amenities and Jean was able to ease her distress in the way beloved of women over the years. She treated herself to a "no expense spared" hair-do!

That and two or three days, just relaxing, worked wonders, although I was painfully aware how little it would take to reawaken the negative vibes.

Attending a Coffee Morning and Bring and Buy sale at the local Anglican Church, we met with a number of people who further restored our equilibrium.

The next stop was Hungerford, the scene of the horrific shootings where a local man had killed a number of town folk. With memories of the "massacre" likely to be fresh in peoples minds, we were not sure what the general feeling would be. The tragedy of the shootings could well have traumatised the towns-folk and it was difficult to assess how groups of people had reacted to such a major event happening within their community. Granted time had passed since its occurrence but how fresh would the memories be.

At that time of the year, the tourist traffic was heavy, and everywhere, including the canal, was crowded.

Some of the local shops had created a ritual of leaving, unsold, stale bread and cakes etc. out to be collected by families wishing to feed the crazy mix-up of ducks, swans, geese, coots, moorhens and terns, that gathered daily at the road bridge and clamoured for food.

The level of inter-breeding was staggering. We were amazed to see just how many Muscovy crosses of various kinds we observed.

Apart from a discrete memorial in the Church, little evidence of the tragedy remained and it was heartening to see how communities coped, with even the most devastating events.

One of the common denominators we found in towns dependent on tourism for much of their prosperity, was the proliferation of antique shops.

Although much more noticeable in the south, it was by no means confined to these areas. Many of the towns and villages in the Midlands and the North, showed a similar bias towards antiques to attract tourists.

From Hungerford, the route passed through the Bedwyns then climbed to the summit up the Crofton flight.

The three mile summit pound, had virtually no sustainable water supply and formed the major weakness on the canal. Any failure of the supply here would effectively divide the canal into two halves and sever the through route.

Wilton Water created a catchment area at the bottom of the flight and the Crofton Pumping Station had been built to lift water from that area up to the summit to replace the lockage.

The amount of water that could be drawn from here was strictly limited, and, even when the Crofton pumps are fully operational, was insufficient to maintain the levels in the summit pound. Two other problems, were restrictions on dredging due to lack of finance, a dearth of dredgings and sludge disposal areas, and the small size of Wilton Water with the need to retain a certain level of water there, to protect its flora and fauna.

Many of the canals problems seemed to stem from the failure of conservationists to recognise that, as an artificial waterway it needed maintenance to live, unlike rivers which to a major extent were self cleaning and had sustainable water supplies and often simply needed protection from pollution.

For two hundred years, Mother nature had worked to make canals into a viable wildlife habitat, aided by the dredging, weed cutting and regular maintenance carried out by man. Now this had to all intents and purposes ceased. Nature was busy returning the area to its natural state, fields with no standing water. No boats, no regular maintenance, equals no canal. Tough luck wildlife!

Long stretches of the canal were practically devoid of wildlife, in fact we saw one lone kingfisher and that was on a short length of river that ran parallel with the canal a few feet below. The difference was that the river bank had a few shrubs and small patches of reed, the canal banks were so overgrown with rank weeds, nettles and massive reed beds that nothing could get into or out of the water easily. An object lesson in what happens when complacency is mistaken for conservation.

I have a "thing" about this and I know that my comments will not be taken kindly by many earnest people. I have yet to be convinced that accumulations of stinking ooze, ten foot high reed beds, mats of blanket weed and carpets of duckweed, create a water environment that is conducive to the continued good health of its flora and fauna, or even invertebrate life-forms.

Reaching Great Bedwyn, we decided to stay overnight as it sounded like an interesting village.

In the main street was an outdoor museum of tombstones and monumental sculpture, which also displayed a number of fossils, stone oddities and weirdest accumulation of "objects d'art." It was difficult to imagine what had prompted such a collection, yet in an odd way it was compulsive viewing.

In common with many others, the church was locked against vandalism and theft. The constant need to locate keyholders and the uncomfortable feeling that you are disturbing their right to privacy, took much of the pleasure out of visiting the buildings and seeking out the facets of local history that hide within their walls.

Passage through the Crofton and Wooton Rivers flights was restricted to a few hours per day, but water levels were not too dreadful.

As we made our way across the summit pound and through the Bruce Tunnel, it was easy to see why this stretch of canal was so vulnerable to water shortages. It was in dire need of dredging both to improve its storage capacity and to ease the passage of the wide, deep draughted Hotel boats that regularly plied the summit.

Once through these flights, the canal entered a fifteen mile long, lock free pound, all the way to Devizes and the Caen Hill flight.

Bishops Canning was some three miles short of Devizes so, as we had a few days to spare, we decided to stay at Pewsey and allow our mail to catch up with us.

The couple in charge of the moorings at Pewsey had a reputation for being very strict, but we found that if they were approached pleasantly, they were fine. We pointed out our situation and the need to stay put for a few days while we awaited delivery of our mail, and they kindly found us a long mooring on the hard standing, forrard of the Trip Boat.

Walking to the village along the main road was fraught with danger but the alternative route along the towing path and across the fields was very pleasant. This became our usual route!

In an area with sights dating back to prehistoric times, Pewsey's claim to fame was slightly less ancient. King Alfred of the burnt cakes is commemorated here and his regal presence gazes out over the modern traffic in the form of a large statue.

The museum of Country Life was fascinating and contained a wide range of artifacts and exhibits in an informal setting. In addition to these displays we were privileged to see an ancient craft still being practised. A thatcher was renewing the roof of a large house using traditional materials and tools.

Calling at the post office, we arranged for our mail to be held for us, then contacted Joan, my sister, by telephone and fixed up with her to dispatch our post A.S.A.P.

Near the end of the wharf, the stonework tapered outwards towards the bridge 'ole. To stop boats colliding with this and guide their bows towards the bridge, a large post and fender structure had been built in the water. On this frame, at water level, a moorhen was sitting on a late clutch of eggs. Overlooked by boaters, children, fishermen and tourists, she sat calmly on the nest, day after day, while her hubby foraged for food.

The behaviour of wildlife never failed to enthral!

Several days went past, still the mail had not arrived. I was concerned as I knew that it had been sent. On the evening of the fourth day, we heard a rap on the side of the boat. Looking out, we were surprised to see the lady from the Post Office standing on the towing path. With profuse apologies she handed over our missing mail. It had been in the office two days but had got slipped behind the franking machine and had been overlooked.

While here we had another rather startling encounter!

The Kennet and Avon Trust had opened a small tea-room and gift shop at the wharf. One afternoon and we had taken advantage of this to have some light refreshments. In conversation with an elderly lady member, we were expressing our concerns about the lack of maintenance.

"If B.W. would grant the canal "cruiseway" status and spend some more money on it we might get somewhere" she exclaimed.

We pointed out that cruiseway status depended to a large extent on the amount of regular boat traffic, of all sizes, carried by the waterway.

She told us in no uncertain terms, that the last thing that she wanted to see on "her" canal was lots of noisy boats, especially large ones like "Athene".

Happy to welcome hikers, fishermen, cyclists, canoeists and at a pinch, small G.R.P. cruisers, she was adamant that large steel boats should be discouraged at all costs. They took up too much space, needed deeper water and were always complaining about reeds and lack of mooring.

Having the temerity to point out that the canal was built for barges, even larger boats than ours, and that if it were not for them, the canal would not exist, did not win us any sympathy or change her opinion.

We left well alone!!

Once our mail had arrived, we set off for Bishops Canning and the Canalfest, with a large white horse, apparently from the Iron age, gazing down on us from the hillside. Our trusty guidebook corrected the impression and gave the information that the figure carved into the chalk hill-side, dated back no further than 1812 and was simply a copy of a horse from another vale.

As we passed the wharf at Honeystreet, we made a note to return to this location and visit the local churches and the pseudo "Iron-Age White Horse." In the oblique, morning light, it was obvious that the hillsides were striped with the remains of mediéval hill farms with their distinctive patterns of field ridges.

By now the grain harvest was just starting to ripen, the waving green acres were lightening and taking on a sheen of gold.

This was the heart of "crop circle country" and we were awaiting news of their appearance with interest. We had seen many curious sights in our travels around the English landscape but we had yet to have a "close encounter." Perhaps the extra terrestrials responsible for the circles would pay us a visit and end our contact famine!

Arriving at the swing bridge where the rally was to be held, it was a little surprising to note the lack of what we would consider to be, "adequate moorings."

No doubt the organisers had things in hand!

Since leaving Honeystreet, the water had become increasingly thickly carpeted with duck-weed, now it resembled nothing more than a grassy lane. We negotiated the bridge and found that, in spite of everything, the water depth was reasonable and we moored close to the rather steep, rough bank. A long gangplank was needed but we were well equipped.

After spending the first evening in splendid isolation, we were visited next morning by Sam Weller, the man responsible for arrangements.

It says much for his persuasiveness that during our conversation, I volunteered our services in any way that would be useful, as part of our contribution to the success of the event, us being outsiders!

My offer was accepted with alacrity, in no time I found myself designated "Harbourmaster" complete with a list of entrant boats and a pile of berthing markers.

My job initially, would be to pace out the banks and allocate berths according to boat lengths and types.

Quite a few cruisers were attending and it was possible to locate them into gaps between trees and shrubs that would not accommodate a long, narrowboat.

I was a little nonplussed at being offered this responsibility, especially as it involves being in charge of an area of organisation that can create controversy. Club members often feel a proprietorial sense about the allocation of positions at Rallies.

I had Sam's reassurance that my authority as Harbourmaster would be respected, in spite of the fact that I was not a local boater, in fact, he thought that my filling the role would be generally appreciated rather than denigrated.

Conscientiously, I paced out both banks, carefully allocated spaces according to the details provided, drew up a large scale plan showing the overall pattern, complete with boat names and berth numbers, then sat back and waited for my customers to turn up.

Jean, apparently gained much amusement from watching me go about my task and was convinced that my persona had changed to accommodate the perceived responsibilities of the role!

Getting newspapers etc. was no problem. The village was quite a walk from the canal but most of this was along the field drive which gave access to the site and the caravan park on the off bank.

Tent and marquee erection was in the hands of the RAF., courtesy of a club member who held a senior position and rank at a nearby Airforce base.

I had contacted Betty, the lady who had worked for me for seventeen years in South Devon, in my days with the Education Department. She had been a perfect secretary, keeping me on the straight and narrow, the diary up to date, all letters, memos and minutes of meetings, correctly spelt and in good English. She lived in Newton Abbot but her son had agreed to drive her up to visit us. The cancer that she had fought against for most of the time I had known her, was taking a serious toll on her health and driving was now beyond her ability. Having never been able to show her the boat, we were both looking forward to the opportunity of putting right this omission.

As Sam had indicated, I was treated with a measure of respect by the boaters and the few disputes that arose were quickly and amicably settled.

A further contribution to the event, made by us, was to offer "Athene" as an "open boat" for visitors. A prominently displayed bowl for contributions towards the funds made this a very practical offer.

The weekend was great fun, we were visited by lots of people whose contributions to the funds exceeded £42; Betty and Duncan arrived, and although I was shocked by her evident frailty, it was good to see that she had retained her mischievous sense of humour; Stuart and Shirley, our elder son and his wife, drove up from Copplestone and spent the weekend with us, then, to place the final cherry on the icing, we were awarded the trophies for Best Traditionally Dressed Boatman and Woman. All in all we had a fabulous time and were impressed by the kindness and friendliness of those involved, both in the Rally itself and those responsible for the arrangements.

After assisting in "Operation Big Clean-up", we moved on down to Devizes to check out the Caen Hill Flight bookings etc. It was disappointing to be told that, although passage towards Bath and Bristol was no problem, B.W. could not offer any guarantees that the flight would still be open for passage on our return. Water supplies were critical and if the weather remained warm and dry, locks could be faced with temporary closure.

Reluctantly we agreed that this was as far as we could go on this trip. Perhaps in a few years time, sufficient work would have been carried out on the navigation to make the return trip viable. That cruise could then include Bath and Bristol.

Footnote.
The K&A is a superb canal with enormous potential. It scores well for natural beauty and for archaeological interest, runs through areas of great historical significance and offers the boater a wonderful cross section of the English countryside.

Unfortunately the positive factors are cancelled out at a rate of 2 to 1, by negative factors relating to the navigation.

Our disappointment at having to curtail our current cruise at Devizes was tinged with a measure of relief that we would not have to continue to face the horrors wrought by poor maintenance. (Although we were led to believe that conditions improved between Devizes and Bath!)

For a big boat with a relatively deep draught, it had not proved to be an enjoyable experience.

We were deeply saddened by this!!

7.
Devizes to Thames

With ample time at our disposal, we gave some thought to exploring the area and consequently fixed ourselves up with moorings for a few days, near to the theatre on the wharf. The Caen Hill Flight was still in operation and every few days boats would congregate ready for the openings. In spite of this we managed to secure a place.

Our first excursion was made on foot. The six locks from lock 50 were not covered by the restrictions so we walked down to the B.W. office at lock 44 from where the boats began the controlled passage. The first sight of the flight was impressive and with the exception of the carpets of duckweed coating the water, everything seemed to be in good order. We visited the B.W. office, but they were only able to confirm their initial comments on the possibility of temporary closure being implemented at some point in the future.

The town itself abounded with buildings that carried the Heritage plaques, indicating their historical significance and the reasons for their preservation.

Among the places of interest was a small museum which was well worth a visit.

A convenient Launderette enabled us to clear our backlog of soiled clothing etc., much to Jean's relief.

Henry, our mascot, a large plastic model of a European Eagle Owl, was showing signs of wear and tear, so, before the deterioration was too evident we repaired to the local pet shop and bought a replacement. At the same time we took a chance by providing him with an attractive model of a Little Owl, as a mate.

She became, Henrietta!

Our lavatory bowl suddenly came loose and began to leak slightly. On stripping it down I found that during its last service the old seals had been refitted rather than replaced. They had collapsed!

There was a Chandlery in the complex of shops next to the wharf, so I thought it would be simple to replace the broken seals. With the emphasis locally, on small boats which did not use pump out loos, spares were just not available. Fortunately the owner of the trip boat plying from the quay had a full set of spares on board and he sold me what I needed. It was not a pleasant job, with a half-full holding tank and hot weather, but it was quickly completed.

At the terminus, we obtained copies of the local bus time-tables. To our great joy, we discovered that Avebury was just a short ride away.

A prehistoric site of great power, it was built astride a major Ley-Line junction and had been a place of worship for many centuries.

Even when swarming with tourists, it is possible to feel the calm and tranquillity generated by the aura possessed by such locations. We had experienced this on Dartmoor when walking along stone rows.

During our visit to Avebury, we felt the latent power that pulsed through the stones. These were not the carved monoliths to be found scant miles away at Stonehenge on Salisbury Plain. They were simply large rocks, erected on carefully plotted locations, and because of this, trembling with energy.

To anyone in the correct, contemplative mood, a visit here could be as spiritually uplifting as a visit to a venerated church.

As we returned to the boat we saw the first of the designs impressed on the fields of ripening grain. This one could not be credited to aliens, except perhaps in the sense that some people choose to alienate themselves from normal society, it had a significance, lost in the so-called mysteries of the crop circles. This was much more mundane, yet in its own way even more revealing.

A single word, tramped into the waving corn in ten foot high letters, "VANDALISM."

An inadequate description of the wanton act that had destroyed so much valuable seed?

Devizes Castle was no longer open to the public and the church was another on the long list of those kept locked to deter intruders. We did in fact find it open at another visit and enjoyed its atmosphere and sense of peace.

The town had made much of its canal heritage and the wharf, with its small museum, was a regular spot for tourists and townsfolk alike to visit. The trip and restaurant boats plying for custom, added to the level of interest.

After one shopping expedition, we arrived back at "Athene" to find that we had another boat breasting up alongside. It was

"Maelstrom" with Jeff and Maureen not forgetting Ben. She was sixty-two feet long, and as they were tying up to await the next opening of the flight, they had moored alongside to conserve space.

Ben was overjoyed to see us again, and, as we opened our forward doors, he leapt aboard, wagging his tail, before disappearing into our cabin for a good sniff around.

He became a regular visitor over the next few days!

With lots of gossip to catch up on, we shared each others company and swapped visits for coffee and cake.

Having pencilled in a number of short stays into our return itinerary we said farewell to Devizes and pointed "Athene's" bows towards Honeystreet.

The "Barge Inn" offered lunchtime and evening meals and as we intended to do a lot of walking in the area, it suited us well and meant that we would have an excuse not to cook.

Mooring was not easy but we managed to tie up reasonably close to the pub, with no need for anything more than our short gangplank.

Two local communities had churches which we wanted to visit. Alton Barnes was a small village, much of which was huddled round its tiny Anglo-Saxon church. Alton Priors had a much more imposing church but was in reality nothing more than a scattered hamlet.

We found both buildings open and, although it was apparently much restored, the tiny church at Barnes with its plain, lime-washed walls and box pews certainly gave the feeling of continuity of worship over the years. The curving pathway leading to the Priors church was like a time tunnel between two ages, so different were the two buildings.

Both proved to be havens of calm in an area which was beginning to swarm with visitors from all over the world, here to view the burgeoning harvest of corn circles.

In order to defray the losses from the damage caused by the circles and the visitors, local farmers were charging what seemed to us to be extortionate, viewing fees. However the foreign visitors we spoke to, seemed quite impressed and forked out the fees cheerfully.

Not wishing to pay the charges ourselves, we walked on through the area and followed the pathway, over the shoulder of the hill, towards the White Horse.

We ruminated on the strange twist of fate that had given this area an ongoing propensity towards creating its own landmarks.

Within a very short time of the first crop circles appearance, the plague had reached epidemic proportions in this area.

Over the previous two hundred odd years, Georgian and Victorian copies of the Iron age fertility symbols marking significant sites, had proliferated and now adorned many of the vales, reducing the validity of the original works.

Having climbed to a vantage point, we were about to take photographs of the amazing collection of circles laid out across the valley, when a group of Americans came up to us. It turned out that they were a family and had made a special trip to England, in order to spend two weeks, walking the harvest fields of Wiltshire and Oxfordshire, visiting circle sites.

Obviously fascinated, they were taking their self imposed pilgrimage very seriously. They talked at great length about sightings, describing the shapes and groupings in minute detail.

In spite of their obvious enthusiasm and the talk of extra-terrestrial activity etc., we felt that the parents viewed the phenomena with a measure of healthy scepticism about the origins of the beings responsible. Their suspicions inclining towards large, reasonably local, seats of learning, whose alumni happened to be at a loose end, just at the time when the fields of grain were beginning to ripen.

On the other hand, their children were much more inclined to go with the theory of alien visitation.

After all, it was much more exciting!

Carrying on upwards, towards the Horse, we found ourselves in chalk grasslands that swarmed with a proliferation of insect and plant life. Fritillaries, Blues and the rainbow hues of many other types of butterfly, filled the air as they fluttered round the fragrant grasses and meadow flowers.

Finishing our climb, we neared the large carving. There was a feeling of size and space but no buzz, no thrill of power that was evident at other sites of antiquity. This was just a rather crude display, seeking attention.

While we had been in Devizes, we had taken a bus to Melksham. This was a town that Jean remembered as home of the RAF. base on which she had completed her basic training.

The area had many links with the Air forces, particularly through the network of Fighter and Bomber Squadrons that flew from here during the Second World War.

At Honeystreet we were to be reminded of these connections. During a conversation in the pub, I was offered an intriguing explanation for the heavy growths of duckweed on the canal.

Local intelligence held that, during the early days of the war, RAF. chiefs were concerned that, on moonlit nights, the rivers and canals would reflect the light and become pointers which could be used, by the enemy, as navigational aids.

This was not a new idea to me as my reading of countless books about the exploits of our pilots over the Continent had outlined the use of waterways and railway lines as aids many times.

What was different was the suggestion that, American Air Force chiefs had introduced a particularly fast growing waterweed or duckweed, native to America, into our waterways to provide cover and prevent the water showing reflections. This weed was supposed to have been released all over Southern England.

I haven't been able to confirm or deny this information, but it does sound feasible.

There is certainly nothing new about species imported to tackle one problem, taking over and producing a whole new range of difficulties, not least for the native flora and fauna who often have scant protection in their established food-chains and environment.

The pub buildings had evolved through a number of incarnations and had emerged as a very popular canalside hostelry, catering for a wide clientele and offering a large selection of well prepared foods and a range of beers, wines and spirits.

Before leaving the area we needed to call at Honeystreet Wharf to take on fresh water, diesel and to get our toilet holding tank pumped out, before we had to resort to issuing the green wellies.

On the final morning, an early start saw us reach the Wooton Rivers Locks in time for that day's passage over the summit.

Just prior to reaching Pewsey, we were amused to be presented with yet another example of the power of local landowners over the engineers who had planned and built the canals.

The route was scheduled to pass through an area of land owned by Lady Susannah Wroughton. She raised objections to this and was eventually placated by a gift of £500, the building of an elaborate bridge, to be named for her and the landscaping of an area of marshland now known as Wide-water. It has been suggested that the bridge was designed by the notable architect, Rennie, who was responsible for the building of London Bridge.

While the canal was in regular use and carefully maintained, this area was a haven for wildlife. Now, even though the canal has regular traffic, lack of care was allowing the area to revert to its original state. The bridge was showing signs of wear and tear but it was still possible to catch glimpses of it's former glory.

Lack of water in the summit pound was beginning to affect passage times and the Bruce Tunnel, under the Savernake Forest, was causing problems, particularly for wide boats.

We completed the crossing with little difficulty and tied up for the night on the public moorings below the Crofton Pumphouse. From here we could visit places of interest locally.

A shortcoming affecting the Pumphouse was the height of it's chimney. Originally much taller, it had been severely reduced in height and now did not produce enough draw on the fires to keep the boilers in steam for extended periods of time.

The canal now had begun its descent towards its meeting with the Thames at Reading. From here it would converge on the River Kennet at regular intervals.

Having enjoyed our first visit, we intended to stay for a few days at Hungerford. We re-acquainted ourselves with the towns large antiques arcades in the main street, but now we held on to our purse strings.

It proved to be a restful two days without any undue exertions, although Jean was now beginning to hunt for material to be used for patches on her latest quilt. This one was designed around a central panel containing an owl, perched on a pentacle surrounded by a gold circle. This was a design we had created for our own logo.

After making another early start, we arrived in Newbury just as the moorings were starting to clear.

Perfect timing!

There was so much left to see in this area that we moored up on the West Mills, for six days.

A short narrowboat, "Maid of Steel", accompanied by a white cruiser tied up behind us. The cruiser belonged to our friend Suzi. In no time her old dachshund, Hemmingway and her grand children, who were crewing for her, joined us on the bank. They had braved the Severn Estuary from Sharpness down to Avonmouth. From there they had entered Bristol Docks, sailed up the Avon to Bath and then completed the Kennet and Avon as far as our meeting at Newbury.

Formidable!

Suzi was a great character and a tireless worker for various canal charities. We had met her on our first outing on the B.C.N. playing her Hurdy-Gurdy at a small Rally at the Walsall Road Aqueduct near Stone Cross on the Tame Valley Canal. Not the most salubrious of venues but Suzi's presence put a smile on many faces particularly those of the children. It was grand to meet up with her once more.

Newbury had been the scene of two battles during the English Civil War. The first, a bloody conflict which ended in the rout of the Royalist forces is remembered through the naming of two locks to the west of the town. Higgs and Guyers Locks are named for two of Cromwell's most able Generals, who were involved in the confrontation. The second battle took place twelve months later. This was an inconclusive affair which involved the Royalists being driven out of Donnington Castle, which they had occupied; retreating to Oxford; returning a week later and re-taking the stronghold.

We made the long, hot walk along a main road, out to the remains of the Castle. They were still quite impressive, dominated by the twin turrets of the ruined gatehouse were substantial, grass covered earthworks defining the area of the original fortifications. After its

There she hung, swinging gently...

"Eyes of Osiris", mounted on her bows

Pooley Hall, Polesworth near to where we moor

Our craft were securely breasted

...to chat and exchange gossip

Loading the boats in Mapledurham Lock

Punk Mallard at Newbury

The level of interbreeding was staggering

Another boat had breasted up to us

...then went outside to record the event on camera

A memorable meeting with "Sarnie" in Triggs Lock.

Carthagena Lock: One of the most colourful and attractive locks.

eventual destruction, the ruins became a source of stone for the locals to use in building or repairing their farms.

Having studied the model of the battle in the town Museum, it was fascinating to attempt to superimpose the model onto the surrounding landscape.

The Museum was housed in an extremely old building that had once been a cloth weaving mill and which had a fleece storage area built onto the end. The exhibits were well presented and recalled the long history of the town. On display were artifacts from many ages including Prehistoric times. Laid out in dedicated rooms, the displays gave a clear, concise picture of the story they portrayed. We were pleased to see the effort the town had put into preserving and interpreting its heritage.

Another plus was, that irrespective of the weather, it was possible to go for a refreshing swim in the large indoor swimming pool at the West Mill Sports and Leisure Complex.

Walking around the town, we had a clear impression that, judging from the large number of imposing buildings still remaining, Newbury had once been very important and wealthy.

In spite of the dire warnings we had been given about the perils attached to mooring too close to the centre of town, these evidently did not include West Mills. Here we felt perfectly safe and did not experience any trouble or meet with anyone who had. The canalside walk was a very convenient promenade for the locals and we spent many happy hours chatting to the young children walking along with their parents. Henry and his new bride, Henrietta were on display and proved to be a popular attraction.

We loved it!

Among the few remaining places between here and Reading which promised good moorings, Aldermaston Wharf seemed to be favourite. Suzi and her friends were intending to stay there for a few days in order to facilitate a change of crews. We would just overnight there and press on.

The lift bridge at Aldermaston, although on a heavily trafficked road, was motorised and traffic-light controlled. It would be no problem but we were getting close to the area of badly cared for swing bridges that had proved to be Jean's bete noir on our outward trip.

She was beginning to get twitchy!

On the Wharf itself was a tiny tea-room and Information Centre run by the K&A Trust where it was possible to buy gifts and souvenirs. The hire-boat company based here had a small, well stocked chandlery which was geared up to narrowboats as well as cruisers.

There was ample time left before the Rally on the Basingstoke Canal but as we were going to get another fifteen day Thames licence we intended to get full use of it without any time restraints.

Next day we moved carefully through the gauntlet of difficult swing bridges and early afternoon saw us tied up at Theale.

This bridge was best tackled in the cold light of an early morning, preferably before too much traffic was on the move.

Although the walk into Theale was not particularly pleasant being along heavily trafficked roads, some sans footpaths, the village itself was nice, quiet with a good range of shops, pubs and cafes.

We cleared the moorings just after seven am. but already the bridge was carrying a reasonable amount of vehicles. Jean closed the barriers and braced herself for the tirade of abuse; it died, stillborn! The fourth car to arrive in the queue was a brightly marked Police car.

Peace reigned!

The operation of the bridge was completed quickly and smoothly. In no time the traffic was moving again and as the Police car crossed the bridge, Jean received a cheery salute and a knowing wink from two amused policemen.

Sighs of relief all round !

The morning was very misty and the banks of the canal were softened by the covering, like a damp, grey blanket. As we approached the lock and began to near the bank; looking for the lock moorings, we saw the loom of a moored boat beginning to emerge, ghostlike, in the cold light. As she took form and substance we recognised the unmistakeable lines of a small, Vee-bottomed, Springer Narrow Boat.

Imagine our surprise as we drew level with her bows, to read the name, "Athene", printed there in large letters.

This was our first sighting of a boat bearing the same name as ours, that was actually being used for cruising.

As we moved slowly past, the curtains twitched and a pair of excited faces appeared, gave us beaming smiles, a big wave and the thumbs up signs.

At that moment, we hadn't really got time to do more than return the greetings.

On reaching Reading we took a chance and moored the boat at Bear Free Wharf. A group of wino's were sitting on a bench a few feet from the boat in a companionable, alcoholic haze. They warned us that after dark the area tended to be frequented by young people who had sometimes ransacked or damaged unoccupied boats, presumably looking for cash to spend on drink or drugs. However they assured us that, during daylight hours, while they were there, no problems would occur.

We chatted to them for a while, took our leave, locked the boat, set the alarm and walked into the town to do our shopping.

True to their word, the wino's were still there when we returned, the boat was undisturbed and everything was safe and intact.

This was midweek and in our experience problems were less likely to manifest themselves, so we agreed to overnight on these moorings. We stayed up late with our music tapes playing to show that the boat was occupied. We did not see or hear anything untoward and next morning set off safely and happily.

Fate had kept one shot in her locker as a parting gift. The drive belt on the Dyno-start of our Geko generator snapped and left us without mains power. I would have to contact Paul in Tavistock for a replacement. Another lesson had been learned, always carry ample spares. Sod's Law always ensures that if a part is going to fail, it will always be at the most inconvenient time, at night or in the middle of nowhere.

Not happy to remain in Reading to await collection we decided to ring from our first scheduled stop on the river Thames, Sonning. Here we could arrange delivery and collection.

We cleared Blakes Lock, passed down between the overshadowing Gasholders and emerged onto the broad, steady flow of the Thames.

Never was a sight more welcome!

8.
River Thames again.

With deep water under our keel and a wide waterway, we were able to open up "Athene's" engine and for the first time in weeks, feel the surge of power and the thrill of unfettered passage. Even though we still had to watch our wake it was good to see the rev. counter showing twenty-one hundred R.P.M. and sense the engine running smoothly, unstrained by shallow water drag.

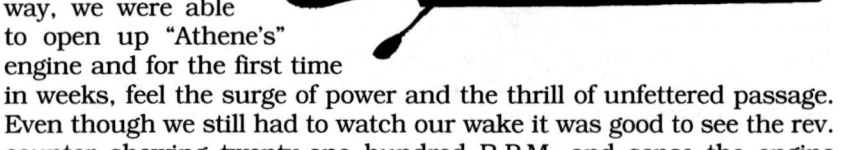

The run down to Sonning was relatively short, there we would be required to buy our second fifteen day licence from the Lock-Keeper.

Henry and Henrietta were safely ensconced in their usual places, now they were each replete with breakfast. In Reading I had sought out a Pet Shop and bought two, furry, toy, white mice. A slit was cut into the bird's bills and a mouse, suspended by the tail from each one. With the movement of the boat and the slight slipstream created by our progress, each owl was rocking gently on its slightly uneven base. The mice, were twitching in the breeze.

A man, riding his bicycle along the path beside the river, caught sight of the slight movement and, fascinated, continued to gaze at Henry until he rode off the pathway onto the rough grass, very nearly finishing up in the water.

It was amusing, especially as it ended without major incident, but the effect was not one that we wished to promote on a regular basis.

We left the owls in position but kept a careful watch for observers, to reassure them that these were indeed, models!

When we were moored up, folk tended to comment and we developed a rationalÈ, that our two companions belonged to U.B.P.G.O., "The Union of Birds of Prey and Guard Owls." This body placed a responsibility on owners to ensure that each one had a meal after each period of duty. Not a particularly onerous task one could say.

The questioners usually seemed amused by the notion!

License bought, we tied up for the night on the free mooring below Sonning Road Bridge.

Our phone call to Paul, produced an unexpected result. It turned out that his brother-in-law lived in Reading and could take delivery of the parcel, then, bring it directly to the boat.

Magic!

We were moored some twenty feet from a substantial sized, flying bridge cruiser, which contained a large stateroom and a number of cabins. As we walked past, we read her name, "Paranormal"; what an odd name for a boat!

All was made clear when we discovered that, inadvertently, we had tied up close to Yuri Geller's house and, of course, his boat!

As we neared London, it became more and more usual to find ourselves in the vicinity of property owned by well known personalities. Not that they were often evident and we certainly had no intention of disturbing anyone's privacy by "rubber-necking".

After receiving the belt, restoring the generator to full working order and, on Paul's recommendation, replacing the water pump impeller, we continued our cruise. A further injunction was, that the Dyno-start brushes should be checked out and the unit serviced. This was a one thousand hour check and was due. He gave us the telephone number of a Geko agent in Weybridge.

It was forty-four miles to Shepperton and the junction of the Rivers Wey and Thames. This gave us a leisurely ten days to enjoy the river and some of its many sights.

First stop, Henley, home of the Royal Regatta!

The sensation of sweeping beneath the wide arches of the magnificent road bridge, with it's carvings of masks of Thames and Isis, then emerging into the broad reach of the Regatta course was stunning. The visitor moorings were on the right-hand side, along the many acres of neatly trimmed grass that host the water borne events.

Some kind of event had recently taken place and the grass was still divided into display areas by tapes, while here and there marquees stood in various stages of dismantling. Fortunately the moorings were only half full and we soon found room for "Athene" to tie up.

Water levels were more than adequate but the clarity of it meant that the bottom was clearly visible. Sitting on the bows, I glanced into the depths, looking, if truth be known, for fish. My eye was immediately caught by the glint of silver. There lying on the gravel, in full view, was a Kings Pattern dessert spoon. Grabbing the small fishing net that we kept handy, I fished it out.

Disappointment!, it was only stainless steel, not silver as I had hoped, this of course being Royal Henley! It did however make an interesting memento of our visit and being quite common, it did not seem to amount to being an indictable offence, to keep it.

In common with many boats, we carried, as an essential piece of equipment, a "Sea-Search" magnet attached to a long cord. Search and recovery of lost ferrous objects like spanners, screwdrivers and winch handles, was greatly expedited.

It does not however work on, Brass, Aluminium or Stainless Steel. Nor incidentally, on Gold or Silver!

We secured the boat and walked along the moorings towards the bridge and the famous Leander Club Boathouse. Crossing into town we found ourselves engulfed in crowds of tourists and assailed by the babble of a dozen languages.

In spite of the towns historic roots and the splendid Edwardian buildings in the main street, we found it strangely unsatisfying. Perhaps it was that we did not react well to jostling people, but, whatever, next morning we were happy to untie our boat and head off, downstream.

For some people, Henley seemed to have become little more than a rather up market venue for a selection of superior boat rallies.

Perhaps they are right!

Gradually the river was becoming converted into a mere adjunct to the buildings on its banks.

Temple island was a perfect example. This small area of woodland, elongated by the steady flow of water all round it, had been "enhanced" by the placing, on its upstream point, of a small, classic temple, for no other reason than to improve the vista for the occupants of Fawley Court, whose beautifully manicured grounds swept down to the river on the west bank.

Over and over again, we were to see examples of mans desire to improve on nature by "enhancing" views.

The Victorians were great builders of follies, architectural gems which often belied the reasons for their very existence. For all their grandiose creations, the Victorians also left a wonderful inheritance in the most mundane of places. In the Midlands and the North of England, we had seen many examples of their work, in the mills that line the canals. Built purely for commercial purposes, they often received the same attention to detail. Four-square and massive, often masking the most appalling conditions, the buildings were still softened by the addition of decorated windows, cornices and lintels. The chimneys alone, were works of art.

From the earliest days of the industrial revolution, the "nouveau riche", riding on the wave of prosperity it generated, went over the top with some of the lavish building projects undertaken to immortalise their names.

Castles, Chateaux, Pyramids, Temples, Pagodas, Tombs and Mausoleums; Greek, Italianate, Roman, Aztec, Egyptian, Indian, Chinese and Japanese all the styles were copied and artifacts looted, then served up as Country estates, in reality, monuments to an extravaganza of dubious taste.

Now, they are mellowed by time, cradled in our native woodland, protected by sweeping gardens and venerated by age and usage. They have become integral with the landscape of the river and as much part of it as the beech woods and the water meadows.

Six miles and one lock, Hambledon, would see us safely to our next destination, Hurley.

This length of the river was flanked by isolated farmsteads and large houses, standing back from the water's edge, to take advantage of the vistas presented.

Among the buildings in this area was one whose name reverberates with notoriety, St.Mary's Abbey. Once the property of Sir Francis Dashwood, it was to become home to his infamous, Hell Fire Club!

Restored to respectability, this lovely group of buildings is also known as Medmenham Abbey after the small village that lies to the north-west.

Apart from the remains of a Benedictine Priory, Hurley had little to offer save peace and quiet, a commodity sought for eagerly after the hurly burley of Henley. We spent the night here and next day set off for Cookham.

Casting off, we soon arrived at Hurley Lock. From here, just a short reach brought us to Temple lock.

Below this was Bisham Abbey, now the home of the National Sports Centre. The water here was crowded with Canoes, skiffs and dinghies, darting in all directions like water boatmen, the insects that play on the surface of ponds in the sunshine. They made passage through the area, fraught with danger. The young people were enjoying themselves but seemingly oblivious to the large steel reef slipping steadily through their playground, threatening them with disaster.

At Marlow, we were able to gaze up the steep, wooded hillside. These were the beech trees of Quarry Wood and the properties amid their shade, were part of Cookham Dene. Most of this area is controlled by the National Trust and one of its famous visitors was Kenneth Graham, author of "Wind in the Willows". He lived here for a number of years and it is possible that Quarry Wood, was his inspiration for the Wild Wood.

With Bourne End behind us we arrived at our overnight stopping point, Cookham.

There were adequate moorings available but now we had reached an area where free moorings were increasingly difficult to find and most sites were charged at figures around three pounds per night.

Quite a change from our canal experience!

The village contained both the home and the final resting place of the noted artist, Sir Stanley Spencer. In spite of this claim to fame, the area had still retained an air of tranquillity and the church was well worth a visit.

Passing under Cookham road bridge at the start of the following day's cruising, we found ourselves faced by a maze of channels where the river described a long loop through Hedsor and past Hedsor Wharf, once an important shipping point. A long canal cut, well marked, led us safely through the clutter of weirs and dead ends.

Between here and Windsor we had noted the existence of service areas and Bray Marina seemed to offer the best opportunity of picking up red diesel at a reasonable price. We would stop there and collect fuel.

Leaving Cookham Lock, we found ourselves once more overshadowed, this time on the left. Steep hillsides covered with beech trees, darkened our vision. Among the foliage, classic, architecture and statuary, began to peep through the leaves, pinpointing the position of Cliveden, once the family home of the Astors but more recently notorious for the antics of the Mitford girls and venue for a whole series of political scandals.

Cliveden Deep a broad, straight reach ended in a jumble of islands. The right of navigation was well defined.

From here, Maidstone begins to make its presence felt on the left bank and the river itself was strewn with islands of all sizes.

Once past the two locks at Boulter and Bray, we cruised between Monkey Island and Dorney Reach on the approach to the Marina.

It's entrance was tucked away down the non-navigable reach that disappeared behind Queen's Eyot. We were only taking on water and fuel so we winded our boat and headed for the wharf, to make the approach into the current, accepted practice on a river where there is a strong flow of water but fortunately not required on the canal system. After taking on fuel we began the search for our overnight mooring.

Wonder of wonders, just as we entered the sweeping left hand curve at the tail of Queen's Eyot, we saw a section of bank with the remains of a concrete wharf. No signs prohibiting mooring, no demands for fees and some evidence that this was regularly in use by boaters. Making a steady, careful run along the bank we found that the water depth was also adequate.

Peaceful, quiet and FREE!

Seated at the table in our cabin, tucking into our evening meal, we were intrigued by the noise and movement in the treetops on the island. Numerous large birds were creating a considerable racket. Gradually it dawned on us that these were not the usual, fairly drab colours of our native species, these birds were bright green.

The binoculars showed us a colony of green parrots or possibly parakeets, who had set up a roost in the wood and were obviously thriving. They were likely to be escapees from a private aviary nearby, maybe even situated on the Eyot itself.

After we had eaten, we took a stroll towards Dorney Reach. Falling in with a local man, out exercising his dog, we were soon involved in a conversation about our lifestyle, which clearly interested him. When I asked about the location of the nearest newsagents, the answer was that it was not within easy walking range. As his dog required a long walk each morning and evening, he offered to collect a Sunday newspaper and deliver it to the boat.

We thanked him profusely and placed our order.

As we continued our conversation, our new found friend pointed out, that along this stretch of the river bank there had been a number of confirmed sightings of a famous pair of "short, fat hairy legs" accompanied by two pairs of even shorter, hairier legs.

In spite of our vigilance we did not add a sighting of Mr. Ernie Wise and his scottie, to our Who's Who of the river bank.

Returning to the boat along hedgerows laden with blackberries, we resolved that, weather permitting, I would spend the following morning, picking fruit for home-made jam and a large blackberry and apple pie to compliment our Sunday roast.

Next morning, true to his word, our friend delivered the newspaper and, in the warmth of a sunny day, I collected blackberries so that Jean could practice her not inconsiderable culinary skills.

On Monday we completed the short run into Windsor and admired the imposing skyline created by the castle as we cruised past Eton.

Leaving Romney lock, we rounded the long bend, passed under the large railway bridge and became guests of Her Majesty, by mooring up alongside the meadows of Home Park, part of the grounds of Windsor Castle.

Our intention was simply to overnight here but, as it was scarcely eleven am. we had lots of time to explore the town. Jean had been in digs in Alma Street and had memories of courting on Eton Wick common then drinking in the local pubs, The Grapes and The Ship.

My only previous visit to the town had been on a school day trip from the Midlands. Neither of us had sufficient memories to create a sense of déja vu.

With the weather staying fine and our mooring, quiet and isolated, we decided to eat "alfresco" and to that end collected the makings of a substantial Bar-B-Que. I had a number of instant B.B.Q. packs on the boat and it would be possible to indulge ourselves, without creating any mess or doing damage to the countryside.

Heading for Runnymede next day, we passed beneath Victoria Bridge and from hereon, although the river bank was beautifully edged, mooring was prohibited. This was a closed area of the Royal Estates. The disused Royal Boathouse, stood in mute testimony to bygone days, giving a poignant glimpse of those yesterdays when Royal Boats plied the river from this very building.

Old Windsor Lock was situated at the head of a long cut, which isolated a large loop of the river from the navigation. The enclosed section of land is now known as, Ham Island.

Odd rumours were reaching us that the Basingstoke Canal had been forced to close due to lack of water. A phone call soon established that the navigation was indeed shut and the Rally organisers confirmed this fact. Assured that our license cheque would be returned to us, we agreed that the best compromise would be to attend, by taking the train from Guildford. This would mean cruising the River Wey and paying the National Trust a fee of forty-five pounds for the privilege.

Tied up safely at Runnymede we were surprised by the large numbers and varieties of water-fowl that were evident. That the local parks and lakes had contributed a number of exotic species was clear from the hybrid ducks which abounded and a number of species of fancy duck that could not be identified via a wild bird spotters's guide. Some we still have not finally identified!

Runnymede was a large area of water meadows, backed by wooded slopes. This area again was entrusted to the care of the N.T. and contained a number of memorials and monuments, including one to that pivotal event which immortalised the area, the signing of the Magna Carta.

Perversely, as a fan of Stanley Holloway, a one time member of an Olde Thyme Music Hall group and a performer of monologues, the over-whelming picture I had in my mind, was the description of the ceremony as it was depicted by that master of the genre, Marriott Edgar;

> *"So they spread Charter out on t'tea table,*
> *And John, signed his name, like a lamb.*
> *His writing in places were sticky and thick,*
> *Through his dipping his pen in the jam.*
>
> *And its through that there Magna Charter,*
> *As was signed by them Barons of old.*
> *That in England today, we can do what we like;*
> *So long as we do what we're told!"*

The final verses of the monologue, The Magna Charter, written by Marriott Edgar and performed by the late, great Stanley Holloway.

Our final stopping off point, prior to reaching Weybridge, was to be Staines, just two miles and one lock below Runnymede.

Moored on the south bank of the river, below the bridge, we left the boat and walked back, crossing over the water. The guide book mentioned the London Stone, situated by Holm Island. An interesting landmark as it indicated the original limit to the jurisdiction of the City of London, over the river.

Sightseeing was not always proving to be simple. Concerns over the safety of the boat's moorings, shortage of time and lack of personal transport while ashore, all mitigated against covering too extensive an area in search for historic and cultural places of interest.

In fact the highlight of our visit to Staines, turned out to be, a visit to the cinema, to see the recently released film, "The Flintstones."

Along this stretch of river we passed a number of enclaves of brightly painted, wooden chalets and bungalows. Built in the Twenties and Thirties, they were originally intended for weekend use. Many of the properties had riverside frontages and next day, as we were heading towards Weybridge, it was amusing to see a number of odd craft moored by some of them.

The most intriguing was a raft, upon which was mounted a Citroen 2CV car. Its drive shaft had been extended and now turned a propeller via a chain drive. I hated to contemplate the problems related to steering the beast should it be got underway.

Although initially built for weekending, it was evident that many of them were now fitted out for much longer periods of occupancy, if not permanent dwelling.

Penton Hook with its massive Marina was built on the Oxbow lake created when the lock cut isolated Penton Hook Island and left the area below the weirs as a back water.

This area offers the nearest moorings to Thorpe Park, possibly the first British Theme Park. Built on an area of flooded gravel pits, the park features our Maritime History.

Once past Pharaohs Island, the complex of weirs and watercourses that mark the confluence of the Wey and Thames navigations came into view. We would need to descend Shepperton lock to enter this section.

Here we would leave the river which we had followed for one hundred and fourteen miles, to explore the much smaller River Wey and its towns, Guildford and Godalming.

Tied up on the wharf, just past the Weybridge Ladies Rowing Club Boathouse, opposite the weirs and the River Police Station, we settled back to take stock of our situation and find out the details of fees, licences and hopeful discounts for long time National Trust members, on a river controlled by the Trust.

9.
What a Wey to go!

The first thing on the agenda at Weybridge, was to contact the agent and arrange to have our generator overhauled. Having arrived there on the weekend that the I.W.A. National Rally was taking place at Waltham Abbey on the River Lee, we discovered that he would be attending and therefore unable to be with us until the following week.

We arranged to meet him, after we had completed our cruise!

As the town boasted a Launderette, we packed our washing into the rucksack and set off to walk to it. After one of the hottest, longest, most tiring walks imaginable, we finally located it and completed our laundry. That particular shop was deleted from our list; we resolved to find out exactly how far away services were sited, before we set out in future, laden down, to walk to them.

River traffic looked like being fairly heavy over the August Bank Holiday weekend, we decided to stay put and settled down to complete a few minor repairs and fit in a few sessions boat tidying.

Notices in the club car-park informed us they were holding a Car Boot Sale there on Sunday morning. It had been some time since my habit had received a fix, by way of a visit to a sale.

Now was the time to end my period of withdrawal.

With a small ferry operating between Weybridge and Shepperton, it was possible to shop in the large chandlery on the far bank and, when the occasion arose, visit the lock-keeper to discuss arrangements for the run down to London.

Picking blackberries at Dorney Reach, had awakened a latent desire within me!

While living in Devon, I had become competent in the art of country fruits, wine making. Now the urge to try out this skill, within the restricted space of a boat, was upon me.

A flash of recall, reminded me of an incident which had taken place, while I was in the country.

Although it seemed amusing at the time, in retrospect it could be construed as cruel, even though no malice was intended. Indeed my respect for the person involved, was of the highest order.

A friend owned a six hundred years old apple press, which he still used to produce fresh juice from the local apple crop, in the time honoured, though fairly crude manner. I usually purchased some to make my own cider at home. That particular year I had taken a whim to prepare an even more ancient brew.

A slightly fermented drink made from honey and called Mead, had been a staple part of the diet of country folk for generations. The addition of fresh apple juice to the honey liquor, before it was fermented, produced Cyser.

The attempt was successful and after an eighteen month maturation period, I was ready to sample the brew.

It was superb, crisp, yet smooth as silk with just a subtle hint of sweetness. It was also potent!

I took a bottle into the office to celebrate both mine and my secretary's birthdays.

My wonderful secretary, Betty, who seldom drank anything more than a small white wine, had celebrated her birthday just nine days previously.

I filled a large whiskey tumbler with Cyser, telling her that it was apple juice and honey water, omitting to mention the fermentation process.

We toasted each others health and Betty downed the drink. For the next few hours she sat at her desk, in complete repose with a dreamy smile on her lips.

Lots of coffee and a large Cornish pasty at lunchtime, saw her back with us and exhibiting no ill effects from her unaccustomed over-indulgence.

Not an incident to be proud of or wish to repeat!

Weybridge had a dearth of brambles within easy walking distance, so the idea of wine making, went onto the back burner.

Though not out of mind!

While shopping in the town, we had been informed by one of the shop-keepers, that this was an excellent area for spotting the famous faces. A regular in his shop, he told us, was Cliff, later to become Sir Cliff Richard.

Neither of us go in for "Celeb spotting", we consider it a gross breech of a person's right to privacy, but along the Thames, so many people pointed out to us, properties belonging to this or that famous body, that the information became part of our subconscious.

Sunday morning, wandering among the stalls at the Boot-Sale, we heard a stall-holder exclaim to a customer,

"You're Sylvia Sims!"

Moments later the lady in question, covered in confusion, disappeared into the crowds, face and hair concealed by a headscarf and a large pair of sunglasses.

If it was Sylvia Sims, that was too high a price to expect an ageing star to pay for her private life.

Early in the week, we threaded our way through the backstreets and arrived eventually at Thames Lock, the only manned one on the River Wey. Here we would eventually be required to buy our license. Enquiries elicited the information that, as N.T. members we were entitled to a ten percent discount. That reduced the cost of the permit to around thirty-four pounds, for seven days, Still, to my mind an extortionate amount.

On Wednesday, faced with Hobson's Choice, we paid our dues and set off to cruise the navigation.

When the Basingstoke Canal was open, boats using only the first few miles of the river to access it, were allowed a concessionary permit, costing five pounds, to cover the return trip between Thames lock and the Canal entrance.

First stop, Ripley, where we moored just through the lock, opposite the ruins of the Augustinian Priory of Newark. These romantic looking ruins are, unfortunately, unapproachable by boat. Crossing over the lock gates still left one faced with the un-navigable channel between the lock and the ruins.

It was an attractive area with extensive lakes, possibly flooded gravel pits, which now support large colonies of water-fowl.

Ripley village was about one mile distant but the intervening walk seemed to offer a quiet, attractive pathway.

What it did produce was an area covered by brambles, laden with luscious, ripe fruits.

On reaching the village we bought a white plastic bucket and lid from the ironmongers and, on our return walk to the boat, picked six to eight pounds of excellent berries.

The bucket could double up as a steeping vessel in which to prepare the must, fermentation could also be started in it, but what was needed now was a basic wine making outfit; demi john, air-locks, yeast and chemicals.

We had bought lots of granulated sugar in anticipation!

At the Boot sale I had been fortunate enough to find an old copy of C.J.J. Berry's definitive book, "First Steps in Winemaking." This was the book I had always used in the past as my information guide.

It would serve me in good stead now!

The river was delightful, the locks were mainly in good order and although reasonable moorings were sometimes at a premium, they were not impossible to find, particularly in the two main towns.

Most of the Guildford moorings were well outside the town, in an area much frequented by walkers and families. It was sufficiently clear of the local pubs, not to be plagued by drunken young people, who often posed the biggest threat to safety.

At Godalming, most of the mooring was on hard standing at the Wharf. It was only able to accommodate a small number of boats, fortunately ours was one of them.

Guildford Castle's gardens were the site of a large archeological dig of some considerable interest and while we were exploring the ruins of the castle itself, we were enchanted by the music being relayed into the building via the loudspeaker at the gatehouse. Wonderful, evocative sounds were soaring and echoing through the ancient stones. Manned by students, the sound system was playing Gregorian Plain Chants, so apposite, clear, dramatic and melodic.

The tapes were not for sale but the name of the supplier in town was being offered in answer to enquiries. We noted the make but due to an unprecedented demand (caused by the students choice of music?), our choice of tape was not available when we tried to buy it.

Approaching Catteshall Lock, just before we reached Godalming, we stopped at the boatyard to replenish our water supply, take on fuel and pump out the toilet holding tank.

The young man who did the pump out, ran into problems when the discharge pipe blocked. With a length of cane and a high pressure hose, he did sterling service in clearing the pipe. When we left, our tank had received the most thorough scouring it had undergone since it was installed.

While he was busy with the operation, we wandered around the yard. The assistant manager, turned out to be an old acquaintance. His boat was credited with Torquay as his home base and we had overwintered with him at Streethay Wharf. Now he had a summer job on the management there at Godalming.

Reaching the limit of navigation for our length of boat, we managed to squeeze into the moorings alongside the hard-standing.

The town itself, though quite pleasant, had little of major interest to offer.

Wine making and Home-brewing did not appear to be high on the list of popular pastimes, judging by the dearth of shops catering for those practitioners of the art. However, we did manage to buy the basic kit from the tiny section in Boots the Chemist. The demi john was of clear glass, not the recommended brown, actinic glass, needed when making red wine, to avoid the colour being leached out of the liquid by the light. We would have to wrap the clear body in light proof material to avoid this happening.

At least now I was able to strain the must, add the yeast and chemicals, then set the fermentation process in operation.

Saturday afternoon saw us back in Guildford, checking out train times and preparing for our trip to Mychett on the Basingstoke Canal for the Bi-centennial Rally the following day. The train service proved to be excellent and we arrived at our destination in good time for the start of the final day's events. These would include our introduction to the popular rally event, Dragon Racing.

In spite of being faced with a long walk through the town to the railway station, we had dressed in full Victorian Boat persons costume. Much to the amazement and possibly amusement of the local populous.

The event was enjoyable and we were able to reclaim our cheque intended for the purchase of the license. We had paid the Rally fee and the organisers were happy to provide us with our boaters pack and Rally Plaque.

As we were the only participants in full costume, with the exception of the actors in the Theatre group which was performing for the event, we attracted a lot of attention and spent much of our time in conversation with groups of parents and children.

One rather precocious child, a boy, was more intrigued by my less than sylph-like figure, emphasised by its broad, embroidered belt, than our careful explanations of the history behind our various items of apparel. His father and I were joking about the amount of beer that went into creating such a spread and I was protesting my status as a non beer drinker, when the boy tugged my sleeve. I looked down and the cherub exclaimed in ringing tones,

"My Dad's got a big willy!!"

His parents looked round for a hole to swallow them and I'm sure I could hear alarm bells ringing among the more vulnerable female members of our small audience.

As it was the final day, the event wound-up by mid afternoon, by four-thirty we were making our way back to the station for the return trip to Guildford.

Our dress was to precipitate one final incident before we reached the boat.

Walking along the station concourse at Guildford, we saw a group of young people approaching us. Unwashed, unkempt, hair in dreadlocks and dressed like drop-outs from an Oxfam rejects Centre, they were a distressing sight.

As we approached, a large male in the group, turned to his companions and mumbled in a bewildered voice;

"Look at those stupid b——-ds! Who the f—k do they think they are!"

Bereft of instant repartee, we ignored them and walked on. I would have loved to have come back with a scathing reply, along the lines of;

"We're Victorian Boat People, out for a Sunday stroll, just who the f—k do you think you are or look like!"

Still, any comment I made would have fallen on deaf ears or have been considered provocative enough to spark off a nasty incident.

Sad!!

Next day we returned to Weybridge where we moored up for a couple of days above Thames Lock.

As we had travelled through the attractive countryside, we passed large numbers of moored craft indicating the popularity of the navigation. The name of the river had inspired many of the registered names, such as, "Weyfarer", "Weyholme" and "Weyside".

In a memorable encounter at Trigges Lock, one of the most picturesque on the river, we met "Sarnie".

Moored at Guildford and piloted by her skipper, a school girl of perhaps thirteen or fourteen years of age. Sharing a lock with this boat was a weird experience.

"Sarnie" was a scale model of a narrowboat and complete with engine, she was capable, not only of navigating the river but also of carrying passengers.

Two sisters were manning the boat and Dad was condemned to being crammed into the cabin, looking for all the world like Alice in Wonderland, after she had consumed the potion that made her grown too large for the cottage. He had bits sticking out of the windows etc.

Alongside "Athene" in the lock, her size was emphasised, she was about ten feet long by around four feet wide.

Lilliputian!

It was used by Dad as a runabout, but the girls for whom it was built insisted, that when they were using it, he kept well out of the way and left the crewing entirely up to them.

Securely moored in Weybridge, we began what turned out to be, a futile exercise; getting the engineer to attend and service our generator.

After a series of phone calls had failed to elicit a positive response we decided that when our Wey license had expired we would leave and make our way down to Brentford as soon as the tide was right.

When we moved onto the Thames moorings, we made one final call, this time it was answered with the promise that the engineer would be with us, next morning.

After a five hour wait, we contacted the office to be told that he was out on another job and would be in contact as soon as possible.

We pointed out their track record on failed appointments and declined the offer. We caught the ferry over to Shepperton, to consult with the lock-keeper.

He informed us that the tides on the following day were suitable for our trip, so we made plans for the run down to the Grand Union Canal, without further ado.

It would be necessary to buy a one day permit from the first lock, but apart from that everything appeared to be set fair.

During the afternoon we took a walk along the Desborough Cut, to see for ourselves the extent of the bridge works.

As we walked, we heard the sound of a boat horn, turning towards the sound we saw the Springer from the K&A. swinging in towards the bank, her name "Athene", clear and large on her bows.

The pair on board had recognised us; (How! I'm sure I couldn't guess!), and were intent on mooring up to make our acquaintance. We caught their lines, helped them secure the boat and were then invited aboard for tea and cakes.

After a round of introductions we indulged in the usual banter and small talk. Eventually it was agreed that we should take their boat back to the moorings for a photo-call.

I was offered the helm for the return trip. The first thing to do was something I had previously never been able to attempt, I was able to turn in the width of the channel.

Not a winding hole in sight!

The drive was quite an experience, she was so much lighter and more manoeuvrable than our sixty-five footer.

On board we opened a bottle of wine, toasted ourselves and the boats, then went outside to record the event on camera. All too soon we said goodbye to two more new friends and waved them on their way.

Boating was certainly proving to be an effective way to get to know people!

Our final night on the moorings left us with one last, less than enjoyable experience.

During the late evening, fishermen began to gather on the wharf. They intended to spend the night, ledgering for carp and bream. Right on our bows a group of three boys set up station. They were around twelve or thirteen years of age.

About three-thirty am., the boat lurched violently and we were shaken awake. From the scraping noises, there was still someone on the roof. I went into the cabin and peered through the window curtains. Two of the boys were by the boat, reaching up to receive the small logs that constituted our winter fuel stock being handed down by the boy on the roof. As I watched he vaulted off and they carried the wood over to a roaring fire that had been lit, towards the rear of the wharf.

I dressed, then went out onto the concrete. I asked the lads what they meant by stealing from my home and they instantly denied having been anywhere near the boat. Further pressure simply resulted in even more vehement denials, the donning of "butter wouldn't melt in my mouth" expressions and looks of hurt innocence, how could I possibly mistake them for the culprits.

I suggested that we go into the boat while I phoned the police on my mobile telephone, then they could sort matters out. Quickly the lads dowsed the fire and returned the partially burnt timber to the boat.

During these exchanges, not one single fisherman raised his eyes or supported my actions.

We returned to the boat, left the cabin lights on, undressed and climbed back into bed. We spent an uncomfortable couple of hours, braced for any sign of retaliation.

Eventually we both dozed off!

Once awake, I redressed and went ashore. In the soft light of morning I saw that, the boys, the fishermen and our shopping trolley, had all disappeared.

Writing it off to experience, I walked up to the shops to buy a daily newspaper.

I found the trolley, intact, pitched into the top of the hedge about one hundred and fifty yards from the boat.

Once the mess was cleared off the roof and we had tidied up the wharf, we said farewell to Weybridge, at least for this trip, and set off for Brentford and Little Venice.

10.
London Layover

In spite of the excitement of the previous night, I had still been plagued with the "colly-wobbles" about taking "Athene" out onto the tidal waters.

Childhood memories of standing on The Embankment, stretching up on tip-toes to watch the water swirling past the barges moored up to the huge metal buoys, whilst the tides were running, came flooding back.

My sub-conscious fed back to me vivid impressions of those currents and the voices Uncle Harry and Auntie Joy Deller, who lived in South Norwood, and with whom I holidayed regularly, warning of the dangers of falling in and being swept out into the North Sea.

To describe my state of mind as, apprehensive, would be akin to depicting Attila the Hun's raiding parties as Sunday School outings.

However, as always, it was a case of all or nothing, and so we untied the boat and set off.

The sights and sounds of that first experience of tidal water, will stay with me for ever, along with the immense feeling of relief when I felt the tug of the current easing and "Athene" gently coming back into my control as we entered the cut leading to the Grand Union Canal, at Brentford.

After our mad dash down the Thames, we felt in need of a break to acclimatise ourselves to the pace of life, back on the canals. Here we found a Launderette that was within easy walking distance of the moorings, we were able to sort out the piles of laundry, which we had accumulated.

The young people in the small cafe by the bridge, agreed to take delivery of our mail, so we made a phone call to set the arrangements in train.

Jean's cousin, Chester, an ex Naval Officer, lived in Ealing, just a short distance from the canal. We phoned him and agreed to meet him and his wife, Daphne, when we moored up at Three Bridges at the top of the Hanwell Flight.

The next few days passed smoothly, we met Jean's cousin, were wined and dined, then managed to fit in a visit to a car boot sale into our programme.

At Bull's Bridge we did our shopping in the large canalside supermarket, finally, a couple of days later, we moored up on the Paddington arm about half a mile short of Little Venice.

Rising early next morning, we were greeted by a heartening sight, on the towing path, just forward of our boat, stood a Heron, gazing intently into the water. I went back into the saloon and collected my camera, then tried to approach the large bird. I was rewarded with a number of posed close-ups of it. It seemed to be without fear. This particular Heron was to become a regular sight in the early morning calm.

A welcome feature of these moorings, was that they offered fourteen days occupation, without payment.

Time enough for us to explore the area more thoroughly.

Two well known markets were within easy reach of our moorings, Porta-Bello Road and Camden Lock. With a regular water-bus service to Camden we decided to make that our destination and set off early in the morning so that there would be sufficient time for us to spend the whole day visiting the stalls.

The visit was an eye-opener and we were surprised at the number of stalls selling ethnic clothing, artifacts and jewellery.

On one such pitch, we entered into a conversation with the young people manning it. Eventually discussion turned to life styles and they were a little surprised to discover that we lived permanently on a narrowboat.

"Ain't yer a bit old fer that sorta caper, Eh! Missus!" One girl exclaimed in disbelief.

Jean pointed out to her that, we had left school at fifteen and had immediately begun to work full time. Having only recently retired we had missed out on our teenage. Now we had chosen to make up the deficit and take that allocation of time, now!

They gave this explanation careful consideration, then one of the boys lurking in the background, decided to agree with us.

"Right on man! That's a real cool idea! Fancy coming with us to a Rave tonight?" He commented excitedly.

Pointing out the limitation of regression and our inability to cope with sustained, loud "music", we declined his offer and moved on.

Leather-wear was very reasonably priced and I was able to buy, a broad leather belt with a large silver buckle and a lovely pair of cowboy boots.

We hadn't quite reached our dotage!

Catching the water bus back to Little Venice, we experienced one of those chance meetings that proved to be of far-reaching consequences.

Finding ourselves sitting across the aisle from a young American couple, we were able to point out various interesting sights and as the "bus" cruised along, to explain to them about some of the boats and other features as we passed by.

Disembarking at the canal basin, we invited Steve and Lucy to accompany us along the moorings to our boat and to join us for tea and biscuits.

It transpired that they were from a small town in New York State, called Hicksville, which was situated on Long Island. They were Jews whose roots went back to Eastern Europe, although both families had settled in North America in the early nineteen hundreds.

From this chance meeting, there developed a friendship that is still going strong, in spite of the difficulties of meeting up with each other.

Steve and Lucy Jaffe were not the only people we met and showed over our home. Many have kept in touch, if only with the annual Christmas card exchange. This friendship however, endured and deepened.

The B.W. office agreed to accept delivery of our mail on a one off basis and once again we were able to catch up on our correspondence.

Among the strange sights along this stretch of canal were the long recesses in the banks at regular intervals. Lined with masonry, they contained pairs of ramps, reaching to the bed of the canal and set in a shallow "vee" shape reaching up to the level of the towing path. We were puzzled but our enquiries elicited a simple answer. In the days of horse drawn traffic, the horses would occasionally slip on mud or frost etc., and fall into the canal. Normally this would mean a major rescue operation to haul the animal out of the sheer sided canals. With the rescue ramps, it was simple, all they had to do was the let the horse walk or swim to the nearest ramp and it could climb easily up onto the bank.

Simple but ingenious!

We celebrated my birthday by spending the day in the Science museum at South Kensington. After a long, full day we returned to the boat where I prepared a celebration Indian meal. A joy to cook and to eat.

Another item on our list of things to do, was to organise a visit to the boat by Theo. She was now, wheelchair bound in the nursing home in Pimlico but we felt that we might be able to arrange something if we hired a large taxi. However the weather had turned cold, wet and windy, we didn't think she would be able to make the trip. Theo felt the same. This had been the last throw of the dice and, unfortunately, we had to agree, that any opportunity to show her the boat for real, had passed.

It left us feeling very sad!

Now that the National rally was over and the visiting boats had returned return to their home moorings or recommenced long term cruising, we decided that it was time to explore the Lee and Stort Navigations.

Moving "Athene" down towards Camden, we spent a couple of nights moored in that area then set off to cruise the two canalised rivers, which entered the Thames at Bow.

Using Ducketts Cut, we avoided the need to travel down to the Limehouse basin, before setting off upstream towards Waltham Abbey.

The first sight of the River Lee was appalling, a thick mat of duckweed liberally scattered with masses of floating junk, covered the surface as far as the eye could see.

It was truly depressing!

The river currents seemed to have a negligible effect on the water condition and for the first few miles we wondered whether it was ever going to improve and allow us to run the engine, without continually reversing the prop.

Conditions stayed poor and it wasn't until we reached the Pond Lane flood gates that we saw any marked improvement.

After overnighting near Highbridge in Clapton, where I was able to open the weed hatch, clean out the trapped duckweed and clear the prop. and drive shaft, we pressed on to Waltham Abbey. Here we found reasonable moorings above the Town lock.

Signs that a large rally had recently taken place were everywhere, we were however a little surprised how poorly dredged and maintained the area seemed to be. One of our main reasons for avoiding National rallies was that boats and boating seemed to be slipping down the list of priorities when it came to choosing venues and confirming or improving their suitability to provide adequate mooring for the five or six hundred boats they confidently expected to attend.

It is difficult to satisfy everyone, particularly when mega numbers are involved but many boaters look to rallies to promote their interests and to seek to protect a way of life and leisure. To me it seemed that the main focus of National rallies had shifted towards commercial interests while the system itself remained under near terminal threat from all manner of agencies.

However, for now we were in an area that abounded with fascinating historical sites and we spent the rest of the day and evening exploring.

The town's history could be traced back to before the Norman Conquest when King Harold developed it as a centre of learning. Its ecclesiastical roots were well represented by the substantial Abbey Church that dominated the town.

Across the country we had seen numerous examples of the artist Burne-Jones work but his beautiful "Jesse" window in the Abbey must be among his finest.

Much of the character of the town had survived in spite of the encroachment of heavily trafficed roads around its centre.

Across on the west side of the canal was Waltham Cross, named for the Eleanor Cross (one of only three that have survived almost intact.) Erected by Edward 1st. to mark the resting places of his queen's coffin on its way to her internment at Westminster Abbey. We had visited a number of these sites in various parts of the country and it seemed to us that her body must have been taken on a provincial tour. The most likely explanation is that the Queen died in Leicestershire during one of the King's "meet the nobles progresses". He would have completed the tour accompanied by his wife's embalmed and coffined body.

Heading for the River Lee's head of navigation at Hertford, we reached, what must be one of the most attractive and colourful locks anywhere on the system, Carthagena Lock.

The lock cottage had a garden that rioted with rainbow hues, while the white paling fence was hung with baskets of blooms whose trailing stems showed flowers of every shade. Every vantage point had been utilised and pressed into service as a platform for supporting yet more plants. It was a real picture, basking in the bright sunshine. An example of how easily our lives and our spirits can be uplifted and enhanced.

The high point of the previous day had been to see the huge sprawl of the Royal Small Arms factory, home of the famous. Lee Enfield .303 calibre service rifle, much respected by our Armed Forces. Today, we were presented with a highlight that offered a much softer, gentler vision, one that was infinitely more uplifting.

We negotiated two more locks and were then looking at the junction between the two rivers. We would continue to follow the Lee which swung to the left and meandered for another seven miles before it reached journey's end, Hertford.

The river had carried water-borne traffic for over two hundred years but was now beginning to get very shallow and the banks, overgrown and broken as the volume of usage decreased.

Between Ware lock and Hertford town is the outlet to the New River; a scheme designed and built by Sir Hugh Myddelton in the 17th. Cent. in an effort to supply London with clean water as the Thames was so polluted. Originally the river was fed by the Amwell Springs but these dried up at the end of the 19th. Cent. and since then the water had been taken from the River Lee.

Since we had been in the vicinity of the Capital, one feature had been a constant reminder of the nearness of the Twentieth Century. The waterways had lost much of their original isolation and a modern form of transport intruded upon our solitude.

Over and over again we found ourselves, under or alongside the take-off and landing approaches to some of the country's major airports. Heathrow, Gatwick and here, Stanstead, shattered the peace of the water with the scream of accelerating or throttling back, jet engines.

Since we had left the Kennet and Avon canal at Reading, right through to Brentford, Bulls bridge and beyond, we had noted the twice daily flights of the "White Lady". Concord has an unmistakable engine note, not so much loud as having a deep resonance that reaches into your body and sets the senses on edge.

We were not subject to the one plane every two or three minutes that had been the case at Heathrow; here the pattern was irregular but in some ways that made it more disturbing.

In Hertford, we turned at the small junction and succeeded in securing the last remaining length of viable mooring.

As we walked towards the road bridge beyond the moorings we could see that silting had reduced the depth of water to around six inches. A large hire boat had either misread or was ignoring the guidebooks directions and was heading towards the next bridge. With much arm waving and shouting we persuaded him to stop and reverse his course before he drove his craft aground in the shallow water.

Again this was an interesting town with a long history but we had become frustrated with the difficulty of finding good moorings on another river navigation. We needed to settle our winter stopover in order to make sure that we had a covered dock in which we could work on preparing and repainting the boats superstructure.

That meant getting back to home waters!

Consequently we restricted our stay to one night and set off next morning to cruise to Bishop Stortford, without exploring the town.

If anything the River Stort was shallower and more badly maintained than the Lee and it was not surprising that Sir George Duckett, it's former owner, had experienced problems making the navigation pay.

A feature we found repeated at most of the locks, were the watermills that took advantage of the weirs. Little was left of the infrastructure that had created them but odd buildings and the names of the locks themselves, bore mute testimony to a long gone era.

We spent our first night on the Stort at Roydon, an area that had developed from being simply a riverside village complete with watermill, which carried the Duckett crest, to a large modern area encompassing a huge caravan site and complex.

Here the mooring was excellent and the riverside walk was much used.

When we reached Bishop Stortford, it was clear that good mooring was at a premium, particularly along the picturesque length through the town and at the fork overlooked by wood clad mill buildings, which was about the only place to wind, and that was a tad tight.

I had some minor repairs and renovating work to do on the boat, so this seemed a good place to carry them out as I had already bought the required materials in the large D.I.Y at Hertford.

We had moored by the hardstanding and in a few days the work was likely to be completed.

The townsfolk were friendly and we knew the owners of a number of the moored craft, these were people whom we had met from time to time as we had travelled around the London area.

One incident that occurred while we were here, served to remind us of the vulnerability of the elderly and the difficulties they faced, if they chose to retain their personal esteem and a sense of independence, by trying to live, more or less unsupported, in the community.

On our walk to and from the town each day, we passed a row of terraced houses of the two up, two down style. They appeared to be tenanted by elderly people and we would make a point of smiling, waving or chatting to the occupants as we passed. Particularly those who were at the front doors or in the tiny gardens.

One particular incident happened, when an elderly lady in a dressing gown, struggled down the short path on painful feet, and asked for our help.

Always willing to oblige we asked, what we could do to assist her. What she wanted doing was mundane and to many would have appeared fairly trivial or even slightly off. She wanted us to call at the super-market off-licence and buy her a four pack of a particular brand, of what she referred to as, Golden Barley Wine.

Nothing loath, we agreed but were somewhat taken aback to be invited into her front room while she sorted out the cash. Her bed was a mound of grubby sheets and blankets, piled onto an old divan base. When she showed us her feet, we found it amazing that she could walk at all.

A locker with a drawer partially open stood by the bed and all across the battered furniture were scattered envelopes containing money. We estimated that she had something approaching three hundred pounds set aside to cover a variety of household expenses.

As we were not regular drinkers, the amount of money she extracted from an envelope to cover the cost of the Barley Wine, seemed excessive but she obviously knew its cost and was happy.

We made the purchase and returned with the cans and a small amount of change. We attempted, tactfully to find out her circumstances, but were unsuccessful and left in a troubled frame of mind.

After discussing the situation, we decided that some action was needed and we decided to report to the Police that she was in danger of being robbed and possibly injured if anyone dishonest became aware of her situation and the amounts of untraceable cash waiting to be picked up.

The Police Station was a long, tiring walk away and when we reached it and made our report, we were informed that this type of problem was best dealt with by Social Services. We walked back into town and located them, only to be informed that they could only take action if the lady in question were identified professionally, as being, "at risk".

In a final effort to make progress we contacted Age Concern, at last we elicited some response. This was to the effect that, the old lady in question was well known for this type of unsafe behaviour, little however could be done to rationalise a support network.

We still felt very uneasy!

Had we been residents of the area, I'm afraid that we would have been prompted to interfere and attempt to organise a rota of people to call at regular intervals. This could have been done without being too obvious and encroaching too much on her sense of independence. We felt that in spite of everything, the lady was in desperate need of regular, no strings attached support. The kind of thing that local Churches could be relied upon to provide.

When the congregations were large enough!

This is not intended as a side swipe at the people of Bishop Stortford, whom we found to be friendly and helpful, It is an indication of the problems created by the Welfare State, whose net is often more full of holes than string, due to their ongoing lack of finance. Today anyone attempting to get involved with the welfare of others can soon find themselves out on a limb.

With our work completed, we set off downstream towards Limehouse Basin where we intended to moor for a few days while we invited Aunt Betty from Gravesend to visit us, on "Athene".

The river still held one sting in it's tail. Leaving a particularly nasty bend, we met another boat, crowding the centre of the channel. In avoiding him, I managed to get our boat under the overhanging branches. In the process we lost the T.V. aerial and mast plus the Radio Telephone aerial. The T.V. equipment was trailing on the co-ax cable but when we hauled it in, part of the antenna was missing. The radio aerial was a total write off.

Near the junction of the Lee and Stort rivers, stood what was left of Rye House and it's estates. It was here that the infamous Rye House plot against Charles' II and his son James, was hatched.

We had a particular interest as one of Jean's ancestors, John Cochrane, Master of Ochletree in Ayrshire, had been involved in the plot. Taken prisoner he was held in the Toll Booth in Edinburgh awaiting the warrant of execution.

His followers could purchase his freedom if they raised £5,000 before the warrant arrived. John's daughter Grizel, obtained the warrant by dressing as a man and holding up the messenger. The delay was sufficient to enable the cash to be raised. In recognition, the eldest daughter of that Cochrane line has always been named, Grizel. My wife's full name is Jean Grizel Elizabeth Lewis, nee Cochrane.

Overnighting at Dobb's Weir Lock, we shopped at the small store attached to the cottage. Here we learned about the history of the Stort Penny. These were tokens, valued at one penny each, which were issued by the operating company of the navigation, to counter a national shortage of small coinage. This way the payment of tolls would not interfere with the country's money supply.

Large replicas, crafted in brass, showed the obverse and reverse sides of one of the tokens. There was also a short history. Purchasing a complete set, I eventually mounted and framed them and they now occupy pride of place on the cabin wall.

As we approached the entrance to Ducketts Cut the following day, we were pleased to find that the duckweed had thinned considerably and were able to negotiate the navigation to Limehouse Basin without meeting any additional problems.

Tide locks on the river help maintain water levels, but along the Limehouse Cut and in the basin itself, levels were still very low. It made tying up and clambering ashore a task not to be undertaken by the fainthearted.

As the basin had originally been a transfer dock, able to accommodate large vessels entering from the Pool of London through the tide lock, it's stone quays were massive. When "Athene" was tied up at the foot of a vertical steel ladder, her roofline was still some two or three feet below the walkway.

The designation of the B.W. moorings was for transit and they therefore carried a twenty-four hour restriction.

Contacting their office, we were given permission to extend that period to one week without incurring any charges. This was because we had repairs to carry out and through traffic was at a minimum.

One thing that had always impressed us about our friends, 'The Jolly Green Giants', was their willingness to listen and to then make every effort to accommodate the needs of the licence holders. Always providing that they were approached reasonably and shown a little respect, One thing was sure, our eighty year old Aunt, was not going to be able to negotiate a twelve foot high, vertical steel ladder to board our craft.

A large part of the basin had been converted into a Marina, with floating pontoons, against which the boats could be secured. Short term mooring was available, with water and electricity laid on but at nine pounds per night, we felt that these charges were a bit rich for our pockets. We had a word with the Marina office and explained our predicament.

Our plea received sympathetic consideration and permission was granted for 'Athene' to move over and tie up against the pontoon nearest to the pedestrian entrance for twelve hours on the day of the visit. There would be no charge. We would need to put down a twenty pounds deposit on a 'swipe card' to operate the lock on the entrance gate, but that was returnable.

Once these details had been sorted out we set about buying the bits and pieces needed to complete the repairs of the two aerials.

It transpired that replacement was the cheapest option and that a qualified engineer would be needed to fix the telephone.

Fortunately, everything was available within half a mile of our berth.

After allowing time for the repairs, we contacted Betty and arranged a time and date for her visit. As she no longer drove a car, it was necessary that she came to Tower Bridge by underground then got a taxi from there to Limehouse.

The repairs and renewals were completed, Aunt's visit passed off well, including a rather nice meal in the Pub which occupied the old River control Headquarters.

The task of getting a taxi to take Betty back to Tower Bridge, almost proved beyond us. Four times we booked a cab to pick her up at the Pub and four times they failed to arrive. Eventually, mine host did the honours and at last a cab arrived.

We were intending to make a run up the tidal Thames to Brentford, which meant that our timings would be controlled by B.W. and their time schedule for lock openings.

Eight a.m, on Saturday seemed to be the first reasonable window so we booked our passage. Three or four other boats had telephoned requests for passage and were listed before us, our locking would be at approx. eight thirty.

This time we would be travelling upstream with the tide under our tail. It promised a much quicker passage than our previous one.

Once through the lock and into the Lower Pool we began a cruise that covered twenty miles to Three Bridges on the Grand Union Canal in a total of five and a quarter hours. This included the ten locks on the canal itself.

The trip up the Thames was magic. River traffic was at a minimum at that time in the morning, as the tour boats were not yet running. Passing a skyline made so familiar by film and T.V, viewing, was an experience not to be missed.

As we swept towards Tower Bridge, the roadway was in place, with the traffic of the morning rush-hour moving swiftly over it's broad span. A tiny fish in a large bowl, we had to content ourselves with steering a central course between the twin towers supporting piers.

Not for us the excitement of hearing the mighty roar of London's traffic, stilled and seeing the massive leaves carrying the roadway, open to allow our passage.

Shucks!!

As we approached the various bridges, we noted the navigation lights on the arches which controlled the right of way of the riverborne traffic

It was a measure of our comparatively small dimensions, that, by ignoring these instructions our main danger would not be running aground, but collision with a large oncoming vessel if we strayed onto the wrong side of the river,

One by one the City's famous sights, hove into view, then fell astern.

We passed The Tower of London, HMS. Belfast, Saint Paul's Cathedral, The palace of Westminster, Westminster Cathedral, County Hall, the RAF. Monument, Cleopatra's Needle, the Royal Festival Hall and Lambeth Palace, all merged into a kaleidoscope of sights that defied order in our overloaded senses. Bridge after famous bridge, loomed up, was negotiated and slipped out of sight into the morning haze.

At Westminster, we received a sharp scare. A tour boat was in front of us on the water and we were closing it. Suddenly it turned across our bows, heading for the landing stages. There was no indication that it was aware of our presence and it certainly did not comply with the accepted sound code and signal it's intention before it carried out the manoeuvre.

I gave them a blast from our twin klaxons and carried on, under Westminster Bridge.

With the unmistakeable bulk of Battersea Power Station on the horizon, we passed beneath Vauxhall Bridge, here we were within about three hundred yards of Theo's Nursing Home in Pimlico. Past Battersea Park and we were in Chelsea Reach with it's jumble of moored house-boats.

Just after Putney Bridge, we passed through the starting point of the River's most famous sporting event, The Boat Race. It's course covers some four and three quarter miles to Chiswick Bridge in Mortlake.

The boat crews cover the distance in just over fifteen minutes, we took well over forty five minutes.

Along this section of the river, lined as it was with the boathouses of many famous Rowing Clubs, we found ourselves surrounded by boats. Single skiffs, pairs, fours and racing eights, all busy on their training schedules and leaving us in their wakes.

With Kew Gardens appearing on our right, it's position marked by it's distinctive Tower, we began to look for the entrance to the Brentford Cut. Passing the Ait, we saw the swirling currents that had almost proved our undoing on the downstream run.

Moving into slack water inshore, we negotiated the entrance with no difficulty. Once more we had entered the man made channel of one of the most successful of England's canals. 'The Grand Union' formerly called 'The Grand Junction Canal'.

11
On the Grand Union.

With our heads still spinning from the exhilarating run up the Tidal Thames, afternoon saw us safely tied up alongside the meadow at Three Bridges.

We knew that on Sunday there would be a Car Boot Sale just down the road, so we decided that this would make an excellent weekend stop-over. That would free us to go and shop for some bargains. As these sales were a regular feature and the actual venue was large, we could expect the numbers of tables to be correspondingly great.

The next day dawned fine, October was living up to it's reputation for providing the occasional glorious Indian Summer.

The crowds took advantage of this and turned out in force. We mingled happily with them. One stall holder was offering electrical goods, among them a carton of factory reject Car Radio/Cassette Players. As they were extremely expensive units at knockdown prices, I took a chance that my son in law who was an electronics engineer, used to working on TV's. C.B.s and radios, could repair it and paid £5 for one. The units were sealed with tape declaring them defective but I felt that if the fault could be corrected relatively cheaply, the unit would be a good buy and would be safe to use.

After making a number of interesting purchases and enjoying a bacon butty, dripping with Tomato Sauce and swilled down with a cup of hot sweet tea (even if it was in a styrofoam cup), we returned to the boat replete and contented.

We had actually made the trip up river on October 1st., now we were anxious to be settled in on a winter mooring by the first week in November. It was time to ratify a base.

Market Harborough had a number of covered docks and our earlier stay had been most enjoyable so we agreed that on Monday morning, I would phone the boatyard and see if they could fit us in. A tentative booking had already been made but now we were content that it would suit our purpose to firm up our commitment. Repainting the superstructure was our major project which made the availability of a covered dock our top priority.

As Jean and I had both had traumatic first marriages we sometimes found the need to lay uncomfortable ghosts in certain areas that had really bad vibes for one or the other of us.

Jean had lived for a time in Langley near Slough; here both she and her two sons were physically abused by her first husband. In an attempt to overlay these bad experiences with pleasant ones, we made a detour and travelled down the Slough Arm to it's terminus. The trip down was enjoyable the water clear and the conditions good. Unfortunately this state of affairs was not to last.

After a night when we had slept undisturbed, we awoke to find that our brand new TV mast and aerial had been stolen, The co-ax cable had been burned through with something like a cigarette lighter to facilitate this amusing act.

We searched the clear water for fifty yards or more either end of the boat on the off-chance that it had been dumped.

We were unsuccessful!

Passing through Langley on our return trip to Cowley Peachey we saw a couple walking their dog. They warned us to be careful as there was a motor vehicle dumped in the water.

With Jean standing look-out in the bows we gently eased our way along. In spite of our vigilance, it was not till the water levels dropped as we approached it that its luggage rails on the roof began to show, this was too late for full evasive action but I did alter course to avoid a major bump.

The vehicle turned out to be a quite respectable white, Ford 8 cwt. van. "Athene" could not turn very far without risking grounding near the bank. In the event, we avoided a head-on collision but did not miss the van entirely, We ground our keelplate edge, fairly heavily along the vehicle's side.

At Highline Yachting, just a little distance further on, we reported the situation to the Police and to B.W.

This was not the most auspicious way to remove bad vibes but little daunted, we pressed on towards Uxbridge. I hoped that we could replace our mast and aerial there.

Our return trip from Slough was dogged with misfortune, Nearing Cowley Peachey, the boat began to get sluggish and each time she heeled, it seemed to be a real effort to regain the vertical.

Jean went below and found that our bedroom carpet was almost awash. Carrying on forward she discovered that the shower tray was overflowing into the bilge. The clothes airier that was kept in the cubicle had fallen against the shower controls and switched them on. Fortunately they were only partially on but the collision with the van had probably initiated the sequence of events and something approaching two hours had elapsed.

The water was turned off and the manually switched shower pump soon cleared the tray. Then, with the access hatch open in the study, Jean set about removing the water, using a bucket and a bailer, We had an automatic bilge pump fitted in the engine room, but that did not clear water from forward of the engine room bulkhead.

Now our first purchase at Uxbridge would need to be a portable bilge pump and a long length of hose.

Thank the Creator, that the shower was not full on or we would have foundered!

With an excellent boatyard and Chandlery to hand, we bought the bilge pump, topped up the water and diesel tanks, then indulged ourselves in an orgy of window shopping around the shelves crowded with the most tempting marine goodies,

The excursion into Uxbridge itself was less successful. We did buy a TV. aerial but a mast was not to be had at any price. We would have to jury rig our set-up for a few days more.

Cruising up the Grand Union, we quickly found the one thing that makes the wide locks on this canal even more of a problem than usual for the lone lock-wheeler,

In a throwback to earlier times, it appeared that the accepted practice was to leave the lock gates open when you exited, in whichever direction you were travelling. This meant that approaching a full lock from below, the unfortunate lock-wheeler would find themselves faced with open top gates. This necessitated walking to the top gates, checking the paddles and closing one gate. Return to the bottom gates, cross on the walkway, back to the top gates close the second one, taking care not to inadvertently open the first gate. Back to the bottom gates, open the ground paddle, cross the gates, open the second paddle, wait for the lock to empty.

I could get the boat into the lock with a single gate open but often this action would push open the second gate. This set up the rigmarole of crossing and recrossing the lock via the walkway on the top lock gates.

These locks are not to be taken lightly by a single boat, but as traffic was light and as we were short of time and unable to wait for another boat, we found ourselves alone on the canal. Jean found the bulk of the locks, against us!

We understood now where the oft quoted figure of 15 minutes per complete lock cycle came from.

The Leicester Arm turns off the main canal at Gayton, between that and our current location we faced the daunting prospect of 85 wide locks. Sod's Law could be relied upon to put the majority against us!

The lock names on the next section were interesting and conjured up strange images, Denham Deep, Widewater, Black Jack's and Coppermill, each one had it's own special ambience.

The Gortex Challenge had some slight similarities with our pastime of "Letterboxing", (see "Athene; Anatomy of a Dream" for details.) without the cryptic clues and map referencing. The idea was to give canal walkers and cruising boaters a series of points along the full length of the Grand Union, where they could obtain rubber stamped impressions on a card. When it was full it would be proof that the whole canal from Brentford to Birmingham had been covered,

We had begun collecting the stamps and as Batchworth Lock near Rickmansworth was the location of one of the stamp boxes, we tied up there. By now Jean was feeling the strain of a days locking so we made it our overnight stop.

The overnight moorings here were excellent and it had another plus it could be added to our growing list of venues with a canalside supermarket complete with hard standing for boaters wishing to shop here.

Famous in working boat circles for the "Ricky" boats, built by W.H.Walker and Bros., the area had become a haven for long term moorers.

Unfortunately, here on the southern half of the canal, we were seeing more and more badly maintained boats. Many were listing heavily and here and there boats had sunk on their mooring, simply from neglect.

We wondered, not for the first time, what induced people to buy a boat and then to allow their investment to deteriorate into a worthless heap.

As the area was only a couple of miles from the B.W., headquarters at Watford, we began to see how the "duckers and divers" of the more remote waterways, seemed to live such a charmed life. Not for them the hassle of rules and regulations, insurance and licenses, Certificates of Compliance and suchlike; those, it seemed ,could be left to the large numbers of law-abiding boaters to comply with or bring down upon themselves the full weight of the Board's attention. Maybe the long threatened advent of the Safety Certificate will start to turn matters round.

Passing through the very attractive Cassiobury Park area, we saw a very sad sight.

What appeared to have been a converted wooden working boat had sunk on it's moorings. A young family with two young children and a toddler in a pushchair, were disconsolately fishing pieces of their personal belongings out of the scum of flotsam in the water filled cabin. Our sympathies were dissipated somewhat, when we were told that the family in question had been warned of the boat's parlous state and imminent danger of sinking, on numerous occasions prior to the actual event.

To no avail!

Here again, it was innocent children who would be bearing the brunt of the suffering created by the disaster.

Jean and I were both pensioners trying to live on a small fixed income. Costs continued to soar but we knew that if we intended to remain on board our boat and to follow our lifestyle, our health and well-being would depend basically on the condition of the boat, its furnishings and its equipment.

With a short day planned, we cruised on through the park and past historic Grove Mill. Just past the buildings ,the canal was spanned by another of the ornate stone bridges demanded by landowners as agreement to allow the building of the canal on their land. This time the name behind the architecture was the Earl of Essex,

Nearing Hemel Hempstead, we reached our stop-over point, Apsley, with its canalside supermarket, good moorings and, at long last, a fresh water supply.

Walking from our moorings towards the main town, we found a TV. repair shop which also did aerial erection. At last we were able to replace our mast.

Pardon what may seem to be an obsession with supermarkets, waterpoints, launderettes and pump-out stations but things that a house dweller takes for granted assume a special importance when one's source of information is as unreliable as that provided by most canal Guide-books. Not that this reflects incompetence on the part of the publishers, rather it is due to the modern change towards a highly mobile population and the high levels of vandalism and shop thefts in some areas which prompts the closure of many small, people friendly businesses.

Our next stop was just above North Church Locks near Berkhampstead. Apparently here were some rather well preserved Norman Castle Earth-works close to the centre of town. We hadn't time for a visit on this trip but made a note to pay a call, next time we passed through the area.

Reaching the summit at Cowroast, the sight of the Marina brought memories flooding back of our late night escapade on the Oxford, what seemed to be aeons ago. (See chapter 4)

Cowroast Marina was on the three miles summit pound, reminiscent of the one on the K&A. Each boat passage drained around 65,000 gallons of water off the summit, close on one third of a million litres in metric values, no wonder the pressure to maintain water levels was high.

Through the Tring cutting towards Bulbourne we suddenly became engulfed in steam. The hot water feed to the heat exchanger had blown off its spigot. Steam and hot water sprayed everywhere. With the engine switched off, the problem was quickly identified and rectified. Sighs of relief that it was nothing more serious!

When the Marsworth flight had been negotiated we found ourselves at the junction with the Aylesbury Arm. It was six and a quarter miles long with 16 narrow locks, still it was there, so we headed "Athene" towards the terminus.

As we had come to expect in this area, the canal abounded with all manner of waterfowl, with one glaring exception. On our travels up and down this waterway we did not see one single Aylesbury duck.

Granted it is a domesticated species but then so were the Mandarins and other exotic breeds which were happily diluting the gene pool of our stock of native breeds.

Our reception by the club members when we arrived at their moorings was fantastic.

After winding the boat, we were allocated a space, connected up to the mains electricity via our land-line, shown where the water point was and given a run-down on all the local facilities and their locations.

The bank-master made us feel thoroughly welcome and was happy for us to share their moorings for three nights.

The quantities of Loo Blu we needed for our holding tank had always proved difficult to obtain. Here they purchased in commercial quantities and were able to supply us with ten litres at a very reasonable price, throwing in a large plastic container into the bargain that would help to keep our storage space neat and tidy.

We are proud owners of Club Tee shirts and a brass plaque which celebrates our navigation of the arm. We wear one and display the other with pleasure in remembrance of a happy three day sojourn.

On our return to Marsworth Junction we tied up to collect their Gortex Challenge stamp. While Jean was hunting for the box, I slipped away to try and make a surprise purchase for her.

The Junction Cottage was a craft studio selling beautifully knitted soft toys in the shape of large Aylesbury Ducks, dressed, among other styles, in traditional Boatpersons costume. Naturally, Jean had fallen in love with them, now I was trying to make a purchase.

Unfortunately the studio was not manned and there did not appear to be any indication of a contact address or telephone number. I had to forgo the pleasure of seeing my wife's face light up when she was presented with her own Aylesbury Duck.

Never mind! Maybe next time!

We took on water and diesel, pumped out the holding tank at Pitstone Wharf, then cruised the short distance to Ivinghoe Lock where we were able to tie up for the night.

Next day, we made the run to Leighton Buzzard, through virtually unspoiled countryside with little sign of habitation until the Leighton/ Linslade sprawl hove into view.

Jean visited the local Health Clinic to get a script for a new supply of inhalers for her asthma. While it was being processed we paid a fascinating visit to the large Parish Church. Among the mediaeval relics in the building was some extensive graffiti just to prove that there is nothing new under the sun.

Among the disgruntled comments of the choirboys about their sadistic choirmaster is an extensive pictogram which depicts the quarrel between Simon and Nell as to wether the Simnel Cake for Mothering Sunday should be boiled or baked.

Wonderful insights into former times!

For years I had regaled Jean with horror stories about the dreaded Milton Keynes, the town that drew hapless travellers into it's coils, never to release them. Tales of benighted souls, wandering through the darkness, their plaintive cries sending shivers down the spines of the lucky few who had had its secrets revealed to them.

In spite of all the praise the designers had received and the awards made, I had spent hours on two previous visits in my car, seeking to escape from the town's insidious clutches,

Jean was not convinced, she felt that my anecdotes were made up on the spot. She insisted that we moor up at one of the regular access points and walk into town. That way she could prove me wrong.

I complied with the request, after all if we ever got back to the boat, we could at least follow the canal out of the town.

Follow the Redways we were instructed. Hours later we found out that the Redways were the footpaths surfaced in a sort of reddish brown asphalt. Each enclave of housing looked the same with their surrounds of tree planted earthworks, even the cars on the drives and the curtained windows looked the same. With no distant skyline and no landmarks we were far more disorientated than we had ever been on Dartmoor, even during fog and whiteouts,

Eventually we stumbled across an abandoned car park covering a number of acres. When we reached the entrances on the far side the main reason for its derelict state seemed clear. The approach ramps were so steep that most vehicles appeared to have bottomed out on the concrete, to judge from the deep grooves in the cracked surface.

Beyond the carpark was a shopping mall, under cover in a large unremarkable barn of a building. It's shops, stores, cafes etc. were no whit different to a dozen other malls except that this one seemed to exude an air of grubby disconsolateness.

Our return to the boat was no less traumatic. We still had little concept of direction or distance. One lady resident commiserated with us and explained that in the first few months after their arrival, her husband had become quite used to searching for her and even on occasions the car when that to had been misplaced.

Once they had settled in and become familiar with the area they had enjoyed the town and were full of praise for its sense of community.

Cresting one last rise we saw the canal beneath us and, miracle of miracles, "Athene" was in sight. We breathed a heartfelt sigh of relief as we boarded her and settled down for the night.

Jean adds her contribution to my Milton Keynes anecdotes now!

One thing we had managed to buy was the remainder of the wine making kit from a small Homebrew Centre in the Mall. Our Blackberry wine was fermenting out well and now needed racking (straining off the sediment.) before the dead yeast spoiled its flavour.

It would be ready to bottle by Christmas!

Half of the month of October had sped by but as we were now well into the last leg before the turn-off into the Leicester Arm, we made a small alteration to our plans. We would be extremely busy with the repaint, almost certainly up to Christmas. If we extended our cruise up to Braunston and then along the North Oxford and the Coventry, we could visit Mum and Joan, before we returned to cruise the Leicester Arm to Foxton and thence to Market Harborough. That way we would not have to break into our work schedule at a later date to make the visit by train and bus.

Heading for Stoke Bruerne we passed through Wolverton, home of what must be one of the most impressive canal-side murals anywhere on the system. For a distance of about a quarter of a mile along the non towingpath side of the canal, a wall had been decorated with a black on white mural of the silhouette of a railway train, At the left hand end it was pulled by a modern diesel-electric locomotive at the right hand end an ancient steam locomotive was connected. A collection of Box cars, goods wagons and loaded flat-beds, the cargo representing local and national products and freight, filled the intervening space.

What was more impressive was that the work was already a few years old and was virtually untouched by vandalism or graffiti. This was due in part to the fact that the land in front of it was not a regular right of way, but more especially, I think, that the mural was the creation of a group of Work Experience youngsters, they were so proud of their work that they let it be known, that anyone defacing it would receive a good seeing too .

Not surprisingly, that seemed to have worked!

Stoke Bruerne had once been a major staging post on the route north/south and handled large numbers of working boats. The canalside buildings had been sympathetically restored and some of them now housed a rather splendid Waterways Museum. Due to the range of buildings available and the interest created by the site, it had developed as a venue for the promotion of old canal crafts and skills.

Colin Jones, who had taught me fender-making, was running a course on the very same craft. We arrived during a short break in the instruction period. Making ourselves known, we thanked him again for the useful skill we had been taught.

With his group well into their course it was obvious that they were enjoying every minute of it, just as much as I had done.

Next day we tackled the Blisworth Tunnel, at 3,057 yards in length, it is the longest, navigable canal tunnel currently in use. Although wide enough to allow two boats to pass in opposite directions, it had no towing paths and so appeared very much narrower than our longest tunnel to date, the Netherton, which has two towing-paths.

Originally this tunnel had to be "Legged" and at each end were sited wooden huts in which the "leggers" could shelter while waiting for the boats to arrive. Having tried this method of propelling a boat for about fifteen minutes in the Dudley Tunnel, I had immense sympathy with the men who had been forced by economic circumstances into doing this backbreaking job, day in and day out in all weathers.

The tunnel was to prove to be a major hold-up on this trip. Unknown to us, a hire boat had entered the tunnel some five minutes prior to our arrival, It's electrics had failed and the boat had, no tunnel light, no navigation lights, not even the basic cabin lighting. Rather than do the sensible thing and wait for a repair crew from the boatyard, they elected to attempt the tunnel passage with nothing more than a small hand-held torch for illumination.

They took over an hour to grope their way through and we found ourselves right up close to their stern at the head of a convoy of boats. Nine boats made the passage in the opposite direction making it impossible to get past and attempt to lead it out. My claustrophobia was not best pleased!

After that, in spite of the fact that we had covered a mere three miles, we moored up at Blisworth village in torrential rain. It was time to call it a day!

The next day was somewhat better, we made passage up the Buckby flight, navigated the Braunston Tunnel, (without a hitch) and completed the six locks down from the tunnel to the start of the moorings.

Our mail was awaiting collection at the B.W. offices in the Stop House. We filled our fresh water tank and moved on to moor opposite the "Boatman Pub."

Our friend Fay was in her usual place with her tiny boat, "Mabs", from which she sold the earrings she crafted. Ivor Batchelor was also on the moorings with "Mountbatten", his "Admiral" class Working boat, that meant we could top up our diesel tank and stock up with coal and smokeless fuel.

We would have to forego heating via the solid fuel stove during the repaint as we would be inside a building.

NO OPEN FIRES!!

With just enough time left to reach Amington and wind before starting our return trip and duty visits, we pressed on, our destination was reached in two days,

Stops to visit, Mum. sister Joan and cousin Dot, added a week to the return. The final leg from Braunston to Market Harborough via Foxton accounted for two more days and we arrived at our destination on November 4th,

A short period of time to get settled in, make our purchases and then, "All systems go!"

We would be in for a few weeks of back breaking work!

12.
"The Harboro' Stripper"

Once we had settled into our moorings and organised the mains power supply etc., we discussed with Peter our requirements for the repaint. The wet dock was currently in use but was due to be vacated in two weeks time. That gave us what we thought would be ample time to get everything sorted out and the materials purchased.

Due to the rather small amount of available storage space on "Athene", we had refrained from buying paint, thinners and brushes from the Chandleries we had visited on our travels, It was a decision we were soon to regret,

The boatyard bought in all its requirements, which were delivered by van. They would have been happy to place an order for me, but I am one of those odd people who find it easier to make choices when surrounded by the physical evidence of the options open. I needed a Chandlery!

We eventually located one on the outskirts of Leicester. It was mainly for G.R.P. yachts and cruisers but carried stocks of the paint we needed and in addition a wide variety of other items we might require.

One lesson that we had learned was that basics like, wet'n'dry flatting paper, garnet paper, bonded emery cloth, white spirit etc., could be purchased far more cheaply from local DIY. stores, than from specialist shops, particularly if they had Marine in their title. We would need all the bargains we could get!

By now we had met a number of "Athene's" and had begun to feel that our boat needed a little extra in the way of a personal identity. As she was named for a Greek Goddess, responsible for wisdom and aspects of War, and as the Greeks had an established practice of adding honorific's to the names, we chose to give our "Athene" one of her Greek honour titles.

"Pallas", we understood to mean, maiden or virgin, in acknowledgement of her chaste lifestyle.

At this "make-over", our boats name would be expanded to "Pallas Athene"

We believed that the spirit of a boat objects to uncalled for name changes, but as this one was a natural enhancement of her name, she would find it acceptable.

S.A.C., were a firm offering a range of computer generated, precision cut, self adhesive vinyl lettering and trim, specially designed for the heavy outdoor use it would be exposed to on a boat. We had ordered Cove lines or as we called them, "go faster stripes", decals, flourishes and canal roses, it would cost a lot of money.

The merchandise they provided was first rate and should have lasted at least ten years but due to our inexperience and over enthusiasm we committed two cardinal sins which anyone using vinyl trim should guard against.

These will be better explained, when the narrative reaches that point

The roof of the boat was looking decidedly tatty due in the main to our practise of carrying coal, logs and other paraphernalia directly on the surface. Water gathering under these items had penetrated the paint and even our excellent etching primer had been unable to prevent some damage. To obviate this in future, we had designed a pair of roof racks, tailored to our roof space, which Peter was going to fabricate for us.

No longer would our goods sit in their own private puddles on the steel plates of the roof.

At the end of the two weeks, we were just about ready to begin work, everything was ready!

Initially we had intended to take the paintwork back to the primer mechanically, using an orbital sander. To do this we would be forced to use a very aggressive grade of emery which could prove to be, too abrasive.

There was a small container of paint stripping gel in the engine room and I tried this out on a small section of the cabin.

It worked like a charm!

Checking out the shops in Market Harborough, we found one that stocked exactly what we needed, at a reasonable price. Wilco's (Wilkinson's) sold their own brand of gel stripper which was first class and did an excellent job,

Just what was needed!,

We moved "Athene" into the wet dock, closed the steel doors and put the draught excluder in place. (A blanket draped over a plank at water level to keep out the night airs,)

As we began the task of stripping a fifty-five foot cabin, it became clear that our consumption of stripping gel would be staggering.

We cleared the stock off their shelves and then Jean began a regular pilgrimage to the shop each time new stocks were delivered. Soon her arrival at the till with the inevitable trolley, would be greeted with shouts from the check-out girls of, "Look out! Here comes the Harboro' Stripper." So much for Jean's fifteen minutes of fame!

Masked up against the heavy fumes, we moved the job along steadily and eventually we had the whole of the upperworks down to her underwear.

What did impress us was the rugged way the International's B.W. Silver Primer had adhered to the metal, after all this time the original coats were almost completely intact. Unfortunately, like many other products it seemed to have fallen foul of its own success like ladderproof nylons and everlasting lightbulbs, any product that appeared to be nearly indestructible was bad news for the marketing moguls. It had been discontinued!

"Hello darlings! You wanted an experienced STRIPPER?

To ensure a stable key we gave the whole of the upperworks, two coats of Yacht primer, well flatted, followed by three undercoats, flatted and washed. Now the cabin walls felt smooth as silk.

Her final colours would be similar to the original British Racing Green and Red. British R.G. was politically incorrect and had been discontinued but for some reason it was okay to replace it with a shade named after an Irish County, so the main body coat would be Donegal Green. Coral Red was the more exotic replacement for the good old standard Pillar-Box Red. As the red pigment was not dense, I had applied a red undercoat to ensure that the coats would be an even colour.

A hundred yards of low tack masking tape to mark out the panels and we were into the home straight.

Her roof was panelled in Cotswold Green Gloss and Green Deck Paint, the gunwales to the first rubbing strake were in C.G. with a green non-slip strip.

She was really looking good!

It was from this point on that we started to over-egg the pudding, as my Dad would have said.

When I put the cove lines and the decorative corners in place, I carefully butt jointed the sections and gave the tape a slight stretch to ensure that it was straight and well bedded down. Finally the boat received two complete coats of Yacht Varnish, to seal the surface and to impart an extra deep gloss over the whole boat.

Some two years later we found that prolonged exposure to the ultra violet rays of the summer sun during our cruises, had done two things. It had shrunk the vinyl by a tiny amount, just enough to open up the butted joints, and the white spirit in the varnish had reacted with the adhesive and loosened the edges. These had lifted, cracked the surface of the varnish and the deterioration really set in.

After three seasons, she began to look like a plate of the old, much maligned B.R. sandwiches; dry and curled up at the edges.

Beware!

Vinyl can do a great job, it saves time and can make the task of achieving a professional looking finish much easier; but, please lay it carefully on the finished paint work, only after allowing it to cure for at least a week, during which time any excess white spirit will also have time to evaporate. Do not stretch the tapes, overlap joints marginally and never, never coat with varnish. A good wax car polish will do the job of sealing and shining much better.

For us, it would prove to be an expensive mistake, maybe we can prevent others from making it!

When she did sail out of the dock, "Pallas Athene" was a sight to bring a lump to the throat, for now at least we had completed an excellent job.

She looked magnificent!

Jean's elder son, Stuart was with us for a couple of days and was able to assist with the float out into the basin.

He was definitely impressed!

The stripping and repainting had left us both with work worn hands, rough and dry from being soaked in thinners so often. One thing was sure, we could not be accused of being folk with an easy employment or one which left the skin, soft and smooth.

We had been befriended by a couple called Elizabeth and Murray, who owned a wonderful, vintage car. We had exchanged visits and had been promised a day out in their vintage open-tourer, when the weather improved towards the Spring

As we had discovered in so many places, people tended to react well to the hand of friendship proffered and in return we had been shown numerous kind deeds.

In the canal cottages near to the basin, lived a man who made pine furniture and a wide range of other objects from a variety of hardwoods. He crafted a deck stool/step for Jean as well as a Jewel Box and supplied me with the timber to make a pair of gang-planks, one short, one long, which we needed in certain "difficult to moor" areas. These were completed with foot-strips and a checkerboard pattern of non slip facing from silver sand. The finished boards were also given two coats of varnish.

Strapped on to our roof mounted pole rack, they looked really smart!

As a final touch, 1 made a pair of cross supports for our life-rings. These were screwed to the roof and carried the life preservers, one at either end of the boat.

These refinements plus the roof-racks served to tidy up our storage area and left the boat looking ultra smart with all the unwanted items tucked neatly away.

Christmas was fast approaching and the town was preparing for it's annual Late night shopping dates. As well as the usual round of late opening by the shops, the town provided, music, street entertainment and fast food kiosks.

Ian and Stuart paid a visit and treated us to a meal at a Lebanese restaurant which was as enjoyable as it was unusual.

During one of the late night shopping extravaganzas, we meet a man in the main square wearing a heavy leather gauntlet; on his wrist, its talons dug firmly into the leather, sat a large European Eagle Owl in jesses, It was a magnificent bird but totally unimpressed when we told him of our own, "Owlus Plasticus", Henry, who was at home minding the boat. With a look of sheer disdain it demonstrated it's ability to swivel it's head through approx. 320 degrees as if to say, "All right mate! Let's see your plastic pet better that then!" On the Saturday before Christmas, we called in on the Coffee Morning being held at the Anglican Church. In addition to tea and coffee they were serving, hot mince pies and spiced, mulled wine.

Very civilised!

We received a warm invitation to the Carol Service on Sunday and to Midnight Mass on Christmas Eve.

While we had been working on the boat, we had tended to put in a seven day week, starting quite often at around seven a,m. Our social life had suffered as a consequence.

One memorable night, I woke with a start at two thirty a.m., I had just had a bright idea of an easy way to construct the pentangle decoration for our engine room roof slide. Nothing loathe, I got up, dressed and went off to complete the task.

In the spirit of; "If you can't beat 'em, join 'em!", Jean had also risen and begun work. When we eventually called it a day at seven p.m., we had put in a sixteen and a half hour day.

Thank goodness I no longer belonged to a Union and could ask for time and a half, double or even triple time for such unsocial hours.

I couldn't afford myself!

Attending the Sunday morning Service, hearing the old, yet ever new message of Christmas and joining in heartily with the singing of the carols, was uplifting.

On Christmas Eve, we walked down into the brightly lit town centre with it's lights, decorations and Christmas Tree. In the ancient Church we joined the congregation in the celebration of Christ's Mass.

The walk back to the boat, our lungs filled with clear, crisp, fresh air, gave us a feeling of great happiness. We felt at peace with ourselves and the rest of the World.

The Parish Church in Market Harborough was magnificent. Built in the 14th.C. it stood large, solid and imposing, in the Market Square alongside the old Grammar School, another wonderful old building, built on brick columns to make room for the cheese market beneath.

Unusually, the Church was dedicated to St.Dionysius. It had grown old and mellow, retaining a splendour and gravitas that reflected its long history of worship and veneration.

Jean's brother, Jeremy, a Circuit Judge, paid us a visit accompanied by his wife, Edna, They lived in Derby, which was relatively close to Harborough.

In the basin, we were plagued with poor television reception and although we could get a marginally watchable picture, it did not afford a great deal of pleasure. The obvious solution was to join a Video Library, provided that we could find one willing to accept our "No fixed abode" status. The large one in the centre of town was amenable to this arrangement and our application was accepted with no trouble.

Now, we could at least watch films on our TV!

Discovering an excellent Handicraft shop in the backstreets we were able to purchase limited edition cross stitch kits of local subjects, designed by a local needlewoman. Jean bought and completed a picture of the Old Grammar School, while I chose a kit commemorating the two hundredth anniversary of the completion of the arm into the Harborough Basin.

With our collection of needlework growing apace, wall space was now seriously at a premium. If we completed too many items we could end up with our home looking cluttered and untidy. Not a situation that we viewed with any relish.

Already our collection of owls; models, embroideries, paintings, and soft toys had reached the two hundred mark. Folk seemed taken by an irresistible urge to present us with an addition to our family when they left the boat.

Now we kept visiting children engaged and busy, by asking them to locate and count all the members of our owl clan.

Typically, one of our priorities had been to locate a local launderette, we now made regular excursions to it, complete with rucksack and shopping trolley. The walk was substantial, around one and three-quarter miles but we had decided that it was worth the expenditure of time and energy.

Like many establishments situated among high density housing, it was subject to high levels of vandalism. Notices informed all and sundry that no money was left on the premises yet break-ins were a regular feature of its life.

At least the damage caused to the machines seemed to keep the hard pressed electrician in regular employment.

Just as we were beginning to look forward to recommencing our cruising, B.W. announced that the stoppage on the Foxton Locks would be extended, now the locks would remain closed until the first week in April.

That was our intended direction of travel, it was inevitable that "Pallas Athene" would be held up until the stoppage was cleared, unless the Board open up a window of opportunity for travel.

The railway station was a fair step from the town but the services were good and I at least preferred the train to the bus. Hence we made a number of excursions into various local towns intent on carrying out large quantity shopping excursions

Leicester was only a couple of stops up the line and trains to Tamworth via Derby were readily accessible, It made visiting Mum, less of a chore. We even managed to fit in a day-trip down to London in order to visit Theo, who was now over ninety years of age and becoming very fragile.

One thing that had concerned us when we began our life of cruising, was the possibility that we might face difficulties in obtaining medical assistance. This worry had proved to be totally unfounded and our experience with doctors, dentists and hospitals, where we attended on a purely casual basis, was that our reception and treatment was consistently of a high order.

Jean needed a constant supply of inhalers to treat her asthma and we found no difficulty whatsoever in obtaining scripts.

As the weather showed signs of improving, we spent some time with Elizabeth and Murray, visiting their house for meals on a couple of occasions. One weekend, towards the end of March, the promised day out in their Vintage car, materialised.

The day was dry, bright and cold. As we would be travelling in the dickey seat, just forward of the tonneau cover over the fold down top, we had dressed ourselves very warmly. I had donned my full length leather coat and was wearing my bowler hat, Jean was equally snugly wrapped against the chill. A short delay while the bonnet mascot was located, (a large chrome hare.) and Murray climbed into the driving seat after we had been safely, if a little tightly, squeezed into the rear seats. We set off to explore many of the narrow country lanes that criss-crossed the area. One visit was a must, a call at the Civil War Battle site at Naseby, another of the Royalists best forgotten conflicts with their Parliamentarian opponents.

After an excellent lunch we took our seats once more and continued the grand tour. Thus was completed a thoroughly enjoyable day out.

As usual, the enforced delay in beginning our new year's cruising was starting to take its toll. I was feeling irritable and unsettled, and there wasn't a thing I could do or say that would alter matters.

"Pallas Athene" was resplendent in her new livery, her roof racks had been fitted and loaded, the roof was tidy, the engine had been serviced, our rudder, swans neck and tiller-bar had each been greased, repainted and the bearings replaced. Everything was A OK. Nothing was left to do.

We were raring to go!!

Fortunately there was one activity progressing in the yard which exerted a fascination akin to fanaticism. A new boat was on the stocks.

Designed by the boss of the company, this boat was of a revolutionary new design.

The main part of the hull showed little deviation from normal, but inside and below the waterline she was amazing. A "canoe" hull was welded where the keel would be on a normal vessel. (Not flat bottomed like a narrowboat.) This was adjustable ballast, filled with water, it could be partially emptied to provide buoyancy and adjust the draught of the boat to suit altered conditions. The bows were sharper than normal and with less hull submerged the power requirement and the wash displacement was considerably reduced.

We studied the build with unfailing interest.

We couldn't wait to see it in the water. Assessing its performance when compared to the projections would be intriguing!

Wether she would enter the water before we left was a matter for speculation. In the event, the day arrived when she was launched, stern first into the basin, as was the practice at that yard. Now she could be tried under power, when she had been checked for leaks.

In her powered trials she fulfilled her designers prophesies in every respect.

At last departure day arrived. We intended to cruise down to Foxton, moor overnight, then head up the flight first thing next morning.

When we arrived in the basin we moored up and decided to check out the locks to see the work that had been done on shoring up the walls of the pounds which had suffered from damage caused by badgers building their setts in the banks.

In a prominent position on the B.W. notice board was a warning that due to subsidence on an embankment towards Watford there would be an emergency closure in operation from the next morning, This co-incided with the date set for the re-opening of the flight.

A short climb took us to the passing pound where the lady lock-keeper was busy.

As there were now two boats anxious to clear the locks before the canal closure was enforced it meant that we would have to climb the staircase that afternoon, or be stuck in Foxton for an indefinite period.

The two flights were still being filled with water and the passing pound was a sorry sight. A small trickle of water between banks of mud, Nothing daunted the lass agreed to lock our boats through and set off to organise the water supply.

The passage through the lock chambers was problem free, negotiating the passing pound was an entirely different story. It was a nightmare but at last we found ourselves safely in the locks themselves,

Arriving at the top, we set off to cruise the five miles to the site of the emergency stoppage so that we could find a satisfactory mooring beyond it,

That five miles proved to be horrific!

The workmen were still preparing the canal for re-opening and knew nothing of the stoppage planned for the next day. We needed to press on but at virtually every bridge work was in progress and mud-boats were moored in the entrances to the bridge holes. We were committed to easing "Pallas Athene" slowly through the narrow gaps, her freshly painted gunwales held clear of the battered steel barges by the thickness of her rubbing strakes.

The tension was heart-stopping, the streaks of green paint left behind on the mudboats, heart-breaking.

We cleared the danger area and moored up for a restorative cuppa. Our mood could accurately be described as dischuffed.

Not an auspicious start to our third year of continually cruising.

13.
Seen that, Got the Tee-shirt!

The territory we were now entering was so familiar that we stood together on the stern watching well known vistas swimming into view. We reminisced on the early days of cruising when everything was new to us.

Then, we would sit quietly among gatherings of canal folk and listen in something akin to awe, to them recounting experiences from their travels, comparing notes and sharing information. The locations of new shops, changes, for better or worse, in the tenancy of canal-side pubs, closures of facilities or the deterioration of regular moorings.

Our admiration of their depths of knowledge and the casual way in which they described routes and venues, knew no bounds.

However would a pair of complete tyros like us ever amass the vast amount of information needed to match these casual feats of familiarity with the canal system?

After nearly two years of cruising we were now able to make valid and significant contributions to conversations about certain sections of the canals and that store of information was growing daily. Our practice of gentle cruising interspersed with in-depth exploration of some areas had given us an almost encyclopaedic grasp of the type of information our fellow boaters were keen to glean.

For instance, we could often give details of excellent local services we had located; "Moor up 200 yds. past the top lock, take the signposted footpath through the hedge, follow it for 400 yds. to the lane. Turn left, then first right, the local butcher is 50 yds. down on the left. His meat is first class, his pies, pasties and cold meats, home cooked and superb. As a bonus, he acts as an agent for the local bakery and can supply "real bread"!

Early in the day it is warm, yeasty and crusty. Delicious!

Often this information was as new and as fresh as the bread!

Up to date information on moorings was always gratefully accepted.

We were cruising the Grand Union and although the tunnels were built to take wide boats, they did not have towing paths and gave the impression of being narrower than they in fact were. Braunston was no exception. It had a number of slight deviations from the straight and narrow, which in earlier days had sometimes caught us out. Our navigation lights had kissed against the tunnel walls before now.

Today, all was plain sailing.

A feature that was becoming more noticeable was the sheer volume of piling work that was being carried out, as damaged and overgrown banks were repaired. What raised the level of our concern was the method employed. No effort was made to re-establish the original line, the Armco pilings were being driven three to four feet inside the channel, encroaching on already severely reduced navigation widths.

With the offside banks left untended, trees overhanging the water and the channel obstructed by roots and reed beds, the towing path side, when the gap between the new edging and the original line was filled with dredgings and consolidated, would make way for a canalside pathway wide enough to accept motor vehicles or at least, a phalanx of Lycra clad, pointy helmeted, all terrain cyclists.

Eventually, some two years later, we had the unnerving experience of cruising down a canal built to pass two 13 ft. 6 in. wide barges, with the reed beds brushing both sides of our narrowboat, simultaneously, so overgrown were the beds of reeds flanking both sides of the channel.

We attended a number of rallies each year and usually managed to tackle some feature of the waterways that we considered to be a challenge or an achievement, such items as the Harecastle Tunnel and the Pontcysyllte Aqueduct etc. .To record these, we had collected a number of brass plates which now adorned our engine room doors.

This practice is viewed in a variety of ways. Some people collect avidly, amassing so much brassware, that periodically the have to shift their ballast to compensate, others view the whole practice as trivial and look upon it with disdain.

We fall between the two camps, we recognise the limitations made on us by lack of mounting space but still seek to mark particular achievements or specially enjoyable events.

An alternative that we sometimes fell back onto was the buying and wearing of Tee shirts, produced by local Canal Societies, Rally organisers or those commemorating the completion of particular Canals, Arms or special features.

As an exercise this could prove to be, not only expensive but obsessive. Our collection was so large that we had special His'n'Her drawers to house it.

One could be loath to wear a special Tee shirt while completing a particularly mucky job, so, they ended up being wore as undershirts and not fulfilling their role as covert advertisements.

This year our itinerary was unusually firm. We intended to complete our courtesy calls and duty visits early, then head east to explore that side of the country. The Trent and Mersey would lead us to the main river and we would be able to explore the Erewash Canal. Continuing along the Trent would lead to Nottingham, Newark, then down the tidal section to Torksey, the Witham and Fossdyke Navigations, Lincoln, Boston and the East Coast. At Lincoln we were looking forward to seeing Brayford Pool which, in Roman times, was a major Inland Port

Returning to the Midlands we intended to head North and our cycle of rallies included, Etruria, Stone, Nantwich and Ellesmere Port. Continuing to head North we would revisit the Wigan Steam Rally before cruising to Stourport where we would enter the River Severn for the cruise down to Gloucester followed by the Sharpness Navigation. This carried boats to the huge tide lock which handled traffic to and from the Severn Estuary and down to Avonmouth and Bristol. (This way we aimed to be well clear of the congestion of National Waterways Festival which was to be held at Chester.) Retracing our steps we intended to leave the river at Tewkesbury in order to cruise the Upper and Lower Avon Navigations, revisiting Stratford, Back onto familiar waters to Birmingham, Fazeley and the Coventry Canal. The Coventry Basin was newly restored and should prove worthy of a visit. We were in need of some small additional items of brassware, so a detour up the Ashby Canal to visit Les at Fenda Products was indicated.

We hoped to round off the season with a visit to the B.C.N and the end of season rally at Stourbridge before returning to Shobnall Marina, Burton upon Trent where we were booked in for a winter of servicing the boat, This should include, dry-docking to paint the bottom, check the rudder and stern gear and the anodes,

It promised to be our most ambitious cruising year yet! Still back to the present!

Reaching Bedworth, we found that Dot and Sid had a young grandson staying with them. He was an avid fan of "Rosie and Jim", so a short trip on a "real" boat seemed to be in order, Sid was thrilled and fascinated to ride the stern at the steering position, although he felt himself to be too frail to take over the helm.

Connor, the grandson, thought all craft should have "Rosie and Jim" on board and spent much of his time waving to other boats and asking after the famous pair.

He was definitely a little wary of the large, white-haired, bearded character steering the boat he found himself sailing in. Gran and Grandad did their best to explain our family relationship but Connor was not going to have any of this.

He did, however, enjoy both the meal on the boat and the sweets his new relatives had thoughtfully provided.

Mum and Joan were pleased to see us again. Joan, if only for the fact that I would collect our mail and she could have her hall cupboard back, just for a short time,

Soon we were heading east for Shardlow and the River Trent.

One last stop at Alrewas to see our grandchildren including the new arrival Harry. As a parting gesture we loaded Mum, Dad and the children on board and cruised down to The Happy Eater at Barton. After Sunday lunch we put them into a taxi back to Alrewas; we were free and clear.

We descended one lock at Barton Turns, moored up and set up our TV., it was Formula One Grand Prix day; one of our very few, must watch, events!

Timing our arrival with our usual care, we arrived at Shardlow on Tuesday so that we could visit the "New Inn" and enjoy the weekly "Traditional Jazz Night" By now we knew a number of the members of the band and the nights always proved to be great fun.

Our Dutch friends were in the pub again so as well as being entertained, we were able to renew old acquaintances.

Next day we did the short run down to the River Trent then made the turn across the current to enter the Erewash Canal at Trent Lock. This waterway is the only remaining navigable section of an extensive network built during the last twenty years of the nineteenth century.

The Erewash was completed in around 1870 and had for its engineer and surveyor, two local men, Smith and Varley. Much of the rest of the network was surveyed and built by a much more well known duo, Jessop and Oughtram. They completed the Cromford Canal around 1794 and the Derby; Nottingham and Nutbrook Canals during 1796. The network was built, amid the usual storms of controversy, to carry coal and raw materials from the coal-fields to the centres of Industry around Nottingham and Derby.

One rather odd feature of a network built to broad boat specifications, was the Butterley Tunnel on the Cromford Canal. This tunnel, over three thousand yards long, was built to the narrow gauge. As it took over three hours for a loaded boat to be legged through the tunnel, a major bottleneck was created

With the exception of the Erewash, the rest of the system was gradually closed down due to subsidence, lack of repair and maintenance and the major fall off of transport demands when rail links were established. Now large sections of these canals are traceable only as marshy depressions, filled in lock chambers or forlorn bridges, spanning nothing, leading nowhere.

With the increasing pace of regeneration, much of this group of waterways is scheduled for reinstatement and renewal.

Slightly under 12 miles in length, the Erewash has 15 broad locks some of which have been fitted with anti-vandal padlocks to protect the waterway from the attentions of the small groups of bored young people that seem to spring up everywhere and create nuisance. In spite of this it did offer a considerable range of interesting factors. Many of the original architectural features are still in place and towards its terminus at Langley Mill, the line of the old Nottingham Canal can still be traced across the countryside, in places paralleling the Erewash and identifiable by the lines of double hedges that once enclosed it,

It was on this canal that we first met up with "The Tilson Giant" and her owners. Tony and Jo were a pleasant couple deeply interested in the history of the canals and the customs attributed to boat people and how they organised their boats. Jo's great grandfather was the "Ilkeston Giant" a man, seven feet four inches tall and after whom their boat was named. Later we were privileged to count this pair among our friends.

Long Eaton had offered a good range of shops and a thriving market, Ilkeston and Sandiacre a fine range of services as well as shops and Langley Mill, good, safe mooring in the basin, which was also the terminal point of the Nottingham and Cromford Canals. In fact it was still possible to traverse the first 300 or so yards of the Cromford, which was now used as long term moorings by the local Canal Preservation Society which was responsible for the upkeep and management of the area above the final lock. We carried on past the moorings, winded and returned to the visitor moorings, taking on water and diesel at the wharf, next to the excellent dry dock facility.

The town of Eastwood crowns the hill, dominating the Great Northern Basin, as the terminal is named. Famous in Literary circles as the birthplace of D.H. Lawrence, it was the setting for at least one of his well known works.

In common with a number of canals whose terminal point is a considerable height above its main junction with the rest of the system, the Erewash depends upon streams and reservoirs for its water supply now that the Cromford no longer feeds it. Levels are supplemented by a back pumping system which returns water from the River Erewash into the basin to retain its level.

The industrial bases of the area were coal and textiles. Some wonderful examples of Victorian Industrial architecture are to be found both around the canal and in the surrounding towns.. After a week in the basin, attending to a variety of small jobs and exploring the area, we headed back towards the River Trent, and our next stopover point, the City of Nottingham.

The Trent carries a considerable volume of water and the locks and lock cuts are an integral part of an essential, flood protection layout. Like many large river navigations, levels are monitored and a rise above a certain height sees the flood gates closed on the canalised sections, passage prohibited and the main water controlled by the massive weirs.

The weather seemed set fair and we were reasonably confident of normal summertime levels for the duration of our cruise. One thing that we always had to bear in mind when exploring areas only accessible via major watercourses, was the possibility of being caught up in or delayed by unforeseen flood conditions. Not a prospect that I viewed with any measure of equanimity.

Once the river had been navigable right through Nottingham and the disused lock at Beeston still gave some indication of its original course. The Beeston Cut had been dug around the same time as the Erewash system, to carry the traffic into the City centre. Along this cut were the remains of the junction with the Nottingham Canal and the wharfs and buildings once associated with it, although inevitably much has now disappeared beneath modern developments,

The name, Lenton Chain Bridge, evoked a stirring in the memory of the hustle and bustle this area once knew.

From this area the Cut became the Nottingham Canal and carried the boats through the city centre to link up with the Trent once again at Trent Bridge. Across the river sprawled the bulks of Trent Bridge Cricket ground and the stadiums of the Nottingham Football Clubs, Forest and County.

We moored just beyond the large Marina, outside a major supermarket. Plenty of time to explore the City and its historic buildings.

Here much was made of the links between Nottingham, its castle, Sherwood Forest and the legend of Robin Hood.

The oft rebuilt Castle and the city's extensive system of underground passageways and caves offer the sightseer an interesting diversion.

Most of the centre is modern with shopping malls and arcades. It owed its prosperity to the textile industry, especially its beautiful hand made lace and latterly to the tobacco industry and the local household famous brand name, "Players"

Once we were past Trent Bridge the river really took on all the aspects of a major waterway and as such demanded to be treated with the utmost respect, especially close to the weirs which dominated the entrances to the lock cuts. Thirty miles and 6 locks would take us to Cromwell Lock which marked the beginning of the tidal section. Once there we intended to cover a further sixteen miles to Torksey and the entrance to the Fossdyke Navigation.

Just downstream of Trent Bridge was the entrance to the long abandoned Grantham Canal, while a mile or so on was the Holme Peirpoint Rowing Centre, one of our premier International Water Sports venues. Here, we were told, a small narrowboat, apparently in a fit of mental aberration, attempted to pass between the large white posts which protected the entrance to the White Water Canoe Course. Fortunately, the water pressure held his boat, jammed against the posts until his rescue was effected.

He never did get to try out his narrowboat on white water. Pity!

There are oft repeated, but I'm sure, apocryphal tales, of boaters bypassing locks, taking boats down the weir slope then complaining to the lock- keepers about the lack of water making the passage bumpy!

The combination of a broad navigation and keeper operated locks, enabled us to make good time and the twenty five or so miles to Newark were soon behind us.

The river would not present any real hazards until the tidal section was reached but it was still large enough to command our respect. Soon we would be meeting with the huge laden sand and stone barges that still ply the lower reaches.

With only two bridges, the rail crossing at Radcliffe and the A6097 crossing at Gunthorpe, the main items to keep us on our mettle were the locks. Along the Trent the small villages seemed to prefer to keep their distance from this unpredictable river often huddled behind flood defence walls,

In spite of the weirs and other control mechanisms the water was still able to overflow its banks on occasions, to devastating effect.

Approaching Newark the aspect changed as industry began to close in towards the river.

Just down stream of Fardon, with its large, off-line Marina built in the remains of flooded gravel quarries, the main course of the river struck off to the west down a massive weir leaving a much depleted stream to carry traffic into the town with its two locks, Town and Nether.

Below Town Lock, the east bank is dominated by the ruins of Newark Castle, now little more than an imposing facade standing less than twenty feet from the waters edge.. Once a Royalist stronghold, it saw a number of sieges before it eventually fell into ruins.

During our approach "Pallas Athene" passed the old windmill and the maltings, reminders of the town's previous history as a centre of the Brewery trade.

Initially we took advice and moored up on the left bank below the lock. For the first time, this advice was at fault and proved to be rather expensive.

Typical of river moorings, these were very high, with an overhang slightly above gunwale height. Cruisers with their extra height and large, fat fenders were fine, our slim, hard fenders were not adequate to keep us clear of the concrete. Before we awoke to the danger, the movement imparted by the passage of other craft, ground part of our engine room wall along the overhang ruining our newly completed livery.

Crossing over, we moored below the trip boats. The walls were even higher but they were flat, it proved to be a very sound move.

One thing that we had discovered, was that, when one or two boaters are gathered together, the conversation will inevitably turn to topics, lavatorial; pump-outs, porta-potties or bucket'n'chuckit, or else, after a convivial drink or three, the sharing of experiences and anecdotes with regard to life on the water. Many, were oft repeated and lost very little in the telling.

A number of years later, after the publication of, "Athene"; Anatomy of a Dream, we were often amused to be regaled with anecdotes that appeared to come straight off its pages, even though they were transposed to different settings and boasted another cast list.

Jean's Aunt used to press for me to include a murder or two, as, in her words, "a book will not sell unless it has a few juicy bits in it, like murders, to pep up the text."

I never did get around to including murders or apocryphal anecdotes, however amusing. If one did seen irresistible, it may have gained its place, provided that the reader was well acquainted, in its introduction, with a statement of its provenance.

While we were in Newark, we found ourselves involved in a minor incident which called to mind some of the discussions we had had in respect of aspects of boating protocol, particularly traditional methods of doing things, which often proved to be based on sound common sense.

A 52 ft. narrowboat was being single-handed through Town Lock. As she began to leave the chamber there was a shuddering thump and her engine stopped. The extra long centre rope had slipped off the roof, fallen into the water and been carried back, into the propeller. With one end firmly round the centre stud, the other tangled round the prop, she was dead in the water. While he and Jean held the boat steady, I lifted the weed hatch cover and cleared the tangle.

The task was quickly accomplished and, although the last six feet of rope was a little worst for wear, the long line was still useable.

As we waved him out of the lock and wished him, "Good Cruising" my mind played back some of the regular discussions we had been involved in relating to rope safety.

I had always understood that the working boaters never moved a motor boat with its stern rope attached. This long rope was stowed on the cabin roof, in a neat coil. There, it was to hand if needed for one of the numerous emergencies which could require access to a rope, coiled ready for throwing. The actual mooring rope was much shorter, with a spliced loop for dropping over the dolly and was usually held secure by one of the cabin strings.

Although overhanging trees and bushes create hazards that were less likely to affect the old boaters. The idea of having an accessible line has merit and the practice of carrying it coiled over the tiller pin, woven between the dollies or coiled on the stern deck would appear to restrict the usefulness of the rope and at worst create hazards.

Whatever the logic of the arguments, discussions over rope handling and mooring techniques fill many a happy hour, and long may they continue to do so.

A relatively short distance below Nether Lock, the transition to tidal conditions was marked by the appearance of Cromwell Lock off our bows.

Now we would be faced with the necessity of timing our runs in order that we arrived at our destination while the locks were still operational. At certain states of the tide it was impossible to clear the lock cills due to the different water levels.

Boaters on the Tidal Trent can be faced with some nasty moments if they are uninformed and unprepared. We had our copy of the Trent Boating Association Navigation Charts and were reasonably confident of our ability to negotiate the river without mishap.

One phenomena we were unlikely to encounter was the "Aegir" or Trent Tidal Bore. This tidal wave could reach heights of up to five feet but was usually only seen at times of high or "Spring" tides in the area between Torksey and Keadby. Currently the state of the tides fell into the low or "Neap" category and we were leaving the river at Torksey.

When I opened the chart and saw how the river twisted and turned it became abundantly clear why there were so many shoals to make the navigation difficult. Boaters more used to the canal system where mud banks were likely to be the major hazard would need to be aware of the vast difference between those and the gravel shoals thrown up by the river currents. These would be far less forgiving and an incautious move on a falling tide could easily spell disaster.

Once again civilisation had stepped back from the river's banks, now it's presence was mainly marked by the regular procession of wharfs, in various stages of use from fully operational to derelict, that appeared from time to time, usually off the starboard bow.

With a 65 foot craft it was essential that the correct course was steered through the difficult bends in order to avoid shoaling water. The flow of the river could quickly turn a mistake into a crabwise passage that was as dangerous to experience, as it was funny to watch; if your own boat wasn't the one in difficulties.

It was at Normanton Stakes, a sweeping right-hand bend, its approach masked by a massive gravel bank to the left and a long, sunken island mid-stream, leaving a narrow port-side passage, that Sod's Law exerted itself with a vengeance. We had cleared the gravel bank, swung to port to line up with the approach to the channel when a massive, stone laden barge entered the passage from downstream. Its approach had been masked by the steep banks lining the next bend.

Although nominally, as the boat travelling downstream, we had right of passage, it was clear that a laden working boat was not to be argued with and common sense dictated that I would have the better manoeuvrability. I was forced to make the passage, keeping well over to the right, which placed us perilously close to the hidden hazard, the position of which was unknown to me.

Fortunately the tide was rising and our draft was relatively shallow and we negotiated the crossing without a hitch. Had my hair not already been white it may have surprised my friends by changing colour during the course of this incident.

The landmarks on the chart appeared on cue with comforting accuracy and navigation was aided by the distance markers that we passed at each kilometre. These coinciding neatly with the distances appearing on our chart.

With High Marnham Power Station dominating our forrard horizon we arrived at the Water Sports Centre where, at various times it was possible to encounter canoes, sailing boats, skiffs and most scary of all, high powered speedboats towing water-skiers. With wet-suit clad figures weaving across our bows and seemingly trying to brush the sides of our boat in transit, we were left with our propeller cavitating as it tried to bite into the waves as we crashed through the washes. To my heightened senses there appeared to be a conspiracy as to which skier could get closest to our boat. This was possibly not the case but as someone lacking experience of these type of antics I was not best amused.

At the huge Fledborough Railway Viaduct, boats travelling down-stream had to steer through the left hand channel rather than to the right of the central support as would normally be the case. This hazard was followed almost immediately by the Fledborough Shoal, a large, solid gravel bank that once again pushed us into a narrow passage off the left hand bank.

This time no gravel barges arrived to dispute passage.

Dunham Rack and the paired bridge and aqueduct, were approached via an enormous 'Z' bend which exited at the base of a cliff face. Here erosion was causing heavy silting and shoal water.

Passage beneath the bridges was restricted to the right-hand channel by the large shoal that had been created by the currents, between the bridge piers and tailing off downstream.

From Laneham Ferry, the river executed a slow, right hand curve that ended in a long straight. Here again power boats and skiers were permitted to operate, much to our concern as we felt very vulnerable to involvement in an accident.

Finally the river made an enormous ess through two 180° bends with the channel leading to the Torksey Lock Cut striking our between shoals just beyond the apex of the second bend.

With a heartfelt sigh of relief we cruised into the placid, if somewhat shallow waters of the cut and moored up below the lock.

For some reason, notice of our passage did not seem to have been passed on by the Cromwell lock-keeper and no-one was on duty. We had resigned ourselves to a night on the lock moorings when the keeper arrived. It seemed we had made very good time against the rising tide and had arrived earlier than expected.

Soon we were safely locked through and we found ourselves on the waters of the Fossdyke Navigation.

This historic waterway had been built by Emperor Hadrian's men to link the inland port of Lincoln with the River Trent.

We were about to follow part of a route laid down by Hadrian's Legions and redolent with the heady breath of history.

14.
In the steps of the Legions.

Clearing the lock at Torksey, we entered the Fossdyke Navigation, reputed to have been built at the order of Emperor Hadrian around the year AD 120. Its purpose was to expand the trade routes by opening up a link between the River Trent and the inland port of Lincoln. This waterway was the oldest man-made navigation still in use. Now it formed part of the flood defences and had the added advantage of being navigable. Of major importance, it was in regular use up until the 17th century, when silting caused it to be abandoned.

As canal mania gripped the country towards the end of the 18th century, it was re-established. The traffic it carries now is virtually completely leisure based but its quiet charm still attracts many boaters.

Our empathy with the historic vibes of area, was working overtime now. Our imaginations ran wild.

Many people tend to find its broad, straight reaches and high flood banks somewhat boring, particularly as there is a dearth of signs of habitation. We were in our element!

No distant hum of motorway traffic, rarely the sound of trains, we were alone with the sounds of nature, broken, for us of course, by the steady beat of our own engine.

In the eleven or so miles to Lincoln, only the tiny village of Saxilby intruded upon the peace of the waterway.

A Celtic settlement called Lindon had been occupied by the Romans who changed its name to Lindum Colonia. Brayford Pool, a large expanse of water at the heart of the area was linked to Boston on the Wash by the River Witham, which they also made navigable. With the Fossdyke open their craft could enter the mouth of the Humber, turn into the Trent at its confluence with the Ouse, then reach Lindum Colonia via Torksey and the Dyke.

Later the stone for those two magnificent Norman edifices, the Castle and the Cathedral, would be brought into the town by this route. The enormous task of manhandling these large blocks of stone, up the steep hillside to the site chosen for the buildings, would have daunted most modern civil engineering contractors.

So flat is this area of Fenland, that the ridge upon which the Cathedral and Castle were built gives them an elevation that dominates the view for miles.

Jean had been based at RAF Waddington for part of her military service and I had attended a number of training courses in the county as a member of the Royal Observer Corps., so we both were on the look-out for RAF planes flying overhead.

Waddington is only some 5 miles outside the city, built on the wide expanse of Fenland that stretches away from the ridge,

At the end of our first day we moored up in Brayford Pool!

The moorings, which appeared to be controlled by Lincoln Boat club, were clearly intended for GRP cruisers and suchlike, they were about 40ft. long finger moorings reaching out into the pool. We were 65ft. long and so over a third of our boat extended into the route of the craft crossing in either direction. This was obviously regular practice and we did not feel in any danger of collision during our stay.

The facilities on offer were excellent, it was even possible to have a shower. Unfortunately the unit on their pump out had a burnt out armature so we were not able to empty our toilet tank.

With so much to see we arranged to spend a few days there, it was not cheap but there was no problem over our request and we made ourselves comfortable.

Climbing the hill to the Castle and Cathedral was a major undertaking for two people almost past their sell-by dates and we were careful to avoid doing it more than once per day. This meant eating out at lunchtimes but as there were a number of pleasant places available it was no hardship.

Except to our pockets, Lincoln can be expensive!

It was still April, the tourist season was not fully underway and we had a reasonably quiet time to do our sightseeing.

Like many similar towns and cities, Lincoln boasted some superb bookshops. I was definitely in my element. Another wonderful find was a specialist Tea and Coffee retailer whose shop was a mecca for people like us who enjoyed different varieties. For instance the shop boasted a collection of around 30 or so Darjeeling teas, from different plantations, heights and seasons

A veritable Aladdin's cave of flavours for the aficionado.

Extensively rebuilt, the Cathedral was still a magnificent building with many architectural features of note. Like so many places of historic importance, including our beloved canals, age was making its heavy hand felt and the costs of restoration and maintenance was evident in the un-subtle requests for cash support. For people on a small fixed income, like ourselves, this created a feeling of discomfort THAT we were wasting our cash eating instead of supporting our friendly neighbourhood Cathedral.

It took something of the pleasure out of our visits!

Sad!

One of Jean's special memories was of the Olde Worlde Tearooms which formed part of the Tudor style buildings, built on the bridge over the River Witham where it exited the Brayford Pool. Known locally as "the Glory Hole" or as Jean insisted on calling it "the Devil's Hole", This must rank as one of the best known, most photographed bridges around. Of the Tudor style river crossings which carried a range of shops and dwellings, this was one of a tiny handful still in existence. It still carried buildings along both sides, in mediaeval times it would have been so crowded that it would not be possible to distinguish it from the rest of the street.

In spite of the large number of shops and stores in modern Lincoln, the city still retained much that was of interest to people like us who had a feel for history and an urge to visit sites of archeological interest.

After a couple of very interesting days, we took our leave of the city. Moving slowly beneath the bustle of the traffic over the "Glory Hole", I navigated our craft while Jean stood in the bows adding to our already extensive photographic record.

Before leaving the built-up area we encountered our first guillotine lock, an odd looking structure with a strong weir-race to one side. Unlike its counterparts on the River Nene, which we understood to be manually operated, this one had electric controls and electronic interlocks to make its operation foolproof.

On normal locks the flow of water into or out of the chamber is controlled by the size of the sluices. Here the full width gate or guillotine was raised vertically by means of steel hawsers winding onto drums and hoisting the gate into an overhead gantry. Lifted too quickly or too far it would allow a dangerously rapid change of water level within the chamber. On a manual lock the gearing between the gate and the operating ratchet was so low that the gate could only be inched upward, effectively controlling the flow. Here a sequence of lifts and pauses was preset into the operating circuits these made sure that all was safe.

Part of the Wolverton canal-side Mural

Foxton Locks on the way to Market Harborough

Snowed up! In our new livery.

Winter ride in a vintage car.

Last remaining Diamond-shaped Lock at Wyre Piddle, Avon

At least the neighbours are quiet

Shobnall Basin. Snowed in.

Shobnall Basin. The blizzard strikes.

Tixall Wide. Just right for Christmas!

Even a boat can look festive!

Snug and warm for Christmas

New Year. Great Haywood Junction

Taking "Pallas Athene" out of the lock, beneath the dripping gate suspended over my head, (like a huge guillotine blade) was quite nerve-racking, for a first time experience.

Moving downstream into the countryside, we had a further reminder of the problems that had been created by the Teenage Ninja Turtle craze of the late eighties. Sitting on a log which was securely bedded into the silt, taking advantage of the warm, spring sunshine, was a large, red-eared terrapin. As an indication of how well these creatures had adapted to life on the inland waterways, this one had reached the size of a small dinner plate.

It presented a strange sight!

This was to prove to be a day for stirring sights.

We had only covered around two miles and the castle and Cathedral still dominated the view aft. Suddenly we became conscious of the thud of heavy engines counterpoised by a faster, lighter beat. Our eyes were drawn downstream. Low over the water, lining up for their run along the ridge, we saw a formation of three, familiar aircraft. The heavy, thudding beat heralded the approach of the famous Lancaster bomber, "City of Lincoln" held aloft by its four mighty Rolls Royce engines. Flanking her, in echelon, came two Rolls powered fighter planes, a Supermarine Spitfire and a Hawker Hurricane.

They were on a practice run for a commemorative flypast due to take place on May Day.

We waved like children from the stern of our boat as the sound washed over us, awakening memories and making the hair stand up on the napes of our necks.

We felt a real surge of nostalgic nationalism as we watched this brave display.

Typically the one object we did not have with us on the stern of our boat, was a camera.

The run down to Boston was 32 miles and as it only featured two locks, one of which was already behind us, we had plenty of time to chat excitedly about the spectacle we had just observed.

Lincolnshire, with its wide flat expanses of countryside had been home to many RAF and American Air Force bases during the second World War so it was not surprising that special displays were staged from time to time.

In contrast, as we cruised along the wide, straight reaches of the river with tall flood banks on either side restricting our visibility, it was easy to imagine an ancient England, sparsely populated. Each slight bend in the course of the waterway could have revealed a rough wooden jetty and a group of Roman soldiers, waiting for transport.

Reminders of the flat expanses behind the banks appeared from time to time in the form of large drains which cut through the banks. Each was closed with a one way valve, in the form of hinged flood gates which allowed the excess water to drain from the land into the river but prevented flood water carried by the navigation entering the ditch and flooding the fields. These dykes and ditches formed an essential part of the area's flood defences.

Some were large enough to be navigable and entry to those was controlled by lock gates. At 65ft long, we were definitely too long to risk any excursions off the main line, except perhaps into the Maud Foster Drain at Boston.

Another navigable section was Kyme Eau, again well down towards Boston. This one was reputed to have a boatyard and moorings but we had agreed not to explore it on this trip.

In spite of the relatively low traffic flow the water was cloudy, this was no bad thing as it did serve to inhibit weed growth. We had found a number of times that where the water was clear, particularly if fed by the run-off from agricultural land, the phosphates carried into the water reacted to the sunshine to produce rampant weed growth. If traffic movement in such waters was low the channel soon suffered from silting and oxygen deprivation.

Shoals of dead fish soon alerted us to the onset of these ecological disasters, caused in the name of progress.

This sense of isolation did not always exist, as a railway could be seen following the line of the river. Half a mile before the village of Bardney, where the railway crossed the navigation on an iron bridge, a weir led the main river away to the left where it described a huge curve and rejoined the channel below the lock. The land enclosed by the water was known as Branston Island. (No connection I'm sure with the well known Richard of Ballooning fame.)

Closed to passenger traffic and carrying only a small quantity of freight, the line could virtually be ignored as a source of noise.

At the lock itself we saw good moorings and a sign indicating a range of services that included showers. A good spot to break our trip on the return cruise. These moorings were not convenient to the village but we discovered a short stretch of moorings near to Bardney Bridge.

A reminder of the perils attendant with mooring on river navigations came as we cruised along the short straight to Bardney. Along this length the private moorings on the right hand side were littered with wreckage and sunken boats; the aftermath of the serious flooding that had occurred in the early spring.

Dykes, drains, ditches, delphs, washways, so many designations for the cross hatching of channels that fed the standing water off the fields into the main navigation.

Between Bardney and Boston, a matter of 22 miles, there were three small villages where mooring was possible; Southrey, Kirkstead and Chapel Hill. These were in the main short lengths of rising moorings provided by the Pubs for the benefit of their patrons. At Chapel Hill the accommodation included a boat club as here one finds the entrance to the Kyme Eau or Sleaford Navigation.

Around half a mile short of Tattershall Bridge we passed the remains of the Horncastle Canal. There were reasonable moorings and Tattershall Castle as well as the disused canal to explore, so we added it to our list of stopoff points for the return trip.

According to our guide the area around Dogdyke must have been quite busy as two boatyards were shown on the map. As we cruised past we searched in vain for the slightest trace of either.

The final ten miles into Boston was broken only by Langricks Bridge which had replaced a ferry crossing. There was no sign of moorings.

The tower of St.Botolph's Church in Boston, known familiarly as the "Boston Stump" could be seen from almost as far away as Chapel Hill.

Two and a quarter miles from Boston at Anton's Gowt is the lock that marks the entrance to the Maud Foster Drain. Navigable into the centre of the town it did not re-connect with the main river. As I was not aware of the length of boat that could be safely winded in the drain and not wishing to risk a three mile reverse, we decided not to venture into the unknown.

The drain was also linked into the network of waterways known as the Witham Navigable Drains. As with the Middle levels that radiate from the rivers Nene and Ouse they had a size restriction of around sixty feet so we would be barred from exploring much of these systems.

Prior to our choosing to live on a narrowboat, we had lived in South Devon and had visited the harbour in Plymouth and read the commemorative plaque to that famous group of people, the "Pilgrim Fathers" who, as everyone knows, set sail for America from that harbour.

Not so!!

Boston in Lincolnshire was the port from which their momentous journey actually started. It was from the surrounding Fenlands that many of the original group that sailed in the "Mayflower", were drawn.

Many river navigations have one fault above all others in the eyes of narrowboaters; the majority of moorings are intended for short boats and cruisers. Linear moorings are space consuming but finger moorings even if arranged in echelon are of little use to a craft whose length is excess of half the width of the navigation. Fortunately in the town there was a mix of moorings with sufficient linear berths for three or four long craft. We were able to slip into the last remaining space. Anchored off our bows, a lovely Dutch sailing barge with side mounted, swing keels.

Two landmarks dominated the area, the town's magnificent parish church, with it's late decorated architecture and tall tower topped with a huge pierced lantern, the filigree stonework looking for all the world like petrified lace, then, a little way from the centre, a well restored, working windmill on the banks of the Maud Foster Drain.

Here then were two musts for our programme of visits!

Our berth was situated as far from the town as it could be. This caused me a little extra effort each morning as I walked into town for my newspaper but it also provided me with an unforgettable experience.

"Walking under the railway bridge that spans the river above the Grand Sluice, I was startled to see a small bundle of fluff fall from the bridge and land with a tiny plop in the water. The girders were some 12 ft. above my head and I peered upward to see what was happening. As I looked two more balls of fluff were launched into the abyss. At that point I saw a Mallard duck standing on the girders marshalling a brood of ducklings. The nest was an untidy pile of sticks, in the junction between two girders and some 8 or 9 inches below the permanent way of a very active railway line.

I stood in amazement and counted as Mama gently persuaded each tiny bird to make this leap of faith. Dad, all this time, was 150 yards up-stream chatting to his mates.

As each little body, skinny legs, webbed feet and tiny wing stubs spread wide, plummeted down into the water, she peered down until the tiny bundle resurfaced, gave a reassuring quack, told it to stay with the others, then turned to give her attention to the next in line.

This procedure carried on until there were thirteen ducklings bobbing around in a tight circle, just out of range of the falling bodies.. At this juncture, Mother left the bridge and flew down to this group leaving the remainder of the brood, stranded up among the girders.

When she had checked out the well being of the first group and marshalled then safely, she called to the remainder to "Come on down!"

Whee! Plop; Whee! Plop; Whee! Plop.

Three more little bodies made the one-way trip to the outside world. This left number 17, alone, squeaking piteously, waddling along the girder. Mother called out to it to get the lead out and join its siblings.

Taking its courage in both stubby wings, it moved to the edge of the girder, did the duckling equivalent of holding its nose, closed its eyes and jumped. His wanderings had put him out of position and the drop ended some 15 inches later, on top of a bridge support pillar. His second effort landed him on top of a support ring for the steelwork some eight inches below. After some more perambulations it was third time lucky. This time the drop was completed, unfortunately, on the wrong side of the pillar. This just was not his day, all that fuss and now everyone had disappeared. There followed a short bout of hide and seek around the pillar, the family was reunited and Mother set off upstream ahead of an untidy flotilla. Father had watched these proceedings from a safe distance, but now he joined the group. 17 hatchlings must be a very large clutch to manage.

One can but admire such devotion to raising a family under such extreme conditions."

I recounted this event in my first book "Athene" Anatomy of a dream and make no apology for repeating that anecdote in its correct chronological position in this volume. I was very impressed and have never ceased to wonder at this event whenever I recall it to mind.

Visiting churches and venerated sites all over the country, we often became aware of how Christianity had superimposed its festivals and dates onto even more ancient Pagan rites and festivals. Many churches occupy sites of power that had been venerated since the coming of man and his first faltering steps towards an understanding of creation and life forces.

May Day was always a major Fertility Festival and many of the traditions hold this significance. The Maypole is a potent Fertility symbol, (the erect phallus) and the dance performed by young people represents the Fertility Dance of the virgins.

In Boston, May Day was marked with a Street Fair in addition to the other events. We attended an open air service in the fairground, organised by the Christian Churches to bless the festival. A Wiccan Sabbat had been superseded by a Christian event, but still celebrating the gift of new life.

With the Church leaders in full regalia and Community hymn singing led by the fairground organ, it should have been an impressive event. Unfortunately, the organ was not on its best behaviour and due to a combination of varying tempo's, microphone lag and some unfamiliar tunes, the congregation struggled. However good humour prevailed, the clerics laughed with us and the fair was duly blessed and launched.

Jean had always permitted me full use of the galley in which to indulge my culinary skills. For some odd reason, I had succeed her as the home baked bread specialist. Not that we went to the trouble of baking bread on a regular basis.

Visiting the working windmill on the banks of the Maud Foster Drain in Boston, we were reminded once again of the varieties and blends of flour that could be purchased. Stone ground flour has a slightly gritty texture that is imparted by the stone grinding wheels being very, very slowly eroded by their own actions during the milling of the grain.

With the sails revolving and the millstones turning, the whole building reverberated to the thud of heavy, slow moving machinery as the gear trains moved the stones. Nearing the milling floor, everything became coated with a thick layer of flour and the air was redolent with the rich, tickly smell of newly ground grain.

In spite of my vertigo we managed the climb up to the milling floor where we saw various grain mixes being fed into the interface between the slowly turning mill stones.

Back on the ground floor, we visited the Mill shop where we were able to purchase 1˙ Kilo bags of a variety of flours specially to bake bread when we returned to the boat.

I was even able to buy my favourite, Malted Granary Flour!

All together the visit proved to be a fascinating interlude and a further insight into a bygone era when life was much more slowly paced than the hectic flurry of modern times.

Thank goodness for life in the slow lane!

Once through the Grand Sluice the River Witham becomes tidal, exiting into the Wash some 5 miles downstream. We were disappointed to discover that the dock areas were restricted and we were unable to walk the area that we imagined the "Mayflower" setting sail from with its cargo of settlers, bound for the America's and the New World.

In St.Botolph's Church, it was possible to climb the tower and look out over the town and the surrounding countryside. On a clear day, the Cathedral and Castle at Lincoln could be seen. However this was one experience I was happy to forego and Jean insisted on staying at ground level in deference to my refusal to make the climb.

For a relatively small town, the Church was imposing and its tower "The Boston Stump" was an impressive feat of architecture, whether viewed from inside or outside the building.

It was well worth the two visits that we paid it!

From the moorings we were able to enjoy the antics of the wildlife and in particular, of Mother Mallard and her large brood.

As the days slipped by our observations took on a more sombre air, as we noted the gaps left in the group via the attrition wrought by the attentions of various predators.

Beginning our return cruise to the River Trent, we planned a number of stops along the Witham Navigation.

Our first stop was at Tattershall Bridge where we moored and set off to explore the line of the derelict, Horncastle Canal. Walking along the navigation towards Lincoln for about half a mile, we discovered the dip in the bank and the remains of the stonework that marked the junction. Following the line into Horncastle we were able to examine the masonry that remained showing the shape and extent of one or two locks and found that some portions of the channel were still in water after all these years. The canal was abandoned in 1885 but the connection to the Witham was not closed until much later, to avoid the problems of flooding.

This was another length of canal that would apparently take a minimum of effort to restore.

Considerable interest is being show nationally regarding canal restoration but I could not help but consider the effort put into some schemes, in terms of work and fund-raising in order to reopen a short length of waterway that goes nowhere and connects up to nothing. Perhaps a more sensible approach may be, to concentrate on those canals that extend, link or complete cruising rings and where combined efforts and concentrated resources could help to overcome some of the problems that are created by landowners, local authorities or Governmental departments who refuse to talk to each other. If this were achieved, support, planning permissions, grants and additional funding applications could be subject to an overall priority listing and realistic time scales imposed.

Currently there are a number of projects that are in danger of stalling due to the intransigence of inter-governmental department groups. Where proposed new roads cross the line of a waterway able or due to be restored, the installation of navigable culverts and aqueducts is surely common sense.

At the edge of the town was Tattershall Castle, the ruin of a moated fortress. Little is left of this imposing structure save for the massive keep. The moat however is still in place, fed from a canalised segment of the River Bain where it passes close beneath the outer walls.

We explored the ruins and while we were on the roof of the keep we enjoyed a further treat. A flight of F1-11's from nearby R.A.F. Coningby, were going through their paces doing circuits and bumps.

One by one they would approach the airstrip, which was only a mile or so away, their swing-wings formatted for slow flight and the air brake flaps down. With undercarriages lowered they waffled down to kiss the runway with their wheels. They would then accelerate to take-off speed and, with their wings swinging backwards into delta format, switch to after-burn. The resultant power-climb was executed while the plane reached for the sky in a tight barrel-roll as it disappeared into the heat haze in a steep climb.

The very air shuddered to the mind blowing bellow of sound as we soaked up the atmosphere, our eyesight blurring and the thunder of the after-burners grinding deep into our stomachs.

It was exhilarating!

When the fighter-planes had completed their exercise, we paused for a snack at the cafe while we took photographs of a rather splendid pea-cock who was showing off his beautiful tail plumes.

Returning to the boat we spent a quiet night and next, day set off to cruise to Bardney Lock. Here we intended to moor up overnight and take advantage of the splendid facilities on offer.

Before that, we had the whole day to explore the village. It boasted a small but comprehensive group of shops and some nice cafes and pubs. On the village green we photographed the unusual RAF. Memorial in the shape of a genuine three bladed propeller from an aero-engine. This was to commemorate the dead of No.6 Squadron, Bomber Command which had been based locally.

As we walked across the green we saw a sight that took us back to our childhoods when such things were common; a group of Romanies, true gypsies, with their horses and traditionally decorated vardo (horse-drawn caravan) trotting briskly through the streets.

Shopping and a quick exploration completed, we return to the boat in the afternoon, more than ready for the long, hot shower we had promised ourselves.

The 50p. we put into the shower meter seemed to last indefinitely and it was wonderful to enjoy a seemingly unlimited quantity of hot water instead of the rather quick showers we had become accustomed to taking on the boat.

We wallowed in the luxury!

Ah! Well; next stop, Lincoln!

After a short, uneventful cruise, we found ourselves moored up again in Brayford Pool. Unfortunately the pump out motor was still in need of repair. Unable to pump out our holding tank and getting just a tad desperate, we were comforted by the thought that at Torksey B.W. had a DIY. Pump out set up that we could use.

Under pressure to complete this section of the cruise we only stayed in Lincoln for the one day then pressed on to Saxilby, where we had promised ourselves, at least one night.

Here at last was a village that did not ignore the waterway, it sat foursquare athwart the channel, its main street following the line of the canal. A little noisy but with an abundance of useful pubs.

Next day we reached Torksey and were able to confirm that the pump-out was working and was available.

Thank goodness!

This news settled our minds and we were able to stow the green wellies back inside their cupboard!

The tides would be suitable for travel to Cromwell Lock, next day and we just had time for a final look around the ruins of the small castle.

We had reached the conclusion of an historically interesting and in some aspects, an amusing couple of weeks.

Now we would head for the main system once more!

15.
Rally Roundup.

Next day we waited until the correct state of the tide before we were allowed through the lock to enter the River Trent. Some boats had cleared the lock late on the previous day's tide and had spent the night on the floating moorings waiting for this moment. These were able to move off as soon as the keeper signalled that the tidal flow was right.

We were the first boat to clear the lock and scraped the cill on our exit as the water was still low. Even so, we were the last boat in a small flotilla cruising upstream to reach Cromwell Lock. With a blustery wind blowing we needed to keep our engine revs, up to maintain steering way.

This meant that we began to overhaul the smaller, slower craft.

One by one they fell behind us until at last, we began to ease past the final boat. We were chatting between our sterns while keeping a weather eye open for water-skiers who were buzzing our boats.

Suddenly, without warning, my engine died!

The skipper of "September Morn." saw my wake die and began to swing towards me. "Pallas Athene" was dead in the water, losing way against the flow.

Out of the blue, a speedboat, clearly not noticing anything amiss, shot between our boats his water skier faced with a rapidly narrowing gap as his boat's wash dragged our boats inwards.

Even his wet-suit turned pale!

We breasted up, tied off our ropes and "September Morn" began, manfully to move both craft against the current.

For 30 minutes we tried every trick in the book to restart the engine. We even topped up the tank with diesel from our emergency containers, all to no avail.

It began to rain. Our very expensive, cloth, golf umbrella was brought out and rigged. All was well until an errant gust of wind, lifted it off the stern and deposited it, handle up in the water. Our final sighting, was of it sailing majestically downstream, bobbing on the broken water.

Eventually I started at the injectors and began to open up each section of the fuel line until I found diesel oil.

Nothing!

At last I reached the main tank and squeezed under the rear deck began to dismantle the final set of joints. I disconnected the fuel line from the top of the tank. There, in the exposed copper tubing, a small grey worm was wriggling!

When the brass filler cap had been fitted to the deck plates which formed the roof of the tank, it had been bedded into a silicon sealant. One of the bolts securing it had extruded a plug of the material as it was pushed into the hole. This segment, 3/16" dia. by 1" long, had dropped inside the tank, where it had lived quite happily for the previous three years, now it had decided to go exploring. It hadn't got very far!

The silicon was removed and carefully set aside, the joints were checked and tightened, everything was ready for the big switch on. Fortunately the engine was self bleeding so we were not expecting too many problems. A couple of turns of the starter motor, a cloud of white smoke and the engine fired. A few moments of erratic running and spluttering, then it settled down to a healthy roar.

The ropes were loosed, the boats separated and we were ready to complete the run up to Cromwell. By now "Athene" and "September Morn" were alone on the river, the rest of the flotilla had long gone.

We arrived at the lock after a long trip to find the tide falling rapidly and the chamber full of boats. The lock keeper was hoping to make a single operation to clear these. "September Morn" was easily accommodated, we were a slightly different prospect. "Pallas Athene" was five feet too long for the remaining space. A large G.R.P. Cruiser could have given us the space but that meant that he would be closer to the top gates than suited him.

Lock-keeper notwithstanding, he was not going to budge!

As time was by now of the essence we reversed out and took up station below the lock. With the craft decanted into the upper stream the lock chamber was emptied ready to receive us.

If the water level was high enough!

We entered the chamber with minutes to spare and moved to the wall where we lay in splendid isolation. Our solitude was quickly broken when a pair of Mallard drakes swam in just as the gates were closing. The chamber seemed cavernous, walls towered over us but the two drakes were perfectly happy.

From the lock edge on the far side we heard a harsh cackle. A Mallard duck began to promenade and call down to the drakes, 'Hello there big boys, Come up and see me sometime.'

Both drakes were galvanised into a hurried vertical take-off and began the steep climb towards the coping. It was like a scene from a "Looney Tune" cartoon. One drake misjudged his angle of climb, smacked into the wall just below the edge and slid dazedly down towards the water again.

The duck however, had immediately vacated the wall, dropped off the edge and dived towards the surface of the water. Levelling out just above surface she flew towards the lower gates lifting over them in a beautifully judged power climb. Two disgruntled drakes watched her disappear with an air of confused dejection.

Alone in the chamber we had to exercise special care to ensure that we had our craft controlled by the bow and stern ropes looped round the vertical chains. Without these we could face a severe buffeting as the water flowed in. It had been a difficult trip and not a little traumatic, so when we had exited the lock we moved up to the visitor moorings opposite the weir channel, tied up securely and checked out the engine room.

Tomorrow would be soon enough to complete the cruise into Newark!

The remainder of the trip to Nottingham proved to be uneventful, with the exception of the passage through the Holme locks. Here, a heavily laden B.W. barge had fouled the cill at the bottom gates and ripped out the electric, hydraulic and mains water lines that ran across the lock entrance just below the bottom step. The gates were jammed open, the lock out of commission and the water point and other facilities deprived of their supply.

Small enough to use the old pleasure boat lock, even if it was leaking badly, we managed to lock through in spite of the difficulties.

The Nottingham Boat Show was now only a matter of days away and a host of boats of varying sizes would be expecting unrestricted passage. Work was already underway to restore the services and frogmen were working to clear the lines and cables that were tangled beneath the barge's hull making it impossible to remove it so that the gates could be shuttered and the lock chamber emptied in order that the work could be completed.

In their usual, efficient manner, the B.W. maintenance crew did restore the lock to full operation in time for the Show!

As we had been unable to take on water at Holme, we left the river and ascended Meadow Lock to reach the water point. After filling our fresh water tank, and much to the amusement of a group of onlookers, we reversed into the lock, descended, then reversed onto the river before turning upstream to reach the Trent Bridge moorings.

This to avoid a long haul to a winding hole in the city!

Having arrived early we were able to take our designated mooring as the inner boat and so tie up to mooring rings against the hard standing. Again we volunteered to assist with the task of preparing and organising the Rally site. This entailed marking out lengths, painting on location numbers and laying a pipeline for fresh water.

The Nottingham Boat Show offered the best of both types of event. As well as a large, commercially orientated show, visiting boaters were catered for at a rally site a little way from the main showground and on the other side of the river.

The moorings were excellent and convenient to the large footbridge over the river. On the opposite bank was the City's War Memorial; a splendid array of triumphal gateways and arches. A very impressive piece of architecture.

By taking the video camera up onto the footbridge each morning, filming the overnight numbers of boats and ending with a fade-out, Jean was able to record the effect of the moorings rapidly filling with boats between fade-ins and fade-outs.

A simple photographic technique used to good effect!

It was possible to walk into the city centre from the site. A rather long, not very attractive walk but as we had been hardened by our many previous shopping expeditions on foot, it did not prove to be too arduous.

On a visit to the large Waterways Museum, we were thrilled to learn that their traditional working boat "Ferret" was due to be moved down to the show site under her own power. That power was provided by a Single cylinder, 15 HP. Bolinder Semi-diesel engine.

As they were short of manpower, I offered to help crew the boat during the short, $1\frac{1}{2}$ mile trip. To my great joy, not only was this accepted but I was given the role of steersman. Me at the helm and controls of a Bolinder powered boat!

I was walking on air!

The morning of the trip, I turned up early dressed in my boatmans costume complete with bowler hat. It was not long before I received confirmation of the correctness of my decision, NOT to fit "Pallas Athene" with a vintage, traditional engine. "Ferret"s Bolinder had decided that it was not going to start. In the confines of her engine room I discovered that arthritic knees did not allow me sufficient flexibility to make any constructive contribution towards getting the recalcitrant motor up and running.

After about an hour and countless abortive attempts, it looked as though "Ferret" would be faced with the indignity of making the trip to the showground, under tow!

At long last the magic combination of settings was achieved. One last despairing kick of the flywheel, and with a faltering stutter, she began to run. A few more minor adjustments and she settled down to the steady, musical, syncopated beat beloved of Bolinder aficionados everywhere. We were ready to go!

After years of handling my own boat it came as a shock to realise just how different were the characteristics of a full length working boat, unladen and with a relatively large, slow turning propeller providing the driving force. My modern four cylinder diesel is comparatively fast revving and not exactly vibrationless. The slow revving, single cylinder Bolinder, advanced vibration onto an entirely new plane of experience for me. My hands and feet quivered to the pulse of the power unit. Looking along the top plank it was alarming to see just how much a 70 ft. hull could flex.

The only way to stop the boat in an emergency, was to slow down the engine in neutral until the revs almost died away, then persuade the engine to reverse its direction of rotation and build up the revs again. Power could now be fed to the prop to slow the boat. Not a skill for the tyro to practice under operational conditions.

It was easy to see why many lock gates were fitted with snubbing posts round which a loop of mooring rope could be dropped to control the forward momentum.

We approached the lock gates very carefully and bled our speed away during the approach. After all we were in no hurry!

With speed wheel controls and a remote clutch it proved to be a totally new experience but one that I would not have missed for the world. Fortunately I completed my task with no mishaps.

Arriving at the moorings, Jean, who had ridden the stern with me, suggested that it would take two weeks for her bust to cease its sympathetic vibrations.

Before I am taken to task by Bolinder lovers let me say, I also love the old engines. This was my first and only experience of a boat powered by such an engine. Techniques such as starting, control and reversing were a closed book. I have some vague, acquired knowledge but please do not judge working boats and their engines by the record of an isolated experience related by a self confessed beginner.

If you attend shows and rallies on a regular basis you will see lots of examples of beautifully restored and maintained working boats, many fitted with Bolinders or similar old engines. Talk to their owners as they bask in the pleasure that they receive from these contacts. Accept the invitation you get to view the engine 'oles, you may even be lucky enough to get the chance to enter the holy of holies. Check out the lack of space for energetic actions: imagine the heat of the starting blowlamp; the reek of oil and grease; then, look at the polished brass and copper and recognise that this is obsessive love not infatuation, commitment not casual interest and above all see the devotion that these craft and engines demand from their owners; and marvel!

A number of our boating friends and acquaintances were among those attending the show and it was good to have a chance to catch up with all the news and gossip. This was a facet of rallying that made attendance worthwhile.

The boaters evening entertainment was being provided by the "Elsan Band", a group of folk musicians from the Wolverhampton Boat Club. They wrote and performed their own songs as well as old stand-bys. Most of the songs were about the canals and navigations of the Midlands, many about the Black Country. Heavily spiced with humour, they dealt with life on the canals, anecdotes about using, enjoying, being frustrated by and all the other facets of the canal boaters life and experience.

Jean's aunt, Theo, used to say to us, "One day you pair will be old and staid. You will sit one each side of the fire like real Darby and Joan's" Certainly our life was settling into a pattern. We both enjoyed cross-stitch embroidery, although now, my main interest was focused on my writing. Winter evenings would find us sitting by our cabin stove rapt in our own separate, yet mutually inclusive tasks. However, for much of the year we had so much to occupy us socially, that we spent very little time in quiet contemplation, as our fingers busied themselves with our hobbies.

A very minor disaster occurred during the weekend !

I had made my usual donation toward the upkeep of the impoverished chief executives of Camelot via the purchase of a lottery ticket. Imagine my amazement on checking it on Sunday morning and discovering that I had won a whole £10. The ticket was placed, not in its usual place, but on the dining table ready to be exchanged for cash on Monday morning when I collected my newspaper. That afternoon we had prepared a meal and tidied up, dumping the plastic bag of junk in the skip on the site.

It was not until I went to pick up the ticket as I left to get the newspaper and found that the rubbish had included the winning ticket.

I wasn't about to climb into a skip full of rubbish for £10!

'Say le vee!'

With a week to go before our next rally at Etruria travelling along stretches of canal that we knew well it made sense to reach the venue early and use the extra time to explore the Caldon Canal, one we had not previously covered. Time out at Alrewas gave us a chance to see our grandchildren then we moved along quickly to Stoke on Trent.

The Caldon was a fascinating waterway with an interesting history. Along the lower reaches close to the junction with the Trent and Mersey at Etruria, small potteries lined the banks and specialist tub boats built for the trade still carried finished pottery to various trade outlets and shipping points. It was possible to identify quite clearly the mechanisms whereby the crated china was handled for transit.

Access to the Froghall terminus is restricted by the tiny bore of the tunnel that spans the approach of the waterway. Our boat was too tall to make the passage. We winded and walked to the entrance. Built to carry limestone from the nearby quarries it was very prosperous for a number of years. A branch leading towards Leek was built to feed water from Rudyard Lake to the summit level. It was not until the early 1900's, some 120 years after the canal was opened that rail freight reduced its efficiency and usurped its place in the economic scheme of things.

It is another canal that owes its existence to the unstinting efforts of enthusiasts bent on reopening it after many years of dereliction.

A relatively short waterway it covers 12+ miles from Etruria to Leek and 17 miles to Froghall, in spite of this it is an interesting route and well worth the effort involved in cruising it with its 17 narrow locks.

We received a sharp reminder of the inhumanity of the human race when we heard the news that the body of a baby had been found thrown onto the bushes lining the canal concealed in a plastic shopping bag.. It was possible that we had seen the bag but had followed our rule, unless its moving don't investigate.

After an enthralling cruise we returned to the junction with the Main Line in time for the rally. As it was linked with folk music and poetry as well as the usual boating interests it promised to be most enjoyable.

The rally site included the arm alongside Shirley's Bone Mill, now a museum showing the relationship between the grinding of bone for the pottery production. Over the years a wide variety of materials have been added to the basic clay in order to modify its normal properties and to produce a wide range of different types of pottery and porcelain. The addition of finely ground bone to the clay base was a technique that dated back to the great dynasties of the Chinese Empire and to the skills of Japanese craftsmen who were developing their own ranges of similar wares. Amazingly, many of these skills and production methods, devised hundreds of years ago, were lost only to be re-discovered by Western potters as they explored the ancient arts.

The wharfs along the arm provided excellent moorings for the small but representative fleet of working boats that had arrived for the event, complete with their advertising boards.

With "Rosie and Jim", the television puppet stars igniting the interest of the very young to the life and happenings around our canals, it was not surprising that a variety of agencies had chosen to take advantage of this burgeoning interest, to sell the concept of canals as a family orientated, leisure pursuit, by targeting the young people.

To this end, many of the working boats were fitted out as mobile classrooms and/or display areas, complete with seating and as an attraction to the adults, the opportunity of a nice hot "cuppa".

The bone mill's boiler had been fired up and regular demonstrations were being advertised. I never truly grow tired of the thrill I get from watching a large steam engine working. Its massive power is produced so effortlessly before being converted, by a seemingly "Heath Robinson" collection of shafts and pulleys, into the driving force that propels the grinding stones in the tubs. The stark contrast between the sense of quiet, efficient power emanating from the engine house and the thudding, rumbling, ear-battering vibrations of the grinding floor.

In addition to the usual array of stands, demonstrations and fund-raising stalls, there was a large, Entertainments Marquee. Here we took great pleasure in sitting and listening to the entries to the Poetry competition, being read to the audience by their authors.

With the rally at Stone on our agenda for the following week-end, we set off early on the Monday morning to avoid any rush of boats that may have been heading in that direction. Actually, most of the boats had chosen to leave on Sunday afternoon, in part, to take advantage of the fact that the top locks on the Stoke flight were being operated by members of the local Canal Society. The fees charged being part of their fund-raising efforts.

Stone has an annual Town Festival and in recent years the Boat Rally had become an integral part of the week-long celebrations. Among the events would be the street Carnival. We were looking forward to this as a real nostalgia trip as it had been many years since either of us had had the pleasure of watching a well organised carnival. We enjoyed particularly the sense of fun and excitement generated by these events.

Many local celebrities and dignitaries would be attending, the Mayor and his special guests would be treated to a sail-past the rows of moored boats and would receive the traditional, siren salute. Among the delights in store for the boaters over the week-end, an opportunity to try our skill at a 'Local General Knowledge Quiz' and another chance to be entertained by the members of the "Elsan Band", from Wolverhampton, who were topping the bill at the Saturday night, Boaters Concert.

After the carnival procession, the opening ceremony was performed by a guest celebrity, when he returned from the cruise past the moored boats.

The formal proceedings completed, we walked over to the showground.

Among the rows of stands was one belonging to a Bird of Prey Sanctuary. Here we met, at close quarters, a number of different species of rescued birds who were mostly sitting patiently on their perches, tethered by soft leather leashes fastened to their jesses.

To our lasting pleasure, we were introduced to a real life "Henry" (in truth, a Henrietta.), a large, female European Eagle Owl. The weather had turned damp, with a soft, misty drizzle hanging in the air. The owl did not appreciate this and had settled down, not on her perch but slumped on her haunches, on the table, feathers pressed against the surface keeping at least one small segment dry. She looked for all the world like a fat, disgruntled model, posing for the design of a novelty tea-pot. Yet, in spite of her obvious discomfort, her eyes remained alert, twin orange and black orbs, burning with a lambent flame, sparkling with intelligence, as her head and those unwinking eyes, followed our every movement.

She was damp, moody and magnificent!

Later we watched the owls, hawks and falcons being put through their paces across the arena as they swooped and struck at lures swung by the trainers.

Even though the weather was less than perfect, the carnival and festival were excellent and most enjoyable.

We filled in our answer sheet for the boater's quiz, finding some of the answers, not to put too fine a point on matters, "elusive". Still it did encourage us to explore the town and the local points of interest, much more closely than we had done previously.

We had entered "Pallas Athene" into the Best Amateur Fit-out competition but in spite of there only being three entries, we were left feeling that we had not even achieved third place. The work we had done in fitting out our boat had been complemented by many people over the previous year, however, it seemed that for the competition the criteria for judging owed more to the standards set by "House Beautiful" magazine than the design we had chosen based on a common sense approach to the rigours of continuous living on board and cruising. That placed a higher priority on comfort and storage space than on shiny surfaces and cutesy trimmings.

Maybe I was experiencing a touch of sour grapes!

We were looking forward to the entertainment and once more we enjoyed the show laid on by our friends from the "Elsan Band" Some of the answers to the quiz turned out to be a little obscure but it was pleasing to note that we were up among the highest scorers, even if we did not quite win.

Our next rally was at Nantwich in Cheshire which would involve us in a return passage up the Stoke on Trent locks to Etruria, another trip through the Harecastle Tunnel followed by the long descent down Heartbreak Hill to Middlewich. This was a stretch of canal that we had traversed on a number of previous occasions and felt that we were beginning to get to know, intimately. Although much of the scenery is beautiful, the Middlewich Arm to Barbridge Junction always seemed to be endless. The shallowness of the channel in many places reduced our speed to little more than two miles per hour, if we were to avoid a breaking wash.

Of all the canals we had covered this was the one where queuing for locks was almost to be expected. Towards the week-end, hire boats returning to their yards at each end of the arm, spend Friday night moored up in numerous locations ready to complete their hire period the following day. To set an example and cruise slowly by so many moored craft is an exercise in patience that takes some learning.

Our booking for the rally had been made early and as all the berths were nominated and marked there was no difficulty in finding where we were to moor. Close to the centre of things and opposite the Club moorings, our only problem was that these moorings were affected by the ubiquitous "Shroppie Step ". Below the water level, a solid edge slopes into the depths. Deep draughted, almost vertically sided boats find themselves held 12 to 15 inches away from the edge with their base plate hard against the sloping bottom. Even the slowest passage of a boat shifted enough water for "Pallas Athene" to be bumped heavily against this "step".

It made for uncomfortable mooring!

The only answer, was to try and hold the hull clear of the obstruction using fenders. Normal procedures did not work but the regular moorers had devised a whole range of ingenious methods for fending off. The simplest and most commonly used were car wheels, complete with tyres floated flat on the water and tethered to the sides of the boat. Simple, but remarkably effective!

Attendance at the rally was good and the majority of the club members made us feel welcome. As it was a bi-annual event it did not fall into the oft repeated error of becoming totally predictable and stereotyped.

Nantwich was only a short car drive from Chester so we rang up Shirley's parents and invited them to spend a day with us. They had accepted our offer with pleasure.

The rally organisers had devised the usual boaters Quiz. This was saved from becoming a bore by our recognition of how valuable participation was to us as it prompted us to re-examine our books and other sources of information for detailed facts about the Shropshire Union Canal and its effects on the history of the local area

The short arm, that was the original start of the canal's intended route before local pressure forced it to be changed, had been turned into a basin serviced by a thriving boat-yard and lined with permanent moorings.

We entered the basin to take on fresh water and diesel fuel then discovered that winding a nearly full length boat in a restricted area, crowded with moored craft was not the simplest of operations. The difficulties were enhanced by the fact that on that day a fierce cross wind was blowing.

It took some rapid fending off and carefully controlled bursts of power to our prop. to complete the task, without decorating any of the moored boats with our nearly new paint work.

Mission accomplished we returned to our moorings!

The major drawback about being moored by the clubhouse, was the distance we had to walk to buy our daily newspaper. Fortunately, for the duration of the rally, a local shop had arranged to stock a small number of different ones; enough at least for the early birds.

The rally proved to be enjoyable but not exceptional. Our one clear and lasting recollection was the amazing vocal talent of a young girl who sang a couple of numbers for the audience during the entertainment Her voice was superb, her confidence and maturity amazing, A really remarkable performance!

Pauline and Tom, Shirley's parents, spent the Sunday with us and we were able to offer them the hospitality of the boat. Tom was particularly taken by the Vintage/Veteran car rally that was held on the rally site during their visit. That and the bric-a-brac stalls were also among our favourite events.

The Ellesmere Port Bicentennial Rally would not take place for two weeks, time for us to take a leisurely cruise to the Port and to enjoy a few days in Chester, en route. Our first fleeting visits had whetted our appetites and we were looking forward to an extended stay.

Our first stopover, however, was at Bunbury Locks were we managed to get an overnight mooring against the hard-standing belonging to the hire boat company based there.

We walked into the village to look at the church and to call into a pub that had been recommended to us, for a meal. The walk was horrific, fast traffic and narrow pavements made for a nightmare visit. We were very nearly involved in a serious accident when a car driven by a woman took a corner too fast and had to drive in the centre of the road. In avoiding on-coming traffic she swerved towards us and as the car began to straighten up the rear end started to break away into a skid. The driver just managed to regain control before we were swept off the pavement.

That was one walk I would not be in a hurry to repeat!

As we had found so often, our visit to the church was in vain, as the building was securely locked against vandals. The meal at the pub made up for this disappointment as it was excellent. Almost good enough to overcome the bad vibes that our narrow escape had caused.

Next day we completed the cruise into Chester and moored up on the short stretch of visitor moorings near the bridge by the City walls. A convenient mooring for visiting the town but the proximity of the large public house was to create problems of noise and stupid behaviour from customers who had drunk sufficient to blunt their senses and produce anti-social behaviour.

In the early hours of the next morning we were awakened by the familiar sensation of someone climbing onto the boat. I walked through the living quarters to reach the front door, this time I had donned my dressing gown. Jean slid open a window and was confronted by a pair of legs. Their owner was standing on the gunwale reaching over to untie our centre mooring rope, which as usual was tied off at the centre stud not at the mooring ring. As I opened the front doors, Jean gave our uninvited caller a whack across the shins. Leaping off the boat he swore at us then legged it along the pathway, away from the pub. I was shoeless so pursuit was out of the question and anyway the hire boat moored in front of us and crewed by a very nice group of Danes, had been completely untied and was drifting in the wind into the wide section created by the winding hole. Attracting their attention was difficult, as they seemed to be sound asleep but eventually they were alerted and able to re-position and re-secure their boat.

Next day we moved down the Northgate Locks and moored up in the lower basin. Hopefully it would not prove to be as fraught with problems down there.

Although we were now less convenient to the town, we had a small measure of confidence that our mooring would be safe. Quite close to the walls and the tide locks down to the River Dee, this area had a wealth of interest including a boat yard that had originally built wooden boats.

On a cold, windy morning we met with Dan who was to take us on a tour of the City's Roman past. Dan was, as usual for the guides, dressed in the armour of a Roman soldier. Jean always did go for large men in uniform, Dan was quite something in his shiny armour, rich cloak and his strappy sandals. The tour was a little strenuous and due to the weather we were his only customers. With our guide's undivided attention we completed our tour confident that we had enjoyed a fruitful and informative hour or so treading in the steps of the troops.

Due to the age of and history relating to the town, other opportunities were on offer for tourists to learn more of the events that had shaped Chester. One such happening was the much advertised "Ghost Walk": Towards evening we found ourselves, with an elderly guide, ready to walk the streets once more and learn the less salubrious incidents of the past which have left psychic scars of the towns persona and some of its buildings echoing to the tragedies of bygone days.

The tour took in a wide variety of sites and associated stories but we were disappointed not to make the acquaintance of even one of the many spectres that are said to haunt the streets and buildings. Just our luck that the Union of Spooks, Spectres and Ghosties was cutting down on their allocation of appearances.

In spite of our declared intention of returning to Chester, out of season, here we were visiting in June. However, the weather was inclement and as the schools were still in term time the situation was not too problematic.

As the I.W.A. National Rally was due to be held in Chester during August, we had hoped that a start had been made on improving the moorings and the waterway beyond the City, if only for the benefit of visiting boaters.

Our hopes were quickly dashed!

As we headed out towards Ellesmere Port it was evident that, not only were water levels abysmal, but also that the amount of rubbish dumped in the water by local residents had reached quite impressive proportions. As the movement of our boat temporarily lowered water levels even further it was clear that up to five feet from the bank the rubbish alone would repel any boat seeking to moor. It was all there, bikes, prams, push chairs, shopping trolleys, countless large plastic toys and a regular Sargasso Sea of floating litter heavily laced with plastic bags and sheeting, ready to engulf the prop-shaft of any boat with too much power on.

We throttled our engine right back to just above tick-over and limped along. Our propeller barely rippling the water. Eventually we cleared the area without collecting any major fouling around our transmission.

It was horrendous!

My sympathy went out to the folk at the Boat Museum at Ellesmere Port, who were doing a magnificent job of restoration and development in the old canal basin only to have its viability marred by the problems affecting the waterway, 10 miles from their site.

While we hoped that many boats would do as we had done and make a real effort to complete the passage, our gut feeling was, that many, including the majority of boat hirers would give up the unequal struggle when they experienced the condition of the canal.

Mid afternoon saw us clear of the outlying housing estates and we elected to moor up along a quiet, wooded area within sight of the magnificent railway Viaduct and embankment. In spite of the fact that this was obviously a regular mooring area we were forced to use a gangplank to get on and off the boat. Our stern was grounded some two feet from the bank and our major concern was, that if the water level dropped overnight we could find ourselves aground and unable to use the prop. to free the hull. On the positive side, the lack of water pretty well ensured that we were not disturbed by passing craft.

Good fortune was with us and on the following morning we set off at a reasonable hour to arrive at the basin as the museum opened its gates for the day.

Arriving at Ellesmere Port just after 10 am., we were welcomed by Russ, the Harbour-Master. He cleared us to proceed to the lower basin where he indicated the general area in which we could moor. Once again we found ourselves tied up just off the bows of the Museum exhibit, "Cuddington" So close that our stern was tucked under the curve of the larger boat's bows and we had to rig fenders to keep us clear of her sheer.

Since our previous visit the number of exhibits in the lower basin had been increased and access to the quayside moorings severely restricted A strong crosswind was blowing and we were not alone in collecting smears of tar on our paintwork from contact with the outer vessel.

Moored in the lee of "Cuddington" all was still!

My daughter Kate and her partner Mike intended to travel down from Newcastle to spend the rally weekend with us.

As usual we enjoyed our stay at Ellesmere Port and the opportunity of becoming part of a truly active, hands on, museum experience.

The rally itself was excellent and we took part in the "Parade of Boats" staged to welcome the visiting dignitaries. We even had a moment of fame when "Pallas Athene" was filmed for the BBC. Local Television News. We were locking down into the lower basin after the parade. That evening, the T V. was carefully tuned and we watched from the edge of our chairs, hanging onto the newscaster's every word. At last our vigilance was rewarded; for all of three minutes during the local news round-up, a report of the rally was shown. There, on screen, white hair flowing from beneath a Breton Cap, we were regaled with a rear view of "Athene's" skipper, slowly sinking below the line of sight as the boat descended into the lock chamber.

Ah! Such is the brush of the fickle finger of fame!

Our guests arrived for their stay but unfortunately this had to be curtailed as Kate was not feeling all that well and Mike wisely took her back home.

During the Rally we were to make our acquaintance with a new country music scene. Cajun music and dancing was very big in the North-West and together with Line Dancing was sweeping across the Country scene. The movement away from the more traditional Country dance into Trans-Atlantic imports was becoming really strong.

Actually, we loved it!

The next fixed date on our programme was the Boat and Steam Rally at Wigan Pier so we had plenty of time to make our way steadily back to the Middlewich Arm and the Trent and Mersey Canal. From Middlewich the cruise to Wigan would be something of a holiday for Jean in view of the small number of locks to be negotiated. (Big Lock, Dutton Stop Lock then nothing until the two Poolstock locks and the lower pair in Wigan.)

Bliss!

Our electrics were still giving trouble periodically and it was obvious that our bank of leisure batteries were not holding the charge efficiently. They would need replacing.

When we reached Worsley on the Bridgewater the replacement of them had become a priority. The boatyard kindly arranged for delivery of a new set and disposed of the old ones after I had fitted the new bank. Disposal of large, heavy, potentially dangerous objects like acid filled batteries always creates a problem which the yard solved for us.

On reaching Leigh we moored up with the Lorenz's at Bedford Wharf and they arranged for us to be on a mains power hook-up for a couple of days while we topped up the battery charge. It became evident over those two days that the fault was located in our Heart Interface Electrical Management System.

That faced us with a serious dilemma!

The only place where we could get the unit repaired was at Hyde on the Lower Peak Forest Canal. There at Warble Wharf was the base of the exotically named Los Angeles and Huddersfield Power Systems, distributors and sole agents for the equipment. The unit needed checking out in situ and so Mohammed would have to go to the mountain.

There were two options open to us; one was to return to Stretford and make our way to Castlefield in Manchester. From there a fee of £29 each way would allow us to use the Rochdale Nine Locks to Dulcie Street Junction The Ashton Canal, six plus miles and 18 locks was "bandit country" as was the three miles from Dunkinsfield Junction to Hyde. The return trip would cover 52 miles and 54 locks plus additional costs of £58 in fees.

Using the second option we could reach Hyde via the Bridgewater and Trent & Mersey Canals to Hardings Wood Junction, the Macclesfield Canal to Marple Junction then the Lower Peak Forest Canal to Hyde. The total distance for that round-trip, 184 miles plus 128 locks, but no fees.

In terms of cost, option one would use 9 gallons of diesel (about £8) but the fees would increase the cost to £66. The second option would use 27 gallons of fuel (about £25) but no additional costs. That together with our reservations about the Ashton Canal now that school holidays had begun, persuaded us to go with the second option.

The short trip could not be justified!

With the weather now scorching hot, comfortable travel could only be achieved during the mornings and evenings. During the afternoons one was liable to be delayed by children swimming in lock chambers and narrows , as well as by the heat.

Under pressure to complete the round trip in as short a time as possible without exceeding the acceptable speed limits imposed by conditions, we were forced to travel during the heat of the day, a practice that I normally eschewed.

While on holiday in Tunisia we had both purchased Arab headdresses, these we unpacked and donned against the heat.

They were amazingly effective!

Standing tall at the tiller I was regularly greeted with comments from startled fishermen. These ranged from "Wotcher Abdul" to cries of "Look-out! Yasser Arafat has hi-jacked a narrowboat , take me to Tel Aviv" Whereupon, I would give the traditional Arab salute, bow and call out cheerfully, "Salaam Allah Kham"

All in the best possible taste, of course!

The 16 deep, narrow locks of the Marple flight, which drop the canal 214 ft., proved to be very difficult for one person to operate, due to their somewhat unusual design. After struggling down the flight and crossing the magnificent Goyt Aqueduct set in the most glorious scenery, we entered the remains of the Rosehill Tunnel now opened up and appearing as a narrow cutting. In the wooded area beyond a tree had fallen across the canal from the far bank comprehensively closing the route. Another boat was approaching the far side and the skipper told us that B.W. had been informed and were on their way. Meanwhile the two crews unpacked the bow saws and we set to work trimming off the upper branches to make the tree more manageable. B.W. arrived in a commendably short time and then their troubles began.

As the tree had fallen, much of its root system had been ripped up, these roots had torn open a wasps nest in the bank.

The inmates were not best pleased and were circling angrily!

In the sweltering heat, one Jolly Green Giant donned, overalls, gloves, helmet and mask. Then, with trousers tucked tightly into his socks, his chainsaw snarling he attacked the splintered trunk. Not a few stings later, the trunk splashed into the water, was dragged round and tied alongside the B.W. maintenance boat. We were free to complete our journey.

Thank you Jolly Green Giants!

Our arrival at Warble Wharf was greeted with a further reminder of the difficulties that can be created by groups of miscreants rampaging across areas. The previous night one or two newly completed boats had been broken into and turned over. We looked quickly at one boat and were sickened by the mindless vandalism that had been perpetrated on a beautifully finished craft. We decided that, if our repairs could be completed quickly, we would overnight somewhere well clear of the area.

The engineer came aboard, checked out the installation, then removed the unit and took it into the workshop to go on test. 90 minutes later, it had been repaired, reinstated, the bill settled and we were on our way once more.

Incredibly, we completed our second assault on the Marple 16 in time to moor up for the night on the visitor moorings just at the start of the Macclesfield Canal.

We had faced one run in with potential trouble, a group of mid to late teenagers crowded the stern as I was leaving a lock chamber. They made vociferous demands to be allowed to board and have cold drinks. I fended them off by tossing ashore a couple of cans of Coke I had with me on the stern and opening the throttle into the pound.

We normally treat horror stories with scepticism preferring to make our own judgements but here our experiences matched the negative reports we had been given. Such a shame, for the Lower Peak Forest is a beautiful, mainly rural canal with many picturesque features and some engineering masterpieces.

Out of season visits, in term time, seem to offer the best bet!

With the weather continuing hot, the return trip was something of a blur. Hot, sweaty days, alternating with restless, sweaty nights. Oh! for some relief. At least our Arab head-dresses, in spite of the ridicule, had prevented our succumbing to the dreaded heat stroke!

Finally, we arrived back in Leigh having taken seven days and eighty-two hours cruising to complete the round trip. The news was that the convoy of local boats was leaving for Wigan next day. Would we care to join them?

The weather had turned slightly cooler now that our marathon was complete and the run down to the Rally site was most enjoyable.

Wigan Pier's Rally was first rate with lots to do and see, including the large array of model steam engines plus a collection of original Steam Rollers and Traction engines. The entertainment on Saturday evening was superb as we had come to expect at this venue and on Sunday morning, Jean and I won the Best dressed Boatman and Woman competition.

That was most gratifying!

With the I.W.A. National Rally due to be held in Chester later that month, now was our cue to head south for the River Severn and Sharpness!

16.
Sharpness. Here we come!

The first few legs of our cruise to Sharpness were through familiar and much travelled routes. We were "au fait", not only with the best mooring sites, but also with viable alternatives, should our first choice prove to be unavailable.

Perhaps we could be excused for feeling a little smug and self-satisfied. Our Nicholson' guides rarely appeared at the stern and we vied with each other as we aired our knowledge of the route ahead.

Childish? perhaps, but great fun!

Nothing untoward happened, the weather remained pleasantly warm and dry while we cruised steadily southward. In spite of the increased traffic of boats heading north towards Chester and the National, we were aware of many boats who, like us, were heading for quieter waters.

The Middlewich Arm and the upper reaches of the Shroppie seemed to stretch out interminably, as usual and it wasn't until we reached the stop-lock at Autherley Junction that we witnessed our first really comic event.

Messages received via the "Tow-path Telegraph", had informed us of our friend Eric Wood's triple cardiac by-pass surgery. We had sent a "Get well soon" card, wished him all the best but were anxious for word of his progress.

From a distance, we saw a boat turn through the junction and enter the stop-lock. As we approached we recognised it as N/b. "Cre-Dal-Wood", it was Eric's boat. Then, wonder of wonders, Eric popped into sight on the stern. He recognised us, dragged open his shirt and exposed a chest sporting enough scars to rival a road map. His cheerful voice rang out, scattering the local fishermen then, as we gently exchanged positions, while "Pallas Athene" entered the lock, we continued our shouted conversation.

Eric was fit, well and heading for Chester to assist with the work of arranging and setting up the rally.

Waving him farewell, we rounded the junction and set off towards Stourport along the Staffs and Worcester Canal. On the approach to the first lock on this section, Compton, we ran into another hold-up. A large section of water-logged tree-trunk had managed to enter one of the upper, ground paddle sluices, or so it was to prove.

All that the B.W. task force knew at that time was that the sluice was comprehensively blocked!

It was amazing to watch the team swing into action. In no time, the stop-planks were in place and the lock was being de-watered. Even when drained it was difficult to identify the problem as the trunk was jammed, inside the sluice chamber.

A workman in water-proofs had the job of clearing the blockage. This was a dangerous task which entailed getting almost upsidedown in the sluice and cutting the trunk into sections with a chain saw. The job was completed with the minimum of fuss, the sawn sections hauled out and loaded into the van, the ground paddle checked, the lock re-watered, the stop-planks removed and the waiting boats were waved on their way.

Two locks further and we stopped at the boatyard at Wightwick to take on diesel before heading for our overnight mooring at the Bratch.

Falling Sands Lock was our next destination. Here we moored up for the night. Next day we could reach Stourport in time for the lock opening of the flight reaching down to the River Severn. It was here we were re-acquainted with our friends from New Zealand and their boat "Kia Ora". It's a small world!

The weather had turned very hot once more and in spite of an early start we were delayed in Stourbridge basin awaiting the opening of the river locks. The first two locks form a staircase and the entrance to the third lock, across a short, awkwardly placed pound was, not to put too fine a point on it, "Bl***y difficult".

Once we had entered the broad reaches of the river, it was abundantly clear that no respite from the sun, by way of shade, could be expected. The river was way too wide and many of the banks shoaled. It was 44 miles to Gloucester, our plan, do it in easy stages.

"The best laid plans o' mice 'n' men, gang aft aglee", said Burns and our plans went "aglee" from the start. The first designated mooring area was the harbinger of chaos to follow. All the spaces were crowded with small G.R.P. cruisers, making the most of the sun and clearly, going nowhere!

With 5 large, manned locks down to Gloucester we were unlikely to get much relief during our passage. As the sun rose ever higher, the day, for me at least, dissolved into a hell of overwhelming heat and blinding glare. Each mooring area presented the same over-crowded scene. On the occasions we saw moored narrowboats, they were tied up two and three abreast, clinging like grim death onto their hard won spaces.

Surely a large waterfront like Worcester would boast some vacant areas. No! small boats swarmed everywhere, a 65 footer didn't stand a snowball's chance in Hell of tying up!

In despair we left the river at Upton on Severn to try and buy a night's mooring at the large off-line Marina. "Very sorry, can't accommodate boats your size. Why don't you try the various Pub moorings?"

After a hellish 30 miles we reached Upper Lode Lock at Tewkesbury. By now I was reeling with heat exhaustion. We tied up against the enormous wooden pilings above the lock and called it a day.

I staggered below and collapsed in a comatose heap!

The next day's forecast offered more of the same but Gloucester was only 14 miles away and with a modicum of luck we would find reasonable moorings there. Then we could relax for a few days.

Our previous visit to Gloucester had been in our Sherpa Van when we had driven up for the weekend to attend a National Boat Jumble. This was before Athene had been started.

Boat Jumbles and Boat Auctions are wonderful venues for collecting odd items for a boat fit-out; provided you have a will of iron and an encyclopaedic knowledge of exactly what you will need.

At a Boat Auction held at Newton Abbot Racecourse, which we attended in the first mad rush of blood following our booking of a building slot for our boat, we purchased the most amazing collection of odds and ends. Much of which proved later, to be totally unsuitable for a narrowboat.

When we became educated in subjects like; insurance, licenses and Certificates of Compliance we became, overnight, considerably more choosy over our "bargains."

Around 7.30 a.m., with the air still cool and fresh we stood on the foredeck waiting for the lock-keeper to open up and finishing our breakfast cuppa. Becoming aware of movement in the air around us, we focused our attention on our immediate surroundings. There, perched on virtually every available point, were dozens of baby swifts. Every couple of minutes they would take to the air, do a few "circuits and bumps" then return to their perches. This was the first time we had observed large numbers of a particular species of bird attending "flying school", that these were swifts and perching within feet of our boat made the experience magic!

Upper Lode was a tide lock and as such marked the upper limit of tidal waters. As the grain mills at Tewkesbury were still supplied by water, huge barges were regular visitors to these waters and the lock chambers were correspondingly large.

The design was new to us. The main chamber was the normal large rectangle with conventional gates at either end. Below this, the lock widened out into what amounted to a tide pool, a large hexagonal chamber with a sloping, paved bottom. This chamber was also gated into the river.

On entering the first chamber we found that the intermediate gates were open. The lock-keeper ushered us through into the tide pool. Puzzled, we enquired the reason and were told that the Paddle boat "Cromwell" was due to lock down with us on her way to Gloucester. She would need all the space she could get and we would need to tuck up small.

15 minutes later, a steam whistle sounded and "Cromwell" nosed slowly into the lock chamber. She was BIG and I could feel "Pallas Athene" cringe away as the wide, bluff bows bore down upon us. Water boiled up from her bow thrusters and our boat tugged backwards against the bow rope that Jean had looped around a wooden frame near the exit gates. This was all that was holding us in place!

As the lock emptied I kept one eye over my shoulder expecting the monster to bear down upon us at any time. Jean struggled manfully to hold our bows in position but it was with a leaping heart that I saw daylight appear at the junction of the gates and finally they swung open to clear our passage to the river.

I opened our throttle and with one last wave to the faces hanging over the steamer's bows enjoying my discomfiture, we set out to put some distance between us and this Behemoth.

The channel was deep and wide, no boats were moored along it so we were able to push on quickly and pull clear. The last we saw of "Cromwell" was her superstructure appearing over the trees half a mile away as we swept into a large bend and out of sight.

Jean pointed out to me later that, while we were locking, just above where our bow rope was fastened, a group of 5 baby swifts were perched and throughout the locking procedure, mama and papa had provided a non-stop breakfast service to their young.

Close to Gloucester, the river divides at the 'Upper parting'. The eastern channel takes one down to the Gloucester docks and we were amazed at how narrow, shallow and silted it was. Particularly as we were aware of "Cromwell" dogging our tracks and certainly intending to moor up in the Gloucester Docks area.

The entrance to Gloucester Lock itself is awkward made worse by the difficulty of mooring to await permission to enter. Fortunately we arrived just as the lock was being loaded. The majority were narrowboats and we were soon sailing in convoy, into the dock area. The rest of the boats immediately began to look for moorings in the basin, we however, had elected to go under the lift bridge and moor against the floating staging of the Llantony public moorings.

The first of our problems came at the bridge, I waited 15 minutes for passage. Jean was put ashore and checked out the moorings, there was space in the quiet area at the far end. She returned to the mooring to await my arrival.

Eventually the bridge was lifted and I was able to proceed along the moorings taking good care not to disturb the boats moored against floating staging. I could see Jean signalling to me as I neared the end of the staging. Suddenly, a boat travelling upstream, accelerated, swung across to the right hand side and dived under my bows to take the mooring. After the stress of the previous day plus the frustration of the 15 minute wait for passage at the bridge, my fuse was rather short.

I went ballistic!

Quite unfairly I blamed Jean for allowing him to take the mooring, though what she could have done to prevent it I, if I had been in a more lucid frame of mind, would not have known.

The boater turned his back ignoring me and getting on with tying up his boat. Jean flounced off in an understandable huff and I was left in midstream.

As luck would have it, the owner of a large moored yacht was planning on leaving in an hours time. There was sufficient room fore and aft of his boat that, when he moved on, the space would accommodate our craft. He kindly offered to let me breast up to him and lowered large inflatable fenders to facilitate this move. Nestled up against the large fenders I sat and fumed; until Jean returned and I made an abject apology for my unforgivable outburst. Later Jean told me that the boat's skipper had informed her that he had no option but to take the mooring as his wife had been injured and needed urgent hospital treatment. The fact that this mooring was as far from the town as possible and inaccessible by road belied the validity of this claim. Much later his wife appeared on deck with a tiny bandage around her wrist and the arm supported in a professionally applied wrist sling. During the two days their boat was moored we did not see her leave the craft except to walk on the decking.

Hardly a case for "urgent treatment"!

After two days they winded the boat and headed back towards Sharpness. This boat, in its distinctive livery was to prove something of a "nemesis" for us over the next few days.

The Gloucester and Sharpness Canal is, in essence, a major ship canal built to link Gloucester Docks to the lower reaches of the River Severn. In many ways this was the event that caused the upper reaches, already difficult to navigate, to silt up and eventually become un-navigable.

Wide, deep and solidly built it was at the time of its construction in 1827 the widest and deepest ship canal in the World. The only hindrances to navigation now are the thirteen swing bridges across its route. The 14th., a swing railway bridge, no longer exists although the remains of its great circular, stone tower are still visible about one mile outside of the Sharpness Docks. At low tide the remnants of the 22 pillars that supported the railway bridge across the river can still be seen. The bridge was closed in 1960 when a large vessel rammed one of the bridge supports in fog causing the centre section to collapse. Later the bridge was demolished and sold to the Chilean Government. It now forms the basis of a road carrying viaduct in that country.

In October 1960 two petrol tanker ships belonging to Harkers were involved in a collision with one of the bridge's stone piers. The accident happened in fog and caused two of the centre spans to collapse. The vessels, "Wasdale H" and "Arkendale H" burst into flames and the river became a sheet of flame from bank to bank. 5 sailors died in the blaze, two managed to swim ashore and another was rescued from the water well downstream. No other casualties occurred.

Visitors to the National Waterways Museum can read about the tragedy from contemporary records.

A few days were spent visiting the local places of interest including the Cathedral and a number of fascinating museums Folklife, local history, archaeology, geology and natural history were all well represented and the National Waterways Museum houses floating exhibits in the adjoining dock as well as extensive displays in the Llantony warehouse that contains it.

Eventually we moved down to the sanitary station next to the lift bridge, which was equipped with a coin-operated D.I.Y. pump-out. After emptying the holding tank we topped up our freshwater and set off towards Sharpness, refreshed by our period of relaxation.

We found the canal a pleasure to navigate!

The water was deep and free from floating rubbish so that we were able to open up the throttle in short bursts to give the engine a much needed clear out under load. It is noticeable that after extended periods running at low revs, the exhaust becomes excessively smoky. Short periods of high rev. running under load when water conditions allow are great for countering this misuse of the engine.

The weather had turned slightly cooler making cruising much less stressful but overnight temperatures were still high enough to make sleeping, hot, sweaty and uncomfortable. Even with the windows, vents and roof hatches open.

The swing bridges were all operated by B.W. bridge-keepers and approach was controlled by traffic-lights. All but one were too low to be navigated safely without being opened and in the majority of cases as we neared the bridge, it opened. Only rarely did we experience any delay and the keepers were unfailingly cheerful and welcoming.

It was only 16 miles to Sharpness but we had no reason to hurry and wanted to explore the canal and its environs.

Reading through the manuscript it must seem that we were often ambivalent about when we were in a hurry and when we had time to spare. The truth is that sometimes, areas that we expected to be interesting turned out not to be or conditions dictated that we cruised for longer periods of time than planned. With the fixed dates on our itinerary widely spaced and a flexible cruising programme the two did not always mesh comfortably facing us with the need to expand or compress it to meet our commitments.

Life was not as chaotic as it must sometimes sound!

We made a stop at Saul Junction where the now derelict Stroudwater canal made a "crossroads" with the ship canal. Originally the Stroudwater linked the town of Stroud, terminal of the Thames and Severn Canal, with the River Severn. From the junction an arm locked the canal down to the river at Framilode. Plans are under way to restore both canals and reopen the link between Saul and the Thames navigation at Lechlade. Currently all would seem set fair for the eventual re-opening of the link.

The half mile of the Stroudwater Canal to the first major obstruction is lined with moored boats. We walked this section and it was heartbreaking to see how short-sighted planners had blocked off the navigation by lowering a road bridge and just leaving a small culvert to carry the water.

This would certainly be one of the restorations that got my vote as it would extend the cruiseable system by opening up another long distance ring. These projects I feel should receive priority.

As the nearest village shop was in Frampton on Severn a little way downstream we moved our boat down to the visitor moorings at Frethern Bridge. From here access would be easier.

Next day we cruised the 4 miles to Patch Bridge the most convenient moorings for a visit to the Slimbridge Wildfowl Trust. The quaintly named village of Shepherds Patch boasted an excellent Pub and a hotel both within easy reach of the canal. The village itself had been in existence for hundreds of years and as its name implied it was the patch where the shepherds who tended the flocks of sheep grazing along the Severn Estuary had their settlement.

The weather had become heavy and humid and as several bursts of heavy rain had swept across the moorings, we felt that a trek down to Slimbridge under these conditions was not sensible so we gave it a miss and restricted our walking to exploring the immediate surroundings. The village itself was tiny but the lanes around it were most attractive. We returned to the boat hot and sweaty as the atmosphere had remained humid but at least the rain had held off.

As we neared our mooring we saw that tied up almost opposite to us was "that boat"!

There was a water point on the mooring so we did not need to be frugal with our supply, we decided to take long cool showers secure in the knowledge that two hundred yards back, at the Bridge, we could top up our tank. A long shower for us meant possibly 5 or 6 minutes each which would consume maybe 8 gallons of water. Even that amount is significant if your supply is limited.

Refreshed we opened up the boat's windows and hatches to catch any cooling breezes that sprang up in the evening, then we settled down for a quiet relaxing session with our books and afterwards, an early night.

Everything was idyllic!

By nine o'clock we were ready to turn in, totally relaxed and pleasantly drowsy, Suddenly our peace was shattered, the boat across the water had started up its generator! On and on the noise droned, drilling into our nerve ends. The crews of the other moored boats were either deaf or had gone away for the evening. After our run-in with this couple at Gloucester we were loathe to remonstrate with them as they obviously considered themselves above normal considerations. We lay in bed praying for relief and trying to concentrate on our reading as a distraction. Nothing worked, in the background the noise continued to nag at our ragged nerves like toothache. Finally at 11p.m. they switched off and closed their boat down for the night.

Blessed relief!

In any situation where other boats are involved this kind of antisocial behaviour is unforgivable, in a quiet, country setting with no background noise from motorways or railways these actions verge on the criminal.

Next day was Sunday but we were more than ready to move on. First we needed to replenish the tank. The water point was partially blocked by a large Dutch Barge which appeared to be unattended. We reversed the two hundred yards to the bridge and managed to squeeze our boat into the remaining space. It was a tight fit! With our ropes secure we ran out the hose to the tap, coupled up and began to fill the tank.

An elderly couple came down the slope from the bridge and began to walk along the towing path. Their eyes were fixed firmly on the ground as they picked their way carefully in our direction. Our hose trailed along the path for a few yards and when they reached it, quite carefully and deliberately, they walked on the hose squashing it flat and interrupting the flow.

We watched in amazement and stunned silence. When they had passed out of earshot we muttered, "They must be related to the pair on 'that boat'." Image our surprise when the couple from the boat stepped ashore, greeted the new comers with hugs and kisses and ushered them on board.

Obviously anti-social behaviour can run in families!

Stated baldly, in the cold light of day, our reactions may sound rather petty but for weeks afterwards any sighting of a boat with that distinctive colouring would set us twitching nervously.

Perhaps we could be perceived as old and crotchety and that our tolerance levels were low but after three more years of continually cruising we have not been involved in similar instances or experienced that level of anti-social behaviour. On the odd occasions when we have needed power in an emergency if our electrics have been playing up, a word with the adjacent boat's crews has invariably met with a positive response. We have found that a smile and a friendly word are the touchstones that open up people and create an atmosphere of sharing and goodwill. It is not a universal panacea but it works much more often than it fails.

A couple of miles short of Sharpness Docks were saw the silted up remains of the extensive log storage pounds. The timber boats would unload their cargo and the logs would be stored; sunk in water "in the round" i.e. before they were sawn into baulks or planks.

The next landmark that appeared off our bow was the truncated remains of the circular stone tower that had carried the swing railway bridge, part of the ill-fated, 22 arch bridge that had been demolished after the tragedy in 1960.

We had arrived at Sharpness!

17.
Bank Holiday Sojourn.

This was Bank Holiday Week-end and the moorings were lined with boats of all sizes. Fortunately we had arrived just as the crews who had decided to cruise that day were releasing their boats and setting sail. We found a berth a little way along the arm leading to the disused tide basin. Most of the area was designated as long term moorings for the local cruising club.

There were permanent moorings on the far side and a few yards farther down we saw a boat that looked very familiar. Our recognition was filled with pleasure as this boat belonged to a couple we had met a number of times while cruising and whose company we enjoyed.

Walking towards the basin, we were hailed from the far shore. It was our friends!

They had recognised us and called us over for a drink and a chat. We crossed on the gates of the lock leading into the basin and made our way along the moorings. Our welcome was warm and genuine. That, after our recent experiences; was heart warming and helped us to justify our belief in ourselves. That we were really were "nice to know".

After two or three hours of reminiscing and putting the world to rights we took our leave but not before extending to them a sincere invitation to join us aboard "Pallas Athene" for a return visit.

Returning to the lock we completed our walk down to the tidal basin for a good look around. One thing that we instantly coveted was the old Harbour Master's house, now converted into a base for a sea rescue group. Standing foursquare and braced against the onslaught of the elements from all points of the compass it was just the sort of property that we would choose to live in and restore, if we had adequate resources.

This was the period for "Neap" or very low tides and the ebb had recently ended. Focusing our binoculars on the mud banks upstream it was possible to make out the ruined foundations of the bridge piers sticking up like rotten teeth across the estuary. The tide had just started to flow and we went to the sea wall to watch. We had been told that the water came in quickly and the tide height is reputed to be second highest in the world but nothing had prepared us for the sight that met our eyes.

Any thoughts that we may have still harboured about making the run down the tideway to Avonmouth and thence to Bristol, died stillborn. We watched in awe at the speed with which the mud banks disappeared and the channels filled with swirling water. To see the power of that tide race and to watch the rips and eddies tearing up the surface of the river certainly made cowards of us and we resolved then and there never to be lulled into attempting such a foolhardy venture.

Pilot or no pilot!

Without wishing to denigrate the achievements of boaters who explore the outer limits of the waterways and push back the boundaries of the capabilities of specially fitted out and equipped, sea-worthy narrowboats. Ours does not fall into that category and 1 am seriously not "sea-worthy".

Initially our wanderings took us into Sharpness village and we were somewhat perturbed at the distance involved in a walk to collect groceries or a newspaper. Luckily we discovered a small sub-post office on the dock estate. They agreed to act as a poste restante address for our mail, offered to get our daily newspaper and collect anything we needed, that they didn't supply, from their stockists. This was typical of the kindness and welcome that we received from the local residents. They also recommended a wonderful place to eat which specialised in providing food at reasonable prices to dock workers and boaters.

A highlight of our visit happened one evening when we had heard on the grapevine that a large coaster was due to dock on the evening tide. In good time we ensconced ourselves on the sea wall near the tide-lock, a good vantage point to observe the ship's approach. The tide was still flowing and the speed of the water flow upstream beggared belief.

The coaster would effect its entrance into the lock without the aid of tugs!

She was at least two hundred yards short of the dock when her profile began to alter as the bows swung towards the lock mouth. In no time she was broadside on to the tide and heading upstream at a rate of knots. Water boiled at her stern as the engines opened up and drove her across the flow to lie up against the sea wall. She was now at right angles to the line of the lock chamber. With her bows inching towards the lock entrance, heavy hawsers were looped over the massive shore bollards.

With the bows held steady her rudder was put hard over and her engines began to thrust the stern out into the current. As she gradually lined up with the lock, the bow hawsers were eased to allow the bows to enter the chamber. All this was achieved to an accompaniment of much tooing and froing prompted by shouts of encouragement from the shore party.

Unperturbed, the pilot slid her slowly into the lock keeping close to the portside. Her bows were almost against the top gates before the bottom gates could be closed. Prior to that happening, the four cruisers that had been waiting to lock up slid in along her starboard side. The final one misjudged his approach and ricocheted between the hull and the lock wall several times before she was bought under control and stopped. With the top paddles opened the lock filled steadily and the coaster held her position. It was almost dark before the lock gates opened to allow the boats into the dock area. Following the usual rules, the cruisers, who had been last to enter the lock, were first to leave and they buzzed off towards the visitor moorings leaving the coaster to exit and make its way to the wharfs.

The morning tide on the following day had been designated as suitable for the flotilla of boats wishing to enter the tideway. We returned next morning and were surprised to find that the lock chamber was almost filled to capacity with boats, so much for our misgivings. Later we discovered that this was in fact a cruising club outing and that the boats were not heading for Avonmouth but simply half a mile downstream to the small remnant of canal at Lydney. It was interesting to watch the large cruisers leave and take up station upstream where they could come to the assistance of any boats that got into trouble. A number of large yachts with auxiliary engines were heading for Avonmouth but these were vessels that could be taken out into the open sea with no problems.

Narrowboats were prominent, by their absence!

During the whole of the time we were there we did not see a narrowboat leave or enter Sharpness via the River Severn and the tide lock.

In our explorations of the area we found the remains of lots of the old Severn Flats that used to ply the river. We were always sad to see such dereliction and to realise that most of the wrecks were beyond restoration. Wooden boats can have a life-span of one hundred years or more but not if they are allowed to rot, full of silt and partially submerged. Along the river bank below the retaining wall, the grassy humps lining the high tide mark showed glimpses of bow sections, stern posts and rudders poignant markers on the graves of many boats from the fleets that once made these waters bustle with life. To us these reminders of the slow demise of a way of life were heartbreaking!

On the club moorings Jean had a not so happy reminder of former days. A 35 ft. yacht was moored, listing slightly, against the hardstanding. This boat had almost certainly once belonged to a family that Jean knew from Torquay and counted among her friends. Her size, layout and above all her extraordinary name, still intact on her stern, all added strength to this conviction. What made it so sad was that now the once immaculate boat was looking severely unloved and uncared for. We never ceased to be amazed by the sheer numbers of boats that we saw all over the country that had been reduced to this sorry state either through simple neglect or worse still by abandonment. It is little wonder that boats have become a favourite target for vandalism. Chances are, that with many boats, such treatment could remain undetected almost indefinitely.

If we had the resources, I'm quite sure that Jean and I would set up a chain of moorings for unwanted boats where they could be repaired and refurbished so that they could end their days with the dignity of being used not abused, in the way in which their original builders had intended.

Sorry! This is another of our hobbyhorses!

As our friends were staying on their boat for a time we were able to invite them over to "Pallas Athene" (they still knew her as plain "Athene") and show them the work we had done since our last meeting. It would also give me a chance to show off my culinary skills by offering them a meal. The visit was most enjoyable. Conversation ranged freely over many topics and among other things we gleaned considerable information about the history of the docks and the Port area.

The importance of the docks in earlier times could be assessed from the size of the railway marshalling yards that had once lined the lower dock estate. A small amount of cargo was still handled by the port but much of the original infrastructure had disappeared and only a vestige of it remained. Here we found ourselves surrounded by disused machinery, quietly rotting away like the hulks lining the river.

With the Bank holiday week slipping away we decided that next day we would head for Gloucester.

As we had yet to record any footage of "Pallas Athene" under way, Jean left me on the moorings the following morning and set off inland to wait for me by the old railway bridge ruins. The canal banks are stone lined and the water deep ,she would have no problem re-embarking after the photo opportunity.

Winding was simple as the junction between the canal and the mooring arm presented a wide expanse of water. I turned the boat and made my way steadily past the row of moored boats. It was still a little early and we did not want to disturb those who were having a lie-in. Once past the boats I opened the throttle and let the revs build up. For a couple of minutes the speed built up then the engine vibrations began to feed back. The bows were dug in deep with six or seven inches of wash being lifted by the bluff bows. At the stern the rear fender was touching the water boiling up from the propeller, spinning deep beneath the counter. The whole hull trembled with unleashed power. With a wide channel and plenty of water below our keel the wash was not breaking and so, for the fifty or so yards left until I reached Jean's position, I gave "Athene" her head.

She seemed to revel in this license!

Once past Jean I closed the throttle and the hull rose as the water settled and the wash died. I glanced round conscious now of being carried away for a short time by the feel of unrestrained power. Jean had recorded my "rush of blood", both on video and still photography, enough to remind me, should I ever need it, how easy it is to be seduced into improper actions, I would be a liar to say I had not enjoyed those mad moments. No damage was done, I was not about to let the experience become habit forming but I could not repress the frisson of pleasure that set my being tingling.

We completed the sixteen and a half miles into Gloucester by lunchtime. After stopping at the lift bridge to take on water at the sanitary station, we carried on into the basin and moored up near to the lock. This meant that we would have a few hours to spare which would enable us explore the points of interest around the dock estate and we could make an early start next day as soon as the manned lock down to the river was opened.

Close to the large graving docks we watched as water surged into the basin pumped up from the river to maintain levels in the dock area. Regular lockings throughout the day were a constant drain on water levels.

As we stood and looked into the vast caverns of the dry docks and saw the size of the vessels that were being repaired in them we noted how much of the capacity of the chambers was unused. This was a stark reminder of how water-borne trade had declined and how few large ships used this port often enough to call on her repair services. Obviously in their heyday these dry docks would regularly house vessels that filled them to capacity and the clatter of tools and machinery would be punctured by the actinic flash of welding torches and the glare of oxy-acetylene cutters.

All that remains of the extensive railway network that serviced the docks are a few lengths of line buried in road surfaces and some examples of rail cars and trucks on display outside the museum.

Almost everywhere we went across the country the same story was being repeated!

Next morning we prepared ourselves to leave on the first locking of the day. Three narrowboats and a small flotilla of cruisers made up the complement for the first cycle. The steel boats were loaded first, breasting-up near the tail of the lock then, festooned with fenders, the cruisers came cautiously into the chamber and looped their lines over the bollards. When the lock was drained and the bottom gates swung open the cruisers began jockeying for position to overtake the narrowboats that had left, in line astern, with "Pallas Athene" in the lead. Until the junction with the main river the channel is so shallow and narrow with a number of nasty bends that overtaking is a hazardous undertaking. However as the cruisers drew much less water with their "vee bottoms" they began to overtake at will using the full width of the channel and to my mind endangering any boat approaching from up stream as visibility was seriously reduced by the bends in the narrow channel. As luck would have it, at this early hour, traffic towards Gloucester was almost non-existent and no problems occurred.

Our plan was to leave the Severn Navigation above Upper Lode Lock and enter the Avon Navigation finishing up in Stratford on Avon. This meant that we could moor up at Tewkesbury for a few days before we entered the Avon.

Such was the speed differentials between the craft, that by the time we reached Upper Lode most of the cruisers had locked through and we had left behind the other two narrowboats.

On a river navigation it had become our practice to take advantage of the higher speed limit and, when conditions permitted, to run the engine faster than usual as this was beneficial to the motor, clearing out the diesel deposits in the cylinders and on the injectors.

Before we entered the lock, one of the narrowboats arrived and we locked through together. Half a mile further upstream we negotiated the sand bars laid down by the flow of water from the Avon and navigated the short channel that led up to the mill wharfs and the short length of public moorings.

Here the lock lifting the boats onto the Avon Upper and Lower Navigations was manned and the lock-keeper tasked with selling licenses to any boats moving through. As we wanted to stay for a few days it was important that we moored up below the lock and out of the jurisdiction of the Avon Navigation.

Tewkesbury was a town steeped in history and had witnessed one of the bloodiest battles of the "War of the Roses", this was an opportunity not to be missed to indulge our morbid passion for ancient battle sites and bloodstained history.

The public mooring below the lock, were full!

Our battered faith in human nature received a welcome boost as the crew of one of the large narrowboats, noted our disappointment, called us over and invited us to breast up with them for the night. They were leaving next day and we could negotiate with B.W. for permission to stay for a few more days. This suited us fine and on that happy note we said our goodbyes to the Severn as we prepared to say Hi! to the Avon.

18.
Puppets and Circuses.

Next morning we were able to exchange moorings with the boat that was leaving and walk into town to visit the Museum. This would be our opportunity to refresh our memories of what we already knew of the Battle of Tewkesbury and to ascertain how much additional information was available. The coverage of the battle plus allied facts and anecdotes was extensive. Even more effective in imparting a feel for the logistics of the conflict was the large table-top model of the site. From this it was possible to identify the pivotal factors that led to the outcome. All in all it proved to be a totally absorbing coverage of a decisive battle. The Yorkists were outnumbered by a factor of 3 to 2 but superior tactics and the successful ambushing of Somerset's troops by a force of some 200 spearmen served to swing the day against the Lancastrians

    The battle began with a charge by Somerset's men against those of Gloucester, who retreated leading the attacking force towards the site of the ambush. Wenlock, who was holding the centre ground should have covered the exposed flank but in fact stood firm. Seeing this and fearing betrayal, Lord Somerset turned his horse, rode back to Wenlock's position and beat his brains out with his mace. This serious "friendly fire" casualty together with the sight of spearmen doing a number on Somerset's vanguard rattled the late Lord's men to the extent that the centre ground collapsed and the forces retreated to the Abbey where they ended up being trapped between the advancing forces of Edward IV and the impassible River Avon.

    Prince Edward of Lancaster, the Duke of Somerset and a number of other nobles were executed on the battlefield and later Queen

Margaret, their Commander, was arrested at Little Malvern and imprisoned in the Tower of London.

Defeated ground troops were allowed to drift away back into the countryside, prisoners of war were too expensive to be economical.

It did not pay to be a "name", on the losing side!

The Museum was housed in a wonderfully irregular, half-timbered building one of many still preserved in the town, often as Inns or Public Houses. A restored Mediaeval house, in a terrace, the others having a new lease of life after being modernised for tenancy, gave visitors an intriguing glimpse into life in bygone times.

The Abbey itself is a magnificent structure and boasts the largest Norman Church Tower in the country. Inside and out the architecture and sculpture is wonderful and the structure leaves one breathless with awe at the sheer scale of its pillars, arches and its mighty West Window with the stained glass figures of the Saints. Inside the tombs and memorials are impressive and include a brass plate in memory of Prince Edward who met his untimely end on the battlefield.

Originally, the Abbey attached to a Benedictine Monastery, it was under threat of demolition by the rampaging forces of Henry VIII during his purge on the religious houses of the Catholic Church. The towns-folk had a whip round, purchased the building for £453 and turned it into their Parish Church.

Thus it was saved from destruction!

The Mill Avon extends along an embankment above Healing's Mill and is lined with private moorings. A rather nice restaurant has been established in what was once the old Water Mill. After a most enjoyable meal we were just leaving when we passed "Rumpole of the Bailey" (Leo Kern) in the passageway. It seemed that his taste of venue matched ours, a fact that we noted with interest rather than overwhelming excitement.

During the next few days we followed the "Battlefield Trail" excellently and instructively marked, visited a number of venerable buildings and generally did the tourist bit. One thing did cause us some concern .At the lock-keepers cottage we saw a number of photographs showing the Rivers Avon and Severn, in flood. Their water levels were equal and the lock itself, submerged. After that each rainy day had us carefully checking water levels, careful for any slight sign of flooding.

If we had needed confirmation that our decision, not to winter or moor up for extended periods of time on river navigations, was correct; this was it!

The night prior to our departure saw us preparing for bed just as the last daylight was fading. We sat back enjoying a last few minutes gossip in the gathering gloom then, suddenly, we were startled out of our reverie by a boat crashing into our side.. "Pallas Athene" lurched as footsteps rang on our gunwales and stern deck. I shot out of the front door onto the foredeck and began to berate the newcomers in no uncertain terms, stating vehemently my views about people with no respect for the property of others. The offending craft was a large hire boat, crewed by young people. They were quick to apologise blaming their status as tyros and the fact that they had been overtaken by nightfall after a fruitless search for moorings on the Severn. Their main concern and the reason they had boarded us was to better fend off their boat and prevent damage. Mollified and keenly aware of the difficulties they had faced in their quest for moorings, we helped them breast up to us as the visitor moorings here were also full. We chatted and I spent some time explaining the etiquette for boarding occupied boats and pointed out that if we had already set our night alarms they may have well have thought that they had walked in on World War III. As it was no real harm had been done.

After a hectic 45 minutes or so all was peaceful once more!

Next morning as we were easing our boat clear of the inside berth ready to lock-up onto the Avon, to our surprise ,one of the young men from the boat presented us with a bottle of wine as a token of their regret for any inconvenience they had caused.

A lovely gesture! I felt a bit of a heel after the "bollocking" I had given them!

The River Avon was much different from the Severn, narrower, with shallow, overgrown areas close to the banks in many places. And it meandered!

Some of the bends were quite demanding and navigation kept me on my toes. Reaching Strensham we found that the lock was no longer manned. The approach was difficult with the weirs creating severe cross currents, sculpting the off bank by their scouring effect and creating areas of sand bars, Even when we had completed the approach Jean found that the lock itself was no sinecure and would have been glad to call on the assistance of the old style "Lockie".

Above the lock an arm of the river flows down towards the weirs and sluices then towards the Mill House with its Mill stream and race. However our route was upstream.

According to the Guide Book one thing that would be in short supply would be the chance to take on fresh water and dispose of toilet waste. Water points and Sanitary stations were definitely at a premium! In common with most rivers, the listed public moorings were mainly populated by cruisers. We found that stopping to explore something that caught our eye or to enjoy a drink at one of the many riverside pubs was not a whim that could be engaged upon on a regular basis.

The river was wide enough to deter casual bridge building but the Defford Railway Bridge carried the main Devon to Newcastle line over the water. A few hundred yards upstream the 16th. Century

Elkington Bridge faced the boater with a bewildering array of different sized arches of which only the largest was navigable. An interesting, stone built bridge it was entirely devoid of the symmetry of more modern structures. Just beyond the bridge the river passes Burlingham Wharf at the apex of the 1800 Swan's Neck bend. The moorings lining the outside of this bend make passage interesting.

The bend is so tight that the possibility is, sometime in the future, the river will break through the spit of land enclosed by the bend and create, first an island then, as the silt deposits build up, an Ox-Bow lake, when the old river channels are blocked off.

Between Nafford and Pershore, the river meandered so much that we found ourselves steering every point of the compass between due West and due East while the river gradually edged its way North.

Defford Road Wharf was not the best of moorings but it had the capacity to accommodate a 65 foot long narrowboat..

The rich, low-lying land around here forms part of the Vale of Evesham, one of the richest fruit and vegetable growing areas in Central England. It provides a weekend mecca for Midland families to pick, plums, damsons, greengages and later, apples and pears. The making of home-made jam and the preserving of fruit is still a skill practised by many local people.

Along the road above the wharf, it was a walk of about one and a half miles into the centre of Pershore. We decided to walk into town and catch a bus back. Keen to take advantage of our location we sought out the green grocers hoping for an extravaganza of cheap, fresh, local fruit.

We were bitterly disappointed!

It may be that P.Y.O. outlets had made local produce difficult to sell in retail shops but as we walked around the displays we could have been anywhere in the E.E.C. Every country of origin was on display with the exception it seemed of England.

We may have "won" the war! We have surely lost the peace!

This phenomena was something we had noted when we were in Boston in the heart of the Lincolnshire fruit and vegetable growing area.

After a quick look around to check out the town and the moorings we returned to the boat armed with the knowledge that he town was certainly worth a visit and that we could almost be sure of a good mooring along the recreation ground bank.

As we climbed the slope above the moorings, we saw that in the hedges lining the road were a number of fruit trees laden down with plums. Over-ripe fruit carpeted the floor attracting wasps. There was no sign of orchards or cultivation and the fallen crop seemed to indicate that these were not under anyone's special jurisdiction. We filled a large bag with plums picked from the low branches; the price suited us fine, free!

As they were simply going to waste we felt that this did not constitute theft!

Pershore Lock and its approach promised an exciting few minutes. The two bridges spanning the river below the lock, one old, one fairly modern, were set at a slight angle to each other and the distance between them was too short to fully counter the slight misalignment of the navigable arches. One thing in our favour was that, as we had had no rain for a while, the water flow was modest and no "fresh" water was expected. The lock itself presented a variation from the "normal" river lock in that it had a single ground paddle to be raised while filling the lock and closed while the chamber was being emptied. To the crew of a narrowboat the combination of ground and gate paddles was pretty much the norm. and offered no real problems.

Timing our arrival at the moorings to co-incide with the morning sailing window we had soon located a berth and were securely tied up, ready for anything.

The town offered good shopping and a launderette and contained some very attractive Georgian properties. The Parish Church had also been an Abbey but unlike the townsfolk of Tewkesbury here the people had allowed it to be destroyed by Henry VIII during his rampage of destruction in which he tore down many of the Catholic buildings. It was only fully restored during early Victorian times although some substantial parts of the Norman building were left standing and are now incorporated into the church.

Taking advantage of the position of our mooring, which was well shaded by mature trees, I seized the opportunity to make another pair of side fenders. An essential part of this process was hanging the partially completed fender from a convenient overhead support while the weaving process was carried out.

The strong overhead branches were ideal, so I prepared and bound the lengths of rope as per the instructions I had received during Colin Jones' course. Lengths of rope were carefully measured, two long and four short; these would be the basis of each fender. I do not intend to attempt a description of the skills and techniques involved, anyone wishing to learn the art need only enrol on a course or simply buy and study Colin's excellent illustrated book, "The Fender Book." the complete D.I.Y. book of Fenders.

With the embryo ropework suspended from a branch, I was busy weaving ropes and tightening knots. A gentleman walking his dog stopped to watch me as I concentrated on making all the weaves, tight and neat.

"Who do you reckon is winning?" he asked "You or that emaciated octopus?"

As is often the case no witty repartee sprang to mind so I just grinned and replied, "I'm not really sure but I think I'm getting the better of the bugger!"

Using whatever supports were handy and working on the bank to make my fenders certainly attracted spectators. The "emaciated octopus" analogy became a standing joke between me and a number of regular visitors who interrupted the serious business of dog walking to share a joke with me and to check on the progress of the project.

Early next morning we pulled our mooring pins and set off towards Evesham. Wyre Piddle lock was less than a mile above Pershore, this being the shortest pound on the Lower Avon Navigation. Almost without exception, the locks on the river had at least one watermill overlooking the weirs and utilising the water flow. The Wyre Mill had collected the epithet of being, "the ugliest mill on the river" if one were to give credence to the views expressed by one intrepid traveller.

The lock itself also had a claim to fame by having the sole remaining, unconverted, diamond shaped chamber left in service. Using it one was left wondering what was the perceived advantage of a design that had patently failed to impress, leading to the conversion of the others into more conventional structures. Certainly, once in the chamber, there was no climbing on or off a long narrowboat during the operating cycle. Again visitor moorings were at a premium, a few on the Mill leat and a short stretch serving the Anchor Inn, reserved for patrons. With little to invite casual exploration of the area and the wide expanse of the flood plain keeping most development at arms length this was certainly the place for people seeking a peaceful few days.

After passing Cropthorne, a village situated on higher ground to the South-East of the river, the stream narrows as you approach Fladbury. Here the boater runs the gauntlet of run off from two Mills before entering the steep sided channel that curves towards the lock restricting visibility considerably. The river's course is almost due South while at Chadbury only some three miles upstream, the channel is heading North-North-West, such is the twisting course carved out by the water. A mile beyond Chadbury the river executes a wide, deep 18° bend in which is situated the old town of Evesham.

It was this loop of water that trapped the rebel forces ranged against the Crown during the Battle of Evesham in 1265 and allowed Prince Edward's forces to wreak such bloody retribution for the defeat inflicted on his army by Simon de Montford at Lewes the previous year. Simon de Montford, Earl of Leicester, his eldest son, eighteen Barons, 160 Knights and 4,000 men were slaughtered by the Royalist troops.

We moored at Workman Gardens just below the lock after a fraught few minutes looking out anxiously for the Hampton Ferry wires. We saw no trace of them.

Perhaps we were just lucky!

At Evesham lock the jurisdiction of the water changed from Lower Avon to Upper Avon Navigation Trust. (L.A.N.T. to U.A.N.T.)

We had little faith in the much publicised (by our Guidebook) bounty of local grown produce on sale in the shops but we would certainly be exploring what we could of the town's historic past.

I felt strange. Being Warwickshire born and bred, I had fond memories of wonderful summer outings to the Vale of Evesham to buy fruit and vegetables, but searching my mind I soon realised that invariably our shopping had been done at large roadside stalls or we had picked our own from the farms and orchards in the vale. My over-riding impression of these stalls was of plump,, rosy cheeked ladies with loud voices calling out their wares to passers-by.

As we walked through Workman Gardens I was reminded of another childhood experience. Each Sunday evening after Church, if the weather was fine, we would set off on a long walk in the beautiful Warwickshire countryside. One route would take us past Dordon Hall, a fortified farmhouse. The farm drive left the lane at the apex of a sharp, left hand corner known locally as "The Jawbones" because fifty yards down the drive, by the duck pond was an arch formed by the massive jawbones of a whale.

In Workman Gardens we found another arch of identical construction!

The lock-keeper's cottage at Evesham was an attractive wooden structure unusual in its shape which was triangular its broad base spanning the mill stream alongside the lock chamber. On occasions flood water had reduced the inhabitants to using a rowing boat to leave the property but had never actually reached the floor level.

Evesham Marina and Boatyard was situated about half a mile above the weir so we walked up to it collect some small items from the chandlery. They also kindly agreed to take delivery of a parcel of mail that was being forwarded to us by my sister.

The town turned out to have everything we had hoped for by way of museums, town trails, churches, ruins and well preserved old buildings. Once the site of a Benedictine Monastery complete with its Abbey Church which, had been so effectively destroyed by Henry VIII during his rampage of destruction of Catholic buildings, that the few remaining portions of them were left freestanding and not incorporated into the latter day Church buildings as was more commonly the case. The 16th. Cent, church of St. Lawrence is still in use and is nicely apportioned, whereas the 12th. Cent. Church of All Saints is unused, partially stripped but still consecrated although it is on the Redundant Churches list.

Walking around the town we discovered a wonderful Antique shop and spent some considerable time looking round the large and diverse range of goods they were offering. In a long glass cabinet I saw a beautifully cared for, Spanish Target Pistol (0.177 Air Pistol) with a carved wooden butt and fully adjustable sights. The proprietor opened the case and I examined the weapon. It was superb and I would have loved to have bought it. However, even at what I considered to be a very reasonable asking price, I still felt that it represented an unjustified extravagance.

An hour later we were in a small cafe finishing off our lunch; or at least Jean had finished, I was just starting my dessert. Claiming to be in a hurry to collect some green-groceries, she left the cafe promising to be no more than fifteen minutes and for me to await her return. Slightly longer than fifteen minutes later she returned, with a few items of fruit and vegetables in a plastic bag. From the way it thumped onto the table, her handbag was heavier now, but I didn't really register that fact.

I had already paid the bill so we were able to collect our bags and walk out onto the street. Our return route to the boat took us past a large hardware shop. The proprietor had just finished stocking the window and was putting up notices advertising a grand sale, starting immediately. This was basically a clearance sale of stock, shop soiled or ex. display. Among the items for sale were a number of electric chainsaws whose boxes had been damaged. They were at a "not to be missed" price. Over the previous winters we had tired of the endless chore of sawing salvaged wood into logs with a bow-saw. Using scavenged timber certainly kept the fuel bills down and sawing wood kept ones body warm and often sweating. For months we had promised ourselves a chainsaw. "If the price was right!", as they say.

Now! The moment had arrived!

With no further ado we marched into the shop. Ten minutes later we hit the streets, the proud owners of a brand new, 14" Electric Chainsaw.

After a few days, we picked our way carefully under Workman bridge, up through the lock, past the weir and cruised up to Evesham Marina to collect our mail. Our telephone had not been checked for messages over the week-end and so Jean dialled up the answer service.

On tape were a series of urgent calls from the Nursing Home in London, please contact them A.S.A.P. as Aunt Theo was seriously ill. We phoned the Home and were advised to come quickly if we wished to see her alive. She was sinking fast!

By now we had just about reached the lock and so we spoke to the keeper explaining our position and seeking his advice on secure moorings if we were to be away overnight. He organised a berth for us in the Mill leat overlooked by his cottage and assured us that he would keep an eye on the boat for the duration of our stay in London.

Lunch time saw us en route for the Nursing Home and Aunt Theo!

Our flustered arrival proved to be something of an anti-climax. We walked into the room to find Theo, sitting up in bed, holding court in her inimitable fashion and looking as bright as a button.

We had booked ourselves in at the Union Jack Club at Marble Arch where we were members. This meant that we could stay with her until after the evening meal then return on the morning of the following day. By now it was clear that, whatever spasm of ill-health had troubled the 90 year old, it had been sent packing in no uncertain terms and Theo was "at home" to her friends and visitors and treating them all in her usual, abrasive manner. Saint Peter had been sent packing, this time at least!

Neither Jean or I enjoyed staying in London, except in our boat, and so next day we took our leave and returned to Evesham. Somewhat, relieved, if the truth be known, that Theo still appeared to be able to soldier on for a while.

Everything was in order, the boat was safe and secure and so, after thanking the keeper for his kindness, we began to prepare ourselves for the next leg of our cruise. Destination, Bidford on Avon.

Although we would be entering the jurisdiction of the U.A.N.T., we would be legal as we had bought a full River license which covered both navigations. The only constraint was the 14 days for which the permit was valid. The visit to Theo had cost us two days but we still had ample time in hand to complete the trip without rushing. From Evesham to Stratford we had a distance of eighteen miles to cover. Bidford on Avon was roughly halfway but with only a third of the total number of locks. (3 out of 9.) The locks on the Upper Avon were mostly replaced in the early 1970's and commemorate a wide variety of individuals, companies and societies which were involved in the restoration and upkeep of the Navigation.

We cruised a four mile reach, heading due North for much of that distance before turning sharply due East. At Offenham we had been warned to keep our eyes open for another cable operated ferry that had replaced the old wooden footbridge. The village itself sounded interesting but if we were to give time to visiting all the places of interest we passed we would have been forced to buy a license for a much longer time period. The cost of such permits was beyond the depths of our pockets.

The first lock we reached had been rebuilt in 1969 and was dedicated to George Billington. It was unusual in that incorporated into the structure was a flood proof lock keeper's hut. Actually added after the completion of the lock, it looks for all the world like a squat lighthouse and indeed is known locally as the "Offenham Light".

Only half a mile of river separate this lock from the Robert Aickman Memorial Lock, another name to conjure with in the annals of waterway restoration. Noticeably most of the locks on the Upper

Avon have lost the mill buildings that used to accompany them. This lock is an exception and is still overlooked by the buildings of Harvington Mill even though the Mill itself has been disused for almost a century. It was re-built in 1982 on a new site when its old location became untenable due to soil erosion and silting of the river channel.

With Cleeve Hill dominating the right bank, the navigation continues upstream past Cleeve Prior and enters a series of bends where the currents have caused heavy silting on the inside banks forcing boats into taking a wide line through the passage.

I.W.A. Lock is the third on this section and shortly after negotiating it our course turned sharply through Marcliffe Corner after which the Bidford on Avon moorings soon hove into view. This is an immensely popular spot and owners of large boats like ours would be well advised to time their visit very carefully as public mooring is in short supply and even fee charged places are not that numerous. We were preparing to moor up at the jetty outside the pub on a fee paying site when a large narrowboat cleared its ropes on the public moorings and departed.

Quickly we crossed over and claimed the berth!

Because the area is so popular it suffers from the usual drawbacks. The site at which we were moored was also used by families as a picnic area and playground. Cars were driven almost to the water's edge and the grass area was dotted with family groups enjoying a day out. The children were doing what they do best; flying kites, playing ball games, throwing frisbees but mainly screaming with all the power of their lungs.

After completing our shopping, enjoying a couple of excellent pub meals and quickly looking round some of the local places of interest, we overnighted then cast off to head for other, hopefully, somewhat more peaceful surroundings.

As we headed upstream, the first structure we met was the rather, impressive, irregular, Mediaeval stone bridge reputedly built in 1482 by monks from Alcester. It is located close to the site of a Roman ford which was only finally removed in 1970. In spite of the profusion of arches displayed by the bridge, only the medium one on the right, approaching from downstream, was suitable for navigation. The approach channels to the other arches were too silted to allow the passage of boats even where the arches were large enough to cater for craft.

After negotiating this bridge we saw a familiar boat moored away to our right near to some overhanging trees. It was "Ragdoll" home of the famous television puppets, "Rosie and Jim." Aware that they were based in the Stratford area we assumed that we had stumbled on the pair's homebase as this appeared to be a regular long term mooring as opposed to a casual one.

With just nine miles and six locks to negotiate before reaching Stratford we anticipated an easy day. In fact as many of the locks incorporate much re-cycled and restored equipment they are not always the most easy to operate and their siting with narrow channels, tight bends and strong cross currents tended to create problems for a boat of our length. The river itself follows a convoluted course which had led to extensive silting in areas making the choice of the safest passage a little fraught. In the main we found that directions were good but occasionally I found myself faced with minor dilemmas, as to the choice of the safest route.

After an interesting transit through the first five locks with our route enhanced by a variety of minor challenges, we finally found ourselves arriving at the last lock before journey's end, the Stratford moorings.

Stratford New Lock was very deep and a large, square framework of girders braced its walls spanning the chamber some 7 to 8 feet above the water level. This structure was necessary because of high ground stresses caused by the depth of the chamber. It certainly ensured that the lock was noticeable. It was also here that the memorial was erected celebrating the re-opening of the Navigation by the Queen Mum in June 1974. Although we were into September and the children had returned to their classrooms, this venue was still popular as the destination for park walks and for dog exercising. It was reached via a very pleasant walk along the riverside and through the extensive parkland.

After running the gauntlet of gongoozlers, who tended to sit on lock beams or stand in the way of their operation, we reached the site and were relieved to find ample designated mooring available along the edge of the park.

We tied up opposite Holy Trinity Church and graveyard. Here in the Chancel are interred the remains of our great poet and playwright, William Shakespeare and a number of his family.

At least the neighbours on that bank would be quiet!

One of the first things to come to our notice were the posters announcing the visit of the Chinese State Circus. This explained the presence of the large, elaborate marquee we could see erected in the park further upstream. As my birthday was now only a couple of days away and we both enjoyed circuses that did not include animal acts, Jean promised me that, if I were good, she would take me to the show as a birthday treat.

The weather was fine and, as there were a number of suitable trees in the vicinity, I got out my ropes and continued with the exercise of fender making.

I was to do this at a number of places and nowhere did it fail to attract an audience and provide hours of interesting conversation. This tended to seriously extend the completion time for each fender as I had never fully mastered the art of working at normal pace while carrying on a conversation. Jean always says that if I had my arms cut off I would be dumb.

I'm sure I can't imagine what she means!

As we knew the town well and had already visited the majority of tourist attractions we tended to restrict our visits to shopping trips rather than sightseeing tours.

One development really saddened us!

Over many years the river at Stratford had become famous for the large groups of swans that lived here. On this visit we noted what appeared to be a serious decline in their numbers. It seemed to us that the establishment of a breeding colony of Canada Geese may have been instrumental in this decline. From the numbers of teenaged goslings evident, they appeared to be much more prolific than the swans and aggressive in their territorial claims.

It was fun to note that a lone White fronted Goose, had been rejected by the larger, more aggressive Canadas' but had been adopted as a kind of mascot by a large group of swans. Whenever we saw this flock sailing regally past, there was the little goose swimming proudly in the van.

Swans are inveterate cadgers and seem to learn quickly which boats are liable to be a soft touch when it came to scrounging. People often expressed amazement when they saw us feeding the swans off the bows, the long necks reaching inboard to take food gently from our fingers. Swans have got an undeserved reputation for violence and we have found that under most conditions they are gentle, if not a little greedy. A cob will be powerful in defence of his mate when she is brooding and get between a pen and her cygnets at your peril but those circumstances aside swans tend to be beautiful, graceful creatures who make friends, sometimes too easily and unwisely.

One fine morning we went out onto the foredeck to find that a young couple in their late twenties were admiring the boat.

They were Japanese!

In conversation we discovered that she was a qualified architect and that he was studying the same subject in the University at Kuala Lumpur. Their home was in Kobe City in Southern Japan but fortunately they were both in K.L. when the earthquake struck their home city.

Yushi's English was virtually non-existent while Toshimi's was hesitant and idiosyncratic, although certainly more fluent than our Japanese which consisted of one word, 'sayonara', As that meant goodbye it hardly seemed appropriate at that time.

We invited them aboard and gave them the V.I.P. tour. They were entranced! As architects they were fascinated by the idea that "Pallas

Athene" was not only a boat capable of long distance cruising, but also a very comfortable home with a comprehensive range of mod cons.

Many photographs were taken and we swapped names and addresses before we parted. Weeks later we received a postcard from K.L. in perfectly spelt but wonderfully fractured English.

"Thank you very much kind for us, last visit UK. You receive this letter!! I never write a mail to ship!! On Stratford, - We were very surprise because your house is just ship and its possible around the UK Never seen such a life. And more inside ship there is plenty "happiness" and pleasure time. We hope to be your happy life in future. So, please take care all of your sailing and hope more happy. Thank you"

Later that year one of the first Christmas cards we posted was to Yushi and Toshimi. We received a beautiful, simple card in reply, gently admonishing us for not realising that as Buddhists they did not celebrate Christmas and wishing us a happy and prosperous New Year.

The one nationality that we were sure to encounter at any of the major tourist locations that we visited were the Japanese. It was mainly the younger ones who found our boats really interesting and those that we came into contact with invariably proved to be polite, considerate and reserved, although quite prepared to respond to friendly overtures.

A buzz of excitement went around when "Rag Doll" in company with her support boat, "The Enabler", arrived to prepare for the filming of a "Rosie and Jim" episode in which the mischievous twosome visit the Chinese State Circus. Filming in the Big Top was scheduled to take place on the final day of the visit. Our tickets had been bought for September 14th; my birthday and the penultimate day.

We heaved a sigh of relief!

It was fun watching the preparations and the filming of short segments of the episode, realising in the process just how crude and basic many of the props are and how much is hidden by the "magic of Television". Still as I have remarked before, basically the shows are good PR for boating even if I still consider that the puppets themselves present an appalling role model in terms of childrens behaviour and lack of discipline. Our own visit to the circus was one of the highlights of the years cruising. The acts were superb, the performances first rate and the performers themselves all seemed so young.

From our ringside seats we could notice the slightly tatty appearance of much of the on-stage costume and props. Seams opening, sequins missing, decorations torn and papier mâché masks worn and chipped. In the seats further back from the arena the magic would have been complete, close-up, the view took a tiny edge off our total enjoyment.

Mind you I have found a similar thing with front row seats at stage performances, plays and pantomimes. Too close a view of costumes, make-up and scenery is not conducive to retaining the special magic. I find that fantasy and performance arts rely to some measure on the imagination of the individual observer, this is often best achieved by being somewhat distanced from the action.

With our river license due to expire the next day we walked up to the basin to check on the availability of overnight moorings. The basin was crowded.

We needed to fill up our fresh water tank before re-commencing our cruise so we moved up onto the hardstanding where the water point was situated. After taking on water we moved a few yards into a berth on the overnight moorings. Now we would be ready to set off next morning following the expiry of our permit.

Before we finally left we were treated to one last comic display by a troupe of swans!

As often happened, the flock of swans swimming on the water outside the Royal Shakespeare Theatre, decided, apropos nothing, to fly downstream. Their take-off technique was spectacular. Running across the water, large webbed feet slapping and powerful wings beating the surface, they powered their way downstream in a phalanx. One swan, despite being squarely in the path of the take-off, declined to move. It was barely clear of the take-off point and swan after swan just cleared it, occasionally brushing it with a wing tip or catching it with a wildly flailing foot, as they strained for height, wing feathers strumming under the pressure of the lift. One large cob, bringing up the rear, appeared to be struggling to achieve lift off. Just as collision seemed inevitable, the large swan heaved itself into the air giving one final desperate thrust of its legs. One large, webbed foot landed squarely on the back of the swan on the surface. It disappeared underwater in a tremendous flurry of spray. Moments later it reappeared, shedding water in all directions and looking in bewilderment at the large rear end now disappearing rapidly downstream.

So much for independence!

The weather had stayed good. No heavy rainfall had raised water levels and caused us problems. Now we were ready to re-enter the canal system and head off, up the locks.

At least there would be ample moorings now and we wouldn't have the problem of weirs at the locks!

19.
Aqueducts and Locks.

After casting off, we negotiated the lock that lead from the river into the basin. Once in that broad expanse of water, the unwary boater could be forgiven for thinking that there was no exit into the canal system. Across in the far corner, diagonally opposite to the lock, it was possible to see, below a major road, what appeared to be a low, square sided culvert, too low to be navigable and impossible to see through as it angled back from the entrance.

However we had been here before and knew that the route below the road was open and navigable so we made our way over to the culvert. Originally it had been a bridge but subsequent periods of rebuilding and strengthening to cope with the weight of traffic on the road had reduced the headroom until now it was quite claustrophobic.

Once through we were on a canal overlooked by the rears of rows of houses and set to climb a flight of locks which lead it deep into the heart of an industrial estate of some magnitude. It was amazing how quickly one lost the feeling of the beauty of the surroundings and fell under the mild depression of an industrial area which did not even pay lip service to providing an attractive backdrop to a tourist highway.

It was thirteen miles to Kingswood Junction with a total of 36 locks to negotiate so this was a difficult length, particularly as the general condition of much of the infrastructure is poor.

The navigation was almost lost in 1955 when the Government Board of Survey proposed a long list of closures and abandonments. Massive Public protests against its closure resulted in the canal being reprieved and eventually leased to the National Trust who undertook to re-instate and maintain it. Considerable sums of money were provided by the trust from its own funds and restoration was completed. To help recoup the monies expended the Trust introduced a license that was to allow boaters to use the newly opened stretch. A canal is a serious piece of upkeep and proved to be a little outside the scope of the Trust's skills and capabilities and so B.W. reclaimed the lease and became responsible for the navigation. For its own reasons, B.W. designated its recently re-acquired property a Remainder Canal which set the level of its commitment to the canal simply as the responsibility of providing the minimum of repair and maintenance commensurate with keeping the navigation "safe".

Now as part of the main waterway system the boater is not required to buy an additional license to use it.

We had contacted Jeanette of Jannel Cruisers at Burton on Trent who had been able to confirm a winter mooring for us and we had booked a session in the dry dock to enable us to re-black "Pallas Athene's" bottom.

With no information to the contrary, we were assuming that B.W.'s normal policy of winter repair and maintenance stoppages would begin on November 1st. as usual. We had until then to complete our autumn cruising.

The Stratford Canal suffers greatly from bank erosion and silting, this means that, even when levels are up to the run-offs, the channel does not hold sufficient water to enable boats to moor up in many places outside of the designated areas. Later, towards the junction, we managed to harvest some of the lovely blackberries that hung in lush clusters on the brambles that cascaded down to the water level on the off-side. This exercise involved steering the boat towards the bank and gently thrusting the bows into the shallows until the first ten feet or so were alongside the overhanging fruits. I would hold it in position with controlled bursts of engine thrust while Jean quickly picked the berries. This was not too much of a chore due to their size and quantity!

Before that however, fate proved herself as fickle as ever. Once more we found ourselves heading north with other boats and virtually no southbound traffic. This put the majority of locks against us with little chance of boats to use the water. A situation we never found easy to live with.

Not in any great hurry, we cruised along steadily, limping through the very shallow water at the approaches to some bridges and taking our time through the profusion of locks in the first few miles.

The Shakespeare legend had spread along the canal and at Wilmcote, 4 miles and 16 locks out from Stratford, we reached the beautifully kept, picturesque Tudor cottage reputed to have been the home of Mary Arden, Shakespeare's mother. Chatting with a group of

American tourists who were avidly devouring any snippet of information to do with the Shakespeare family, we succumbed to a base urge.

We commented on how humble we felt when faced with the closeness of history and how wonderful it was to live surrounded by reminders of bygone times. As we cruised along this stretch we imagined Mary wheeling young William down to the waters edge in his McClaren Buggy to watch the narrow boats passing through laden with coal. For a while they savoured the thought then, gradually, clarity dawned. They laughed with us commenting;

"Gee buddy I guess you must be funning us, they wouldn't have Buggies would they!"

We had not intended any malice and they were quick to see the humorous side of the exchange, but we did find them very earnest and open to believing almost any statement delivered with the appropriate brand of blue eyed innocence.

Many of them seemed to be involved in what almost amounted to a national pastime for them, the game of, "Spot the Relative!" One would often meet small groups of our Trans-Atlantic cousins busily getting in touch with their roots. They would scour churches and graveyards searching for references to their family name on memorials and tombstones.

Our cousin Yoma from New England was a prime example of this obsession. No visit to England would be complete unless it involved an intensive round of "relative spotting."

Born in Burma, married to an American she has spent most of her 80 odd years living abroad, yet she knows more about her and her husband's extended family ancestry than virtually any other person alive.

Our American cousins; We love 'em!

After Wilmcote there was only one more lock before we reached our projected mooring at Wooton Wawen. However two of the three aqueducts of a type virtually exclusive to this canal have to be crossed. The Edstone Aqueduct was something of a bogey to me. It is about two thirds the size of the Pontcysyllte in terms of height and length but was narrower and seemed to suffer permanently from an awkward cross wind. Still I had begun to get my feelings of unease under control and so we entered the channel with only the slightest of hesitations.

Once more the feeling of crossing was horrendous, again we reached the far side in complete safety ready to cruise on to Odd Lock. Next stop, Wootton Wawen.

We would be mooring in the basin created when the canal building programme had been temporarily halted. It's unusual in that it is built on an embankment and boats from Stratford enter it through a narrow channel leading directly from the aqueduct that carries the canal over the A34(T). It now houses a boat yard which runs one of the few hire fleets operating on the Stratford Canal.

The village itself was situated some small distance away and was very scattered. It promised some interesting features that we hoped to explore during our stay.

The small area of public moorings were available on the towing path side and we were fortunate enough to be able to select a pleasant if somewhat shallow berth.

The Navigation Inn, hard against the basin, was one of the first canal venues I had introduced Jean to during our visits to see Mum and Dad, before we had finalised our plans for a life afloat. Then, we had been impressed by their catering standards, now we were looking forward to re-establishing our acquaintance with their cuisine. We were not disappointed!

From our reading of the guide book, the Church sounded like a gem and its setting was in a beautiful rural area with half timbered houses completing the picture. It had been declared a Conservation area which gave us a slightly ambivalent feeling as this sometimes seems to be taken as an excuse to do nothing. For us little could be worse than seeing beautiful, old buildings mouldering quietly away in the name of conservation. Here, however, we were pleasantly pleased with what we saw and impressed by the quiet ambience of the village in spite of the proximity of the noisy A34 trunk road.

There were a number of areas of woodland and a couple of well preserved Manor houses but rightly, pride of place must go to the Church of St. Peter, which overlooks the scattered houses. Its buildings were an intriguing mixture of dates and styles with sections dating back to Saxon times. The Sanctuary is intact and original and still forms the focus of worship. Much of the structure is refreshingly plain and the enormous Lady Chapel resembles a barn with its uneven flooring and roof.

It was what the guide books had promised, "An intriguing building!"

Next door to the pub was a large farm with an extensive range of outbuildings. At least that was what it had been originally. Now the buildings on three sides of the old farmyard had been converted into workshops and formed the basis of an active, thriving Arts and Crafts Centre. The range of skills being displayed and the variety of goods on offer was astonishing and we were able to buy small gifts for members of the family. These would be distributed next time we reached the Coventry Canal.

Just over half our journey to the Kingswood Junction had been completed and still the traffic was mainly northbound, it looked like the remainder of our trip would be dogged by many of the 18 remaining locks being set against us.

On this section the locks only have single gates top and bottom but the paddles are small which makes the chambers slow to empty and fill. This adds to the sense of difficulty which pervades this flight.

In general terms, the area is very attractive with trees and bushes encroaching on the water, giving it the aspect of a small river rather than a canal. Aesthetically, this creates a feeling of beauty but it has attendant problems of silting and weed growth. Unlike a river, it is not subject to scouring with fresh water following heavy rains. The canal, basically, is devoid of any useful water flow.

Barrel roofed cottages and split iron bridges at some of the locks add charm to the overall scene, especially as most of the canal buildings are either occupied or in use.

Not having confirmed the information, I must qualify the following as possibly apocryphal. I was told by a man at one of the locks that the reason for the barrel shaped roofs on the lock cottages was due to the thrift of the builders. When bridges were built a support arch was needed for the bricklayers to form the shape over. Not wishing to break up the frames but finding them to awkward to transport over long distances, they collected them at fixed points such as locks and used them as roof beams when building the lock-keepers cottage.

It seems such a lovely idea that I haven't tried too hard to discredit it!

In such rural surroundings, devoid, to a major extent, of signs of habitation, it is not surprising that canalside hostelries like the "Fleur-de-Lys" at Lowson Ford attract, not only boaters but large numbers of adults and also families with an interest in watching the boats.

Pubs and locks are an irresistible attraction to Gongoozlers!

The aqueduct at Yarningdale, hard by lock 34, is quickly crossed but is built to exactly the same pattern as the others on this canal with the towing path fixed at the level of the base of the iron tank which carries the water.

Towing path walkers get an extraordinary view of the boats as they cross the tiny stream!

With fresh water available at Kingswood Junction we could afford to pause awhile and get our breath back before cruising the stretch of the Grand Union Canal leading into the heart of Birmingham, a length which we had yet to explore.

From here on we would be faced with wide locks with their instantly recognisable paddle operating gear, which we knew so well from our excursions up and down the Hatton Flight. All being well we would meet up with boats of a compatible length and travelling in our direction, then we could breast up and share the rigours of lock wheeling.

As an area, Lapworth had little to offer beyond its industrial connections with the canals. Here the Stratford and the G.U. pass within 300 yards of each other and are connected by a short arm lined with wharves. The lock at the end of the arm that lifted the G.U to the level of the Lapworth feeder lagoon had been by-passed, now a narrow cut linked the canal direct to the pound above lock 22. When this excavation had been completed the lock-keepers cottage was left isolated on a small triangular island. The actual cut was quite narrow and as it was angled towards lock 21 boats climbing the flight from Stratford and wishing to enter the G.U., found the turn extremely tight, particularly if they were as long as "Pallas Athene."

The area between Kingswood and Knowle is relatively flat and featureless, dominated, like so much of the edges of the industrial heartland, by sprawling networks of electricity pylons.

Re-reading our guide book we had been pleased to note that, in fact, the 5 lock flight at Knowle would be the last of the wide locks and after that our proximity to Birmingham would establish narrow locks as the norm.

Arriving at the winding hole below the flight we saw a long hire boat taking on water. It was pointing in the wrong direction to be of use to us as a partner but as she seemed to be experiencing some slight difficulty we pulled over and offered our help. It turned out to be a crew of young Americans, two couples. They had overnighted in the basin and were almost ready to set off up the locks towards Birmingham. Ace!

The cross wind was giving them problems and they were pinned against the wharf unable to hold out the bows long enough to begin winding the boat. We dropped a line across to them, started their boat into the turn then cast off before we got ourselves into difficulties. The flight was in our favour and with Jean and two of their crew members ashore the bottom gates were soon open to receive the boats. We entered first as their boat was still winding but they made it in to the chamber with little additional difficulty. With the gates closed and before the lock wheelers began to flood the chamber, I did the honours and secured the two boats firmly side by side. When the lock was filled and we were preparing to leave I suggested that they switch off their engine and the whole crew could help with the main task of operating the locks while I handled both boats as a single wide beam craft.

This flight had originally consisted of six narrow locks and the remains of these chambers still flanked the flight. Typical of many hire boats they appeared to be short of equipment and had just two windlasses, this meant that a certain amount of "Pass the Parcel" was involved. One paddle got left open and a young man noticed this as he was preparing to head for the next lock. As he did not have a windlass, he called to his friend to throw one over.

Jean's warning cry and the windlass arcing towards the young man were simultaneous. Seeing two pounds of awkwardly shaped steel wheeling towards him, discretion became the better part of valour, he drew back his hand and the windlass clanged against the concrete. Seconds later, it had ricocheted over the hard standing and flipped gently over the edge into a disused lock chamber.

His, "Just a second, I'll jump in and retrieve it." provoked a further shout from Jean, this time, thankfully, it had an immediate effect. His expression was puzzled until we walked over to him and pointed out that the chamber was actually 12 to 15 feet deep, not the six feet that it appeared to be. The surface of the silt looked fairly firm but as we explained if two pounds of steel could disappear so completely, without leaving a trace how much more effectively would the ooze swallow up a six foot tall, 12 stone man

We kept a "Sea Search" magnet on board for such emergencies but the idea of fishing in the semi-liquid morass did not appeal. To make up their complement of equipment, we donated one of our spares to avoid their being charged for it and forfeiting part of their hiring deposit.

When we began our life on the canals I had bought two standard windlasses. The second purchase was one with a long shaft to aid Jean on locks were the paddle gear was stiff. Later I bought a windlass with a special roller handle to reduce the calluses raised by the usual handles. Over the years we lost a couple and gave two away, currently we have eight assorted windlasses in the engine room.

It's not that they are particularly prolific breeders but they are adept at escaping from custody at locks and waiting to be found by the next boater along. Perhaps they are looking for a really good home!

It may sound a little harsh that boaters collect windlasses in this way but there is rarely any indication of which boat they belong to or even which direction it was heading in.

Some folk seem to be very lucky trawling lock exits with their magnets but we have never found any extra bits and pieces when we have been fishing for lost tools etc..

We have lost a couple of stainless steel "Chinamen" overboard, but as they were non-magnetic, they are still nestling in the mud somewhere.

The idea of the magnet is wonderful, unfortunately many of the things that disappear overboard are neither buoyant nor magnetic. Water, fuel and pump-out caps, tiller pins etc. are often crafted in brass or other non- magnetic materials. Increasingly, stainless steel is taking over due to its ease of cleaning, Pins and shackles used on ocean going yachts are quickly finding there way into the inventory of narrowboats. The old favourite cast iron also defies attempts to fish it out using a magnet.

In your travels, if you meet someone swinging a large bunch of keys, dangling from a cork float the size of a billiard ball, it is a fairly safe bet that you have made the acquaintance of a boater.

Our American friends were not a little surprised at how easily the flight was climbed, under Jean's expert directions. On the way down the locks the previous day, a number a difficulties had arisen mainly due to their not having access to informed advice.

The comments in our guide book were amusing, it suggested that, though the locks were heavy and difficult to operate, they were beautifully painted!

I'm sure we all felt uplifted by that gem of knowledge!

My sister-in-law managed a Building Society office in Knowle, so we said goodbye to the Americans after we had untied the boats. While they continued their cruise we set off to surprise Margaret. The walk was for nothing, our information was out of date and the office had been closed down and relocated in a town near to Coventry.

During the short time we spent there we could not do much exploring but we felt seriously under-whelmed by our impression of the village. It may be that the folk who live there find it great and that our tiny snapshot was totally unrepresentative, if that is the case, please accept our apologies to a community struggling to cope with traffic flow and the other blights that mar life in areas close to major cities.

Returning quickly to the boat we continued our day's cruising. After covering only four or five miles we saw our American friends moored up near the pub where they had lunched. Now they were back on board so, following up on a conversation between us regarding the possibility of their completing the "Gortex Challenge" at some time in the future, Jean had decided to give them our duplicate stamps and some additional details.

Sounding our air horns to alert them to our approach I throttled back and began to close up on their boat. We coasted forwards very slowly and "Pallas Athene" was alongside long enough for us to complete a short conversation and to hand over the odds and ends we had looked out for them. Our efforts were gratefully accepted and they waved us on our way.

There was no point offering to travel in convoy as, from here, all the locks were narrow gauge and in any case they were continuing into Birmingham while we intended to turn off at Bordesley Green Junction. We had reached the City suburbs but for long distances the canal travelled deep in tree lined cuttings with bridges arching high over us carrying both roads and railways. The traffic noise was remote and in spite of our own engine's steady beat we could hear snatches of birdsong in our peaceful surroundings.

Suddenly our route emerged into an inner City landscape with housing estates sprawling right up to the canal. Here and there large factory buildings reached towards the canalside as we thrust our way deeper into the city's industrial heart. As they became more numerous our course became crowded and the towing path seemed to make little contact with the outside world..

At Tyseley the huge goods yard spoke eloquently of the part the railways had played in the growth of the area. Now, however, like many other sectors of our industrial heritage it is vastly underused and much of the infrastructure is derelict and rusting. Buildings continued to crowd in on us, enormous, low bridges carried railway lines and roads across our route making the whole ambience of the area grim and claustrophobic.

In spite of the work that had been carried out at the Camp Hill Locks, water levels were still low and the water quality poor. Rafts of floating rubbish swam in the chambers waiting to clog the propeller of any un-wary boater's craft.

It became a case of throttling back and slipping gently through the water in an attempt to avoid the heavier shoals!

Arriving at the Camp Hill flight, we were amazed to find that they lead down hill. I had assumed that all the locks climbed towards the Birmingham summit and hadn't really noticed which direction (up or down) the guide book had indicated.

Again the locks were not in our favour and Jean had a extensive lock-wheeling process to carry out.

While the first lock was filling, she walked forward and drew the paddles on the next one or two, depending on distance. Meanwhile, I would open the top gates when the chamber had filled, enter, close the gates and paddles, then draw the bottom paddles and climb aboard to control the boat during the descent.

Jean would return, open the bottom gates, lower the paddles and when I had exited, close the gates.

The next lock was prepared and the process repeated!

A little more time and energy consuming than climbing a flight.

Although these were narrow locks, the gates were heavy and the rubbish in the water often made it difficult to open and close them without jamming the gates. As this flight had recently been worked on we feared what we might find on the Garrison locks which lead from Bordesley down to Salford Junction. That particular flight had a poor reputation and was a group of locks that many people had advised us to treat with caution if ever we were unlucky enough to have to traverse them.

This was definitely an area where it was unwise to leave a boat unattended, even for a short time and some of the locks were secured with anti vandal devices to deter mindless acts which often take the form of draining the locks or better still the pounds.

Well into the afternoon, we needed to press on if we wished to moor up in an area that offered a reasonable measure of safety. We felt that this would involve us in clearing the Minworth locks on the Birmingham and Fazeley Canal, before we moored up for the night.

With 5 locks in the Garrison Flight on the Birmingham and Warwick Junction Canal, and the three Minworth locks we would be covering another 8 locks and 7 miles. Added to the total we had already completed that would bring our total from Kingswood to Minworth up to 17 miles and 20 locks. Our estimate of the cruising time was around ten hours.

A heavy day's travel but infinitely preferable to mooring in an inner city area that had no recognised mooring sites and was poorly frequented.

Dame Fortune smiled on us and the passage down to Salford was much less eventful than we had feared. In no way could these be seen as a "tidy flight of locks", a description offered by our guide book.

Ours was the 1991 edition but we had a distinct feeling that when the material in the original, 1983 edition was revised a large number of items slipped through the net. This was clearly one!

Arriving at the final lock in the flight, we saw an apple tree, laden with delicious looking fruit. It was obviously a throwback to the times when locks had resident keepers who worked hard to keep the whole area tended and attractive in addition to the normal job of maintaining the flight. We picked one apple and tasted it confirming that they were as good as they looked but we refrained from filling a bag in case B.W. still laid claim to fruit growing on their property.

From here our route would be familiar!

Navigation hazard! Nottingham Canal.

Boats have allegedly negotiated weir slopes.

Canal in Lincoln. Glory Hole in distance.

Taking on water! R.Witham at Boston.

"President" at Black Country Show. She was built in 1909.

Sunshine at Gloucester Docks

The Lock-Keepers House. The Old Tide Basin Sharpness.

Attempt on Water Speed Record. Sharpness.

May Day Service, Boston on the Wash.

Unplanned break. Rosehill Cutting Marple.

European Eagle Owl at Stone Show.

Rally at Etruria Stoke on Trent.

20.
On Home Ground.

Once through the permanently open stop lock near the end of the canal, possibly a location for toll collection, we could see the giant concrete cat's-cradle of the M6 motorway intersection, rearing up in the background. Known nationally as "Spaghetti Junction" it towers over the Salford canal junction dwarfing everything. Here, amid the forest of giant support pillars, the canal plunges into a netherworld, its presence un-noticed by drivers, crisscrossing in multi-layered abandon, carried on concrete ribbons slung at dizzy heights above the boats. This was familiar territory to me and down here I encountered none of the problems that assailed the motorists as they sought to weave their way through a maze of roads, juggernauts bearing down on them from all points of the compass.

I never visit this area without experiencing a shudder of remembrance recalling the pointless hours spent in my motor car, picking my way through rush hour traffic, eyes streaming, throat sore from breathing the noxious fumes. From here the frenetic pace seems to have slowed somewhat, traffic appears lighter, emission levels down.

At least that was what it looked like from the safe haven of "Pallas Athene's" stern!

Amazingly, the roar of traffic is muted and it is possible to imagine how the old working boatmen would have reacted to the pace of life which sends vehicles racing across this country and the Continent in search of trade.

We were well into the evening and still had three locks to pass through but at least we were off the worst section and on water that we had cruised on a number of occasions. The first section passed through a heavily industrialised area which only began to take on a less depressing aspect once we had passed the Cincinatti works. A small group of boys on a bridge threw stones at the boat as we attempted to moor at Minworth. No damage was done but after we had made a pantomime of radioing for Police assistance on our tiny walkie talkie set with its long whip aerial, which sent them scampering for cover, we carried on for a further half a mile and moored, out of sight of the bridge, against the remains of a wharf which had once served an arm leading into a foundry.

This was an area where the tide of industry had receded, leaving a truncated entrance, bricked off and silted where once the clamour of commerce had reigned supreme. Here raw materials for manufacture were discharged and finished goods loaded for distribution.

In many parts of the country we had seen where arms used to disappear into buildings, where gantry cranes would load and unload goods, whatever the weather. Now these huge portals are bricked up and most traces of the channels all but obliterated. Future generations may discover that so much of our industrial heritage has been lost that they will find it difficult to witness at first hand some of the multifarious and ingenious devices that our forebears devised to keep their canal system, not only working, but showing a profit!

With the advent of modern technology, the great plants and factories have become more streamlined. Instead of huge, grimy buildings emitting a mixture of noise, smoke and fumes, many have disappeared to be replaced by featureless edifices of stainless steel and smoked glass. No doubt they offer a more efficient, healthy and safe environment for the relatively few workers they employ but where is the workforce that powered the wheels of the great Industrial Revolution? In areas that had once relied on heavy industry, all we find are acres of derelict sites covered with rusting steel work, marring the landscape, while in the towns, thousands of displaced manual workers (and not a few managers.), crowd the job centres seeking employment.

I don't see myself as a dinosaur, but this does make me sad and I can't help but think, that somewhere along the line, we've thrown the baby out with the bath water and opened the door for all and sundry to plunder our once prosperous land.

It is a sad commentary, that with so many people out of work, the environment continues to deteriorate because Government is unwilling to earmark the manpower and the capital required to restore and regenerate it.

For instance; to develop the potential of the canal system, even for leisure pursuits, requires a major injection of capital but in return could provide valuable work opportunities for many who currently languish on the Nation's scrap heap.

Whoops! Another of my hobby-horses!

Next day we descended the Curdworth locks and made our way towards Fazeley Junction and the Coventry Canal. With the weather staying really warm we were glad of the brisk breeze blowing across the open countryside. The flooded gravel pits that formed the water sports complex and nature reserves at Bodymoor Heath seemed to cool the air and keep it moist. This certainly made a break from the baking heat of the inner city, where concrete, glass and brick created a heat-sink that made life uncomfortable, even on board a boat.

Back on familiar territory we were able to recognise many of the boats as we approached their moorings. We swapped comments with folk who were taking advantage of the prolonged dry spell, to work on the external paint work of their craft and to polish the brightwork. Something that I occasionally let slide.

I needed to work on my brasses!

Just past the swing-bridge at Drayton Manor, a new Marina was being planned, up to now it seemed to be restricting its development to an area of the off-bank near to the winding hole. It would be interesting to see how it progressed.

We intended taking a short break at Amington and Polesworth, to shop, to do our laundry and to visit friends. If we stayed over the weekend we would be able to attend Morning Service at Tamworth Central Methodist Church. Mum and my sister's family always enjoyed this.

To be sure our fresh water supply, would hold out we stopped at the B.W. point at Fazeley to replenish the tank. After climbing the two locks at Glascote we kept an eye open for a sighting of the rather splendid, Vietnamese Pot-Bellied Pig that roamed the gardens of a large house near the Tamworth Road Bridge in Amington. When the "Gate Inn" appeared off our starboard bow we knew that our regular mooring was close. We pulled over and moored on the towing path side.

This was as near as I would get to my roots!

It was strange that, having spent the majority of my adult life living in various parts of the country and of all the properties I had owned, only one was in this area, I still felt more at home here than anywhere else. Obviously, having parents, relatives and friends in the vicinity made a considerable difference but in a special way I felt a much closer affinity with the people of the Midlands and the North than with those to the South. There is a strange chemistry which binds us to our roots.

Coming from a coal mining family and having been touched by the brutality of that life, having experienced at first hand something of the injustice dealt out to miners and their families by those in authority, I was keenly aware of the North/South divide. Not that I harboured any enmity, I had become, through the experience of travel and having lived in many areas of the country, cosmopolitan.

Yet! my blood is still stained with coal dust!

Jean, having been born into an Army family, spending her formative years with an Aunt and Uncle in Cyprus and India, did not have the same feeling of belonging, unless it was towards Devon, where she had spent her adult life and bought up her two boys, as a lone parent.

The welcome she had received from my family and friends, then later, while we living in the area while the boat was built, from the people who surrounded us, had endeared the Midlands to her and almost everyone who met her, came to admire her, in spite of the fact that she talked, "cut glass!"

From Amington we had a choice of Launderettes. We could walk the mile or so back along the towing path and through the housing estate, to the one in Glascote, not forgetting to say "Hello" to the adorable Vietnamese Pig that roamed the large lawns of a canal side house. Alternatively, we could catch a bus into town and use the one in Lichfield Street almost next door to the R.A.F.A. Club. As an ex-WRAF, Jean was a member and it offered a venue where one could get a good meal at a reasonable cost.

Having collected our mail when we arrived; next morning saw us hiking into Glascote with the laundry. I was carrying the bulk of it in my large rucksack. Most of the route was fairly level yet I was experiencing the occasional stab of chest pain. I wrote this off as the effect of unaccustomed exercise, I hadn't carried a loaded rucksack for some time.

It was Friday and that meant, Market Day, an irresistible magnet for us, we spent the afternoon there after returning the washing to the boat. We left the living area looking like the archetypal Chinese laundry with washing airing on a variety of frames. At least it meant the process would be completed without our being unduly disturbed.

I believe we saw a film at the Multi- Screen Cinema later that afternoon, sitting in splendid isolation in an empty auditorium, surrounded by our purchases. We did not normally choose to see films that we were not keen to view but this one seems to have made a negligible impression. I can't recall the title and we didn't record it in our diary!

At least in Tamworth the cinema was within an easy walk of the town centre. Nowadays, the tendency seems to be, build all the shops in an "out of town" centre and site the main areas of entertainment there. Without a car or intimate knowledge of the local Public Transport system, one was hard put to reach the venues. To use taxis' put the whole exercise beyond our pockets, even allowing for reduced admission for pensioners.

That evening, Pam and Maurice paid us a visit and stayed for supper. We spent an enjoyable couple of hours, reminiscing about old times. Jean was not excluded but was able from time to time, to regale us with anecdotes dredged from her childhood in India. In some ways far more exciting than our fairly commonplace recollections.

We spent Saturday afternoon at Joans', catching up on local developments and making arrangements for Sunday. Next day Mum would be picked up and taken to the service with us and we would all have lunch at the "Gate Inn" to relieve Joan of the chore of cooking for such a large group.

Towards evening, we made the one hour cruise to Polesworth, mooring up at our usual spot near the "Royal Oak". Here the moorings were overlooked by a block of flats and some of the folks living there knew us well enough to keep an eye on the boat while we were away from it.

Joan had telephoned details of Sunday's arrangements through to Mum so we relaxed and enjoyed an evening watching television. Next morning we climbed the hill to see Mum and await transport.

We received the usual warm greetings from the church folk, many of whom were childhood friends, and enjoy an hour of worship with them. The pub had been telephoned and a table booked, everything was ready. When the meals were ordered, Mum chose to have child's portions as her appetite was no longer great. She ate well and finished off with a sweet course. Alarmed by the size of the adult portions, Jean and I acutely conscious of our waistlines, were the only ones to forgo the sweets, rounding our meal off, simply with a cup of tea.

Having spent most of Monday and Tuesday at Mum's, we rose early and set off to Grendon and the Atherstone flight, aiming to get there before the day's traffic began. These locks are notoriously slow to fill and we never climbed them without wondering at the shortsighted policy which had caused the side-pounds to be abandoned and the operating mechanism that linked them to the lock chambers, removed.

These side-pounds were built as an integral part of the flight and served two distinct purposes. First, to reduce the amount of water removed from the flight by lock operations, secondly to increase the speed of the operating cycle. Both purposes were now sorely missed.

All things being equal and using our tried and tested lock wheeling system, we could complete the eleven lock flight in one hour forty-five minutes.

Not bad for a pair of "old wrinklies!"

With the flight behind us, we moored up in Atherstone, bought a newspaper and treated ourselves to a belated, cooked breakfast at a snack bar. That was the problem with boating, all that healthy fresh air left us with an appetite but without the willpower to turn down the opportunity to indulge ourselves with an unhealthy fry-up.

Jean could relax now, from here to Coventry, the pound was lock free right into the terminal basin.

Here we were passing through countryside that my Dad had known as a young boy and where I had been taken with our Jack Russell terrier, a pair of ferrets and a large net, to trap rabbits in the warrens that abounded on the wooded slopes. This was pre-Myxomatosis. I also remembered attending Point to Point horse races here.

It has been a long time since I saw Point to Point on a sporting calendar. I believe it took place outside the hunting season to give riders the opportunity to exercise their "hunters" by riding them competitively on a cross country course that picked its way from, "point to point". Covering considerable distances the courses included natural and man made obstacles and jumps. It was a real test of the skill and stamina of horse and rider. Large crowds would attend, lining the informally flagged course at various vantage points.

Another childhood memory was of being taken on the cross-bar of Dad's bike, and later riding my own cycle, to see the Boxing Day Meet of the Atherstone Hunt.

Without wishing to get involved in controversy ,I am country born and bred and I would hate to see the Hunt disappear along with Point to Point racing.

After passing through the moon-scape of spoil tips at Hartshill and Tuttlehill, we entered the town of Nuneaton. From here we re-entered an area which had been dominated by coal mining and which still bore the scars. After cruising past these crumbling remnants of a community's Industrial base we passed through the basin at Marston where the Ashby Canal began it's winding, but lock free passage. Then we were at Bridge 13 in Bedworth.

This was another of our established mooring places. We usually chose to stay here when visiting Sid and Dot as the moorings near to Bridge 14, were a little too close to the Pub for comfort. Although it was a long walk, the town offered excellent shopping, a small street market and a group of rather splendid Alms Houses built in 1840, which extended a warm welcome to visitors attending their daily Coffee morning. The people there were really friendly.

Paying a visit to my cousins was always enjoyable. They were always pleased to see us and seemed to like coming on board for tea and cake. It was lovely to see how Sid came alive while talking about the old days of the working boats and we loved sharing his memories.

On this cruise we were aiming to reach the re-furbished basin in the centre of Coventry. We had not yet seen what had been achieved and were keen to find out at first hand. When we left, the Council had just fitted a new gas fire in Mum's front room. They had removed the old fireplace, the tiled surround and hearth. What they had failed to do was to refurbish the raw concrete area that this had left. We intended to buy some tiles and the other essential materials and complete the job on our way back.

First we needed to buy the supplies!

The basin had been well restored, unfortunately, the canal leading to it, hadn't. We really struggled! Our wake showed the consistency of liquid mud as we ploughed through, the flat base scraping a wide channel along a bottom silted with slurry. At the bridge holes we would stop the propeller and allow the boat to drift forward, avoiding pulling rubbish into the blades. The technique consisted of gathering as much speed as reasonable in the relatively clear areas, switching the drive off and using the momentum to send "Athene." gliding through the bridge holes. Not the fastest method but one which gave me a more than even chance finishing up at journey's end, without plunging my hands into the stinking water in the weed hatch to clear the propeller

The refurbishment of the basin had been thoughtfully accomplished but it been left a little too accessible to the roads in the area. It was well supplied with security lighting and covered by C.C.T.V. but still managed to give the feeling that security was not that high on the list of things you could expect. Arriving at lunchtime we were able to explore the area during the afternoon and to locate Tilecentre. After a lot of consideration we decided that the most appropriate tiles would be inch square mosaics in shades of brown to blend in with the carpet. We did hope Mum would like our choice!

Overnighting was weird. The security lighting stayed on and we assumed that the scene was watched by the cameras. However pedestrian traffic around the basin continued into the early hours and the interior of the boat was so light that it was almost impossible to settle down to sleep. Not the most comfortable of experiences.

Early next morning we returned to Hawksbury Junction where we filled up with water then headed for Marston Junction and the Ashby Canal. We moored at Hinckley having arranged to visit Les. at Fenda Products. We had seen a tiller pin with an Owl and chick on, and we coveted it. Les. was going to get us one, it would be worth the effort of the detour. On October 1st. we winded at the bridge before returning to the Coventry Canal, weaving our way back to Atherstone, negotiating the eleven locks, before mooring in the late afternoon at Polesworth. Next day we were able to walk up to Mum's, sort out the hearth and fix the tiles. She was pleased both with the tiles and how it looked when finished, with the tiles in place and the carpet carefully fitted. It was a good feeling to know that when we left, Mum's life would be that tiny fraction enhanced and more comfortable. Showing our love through deeds and not just words was a wonderful feeling.

We paid a fleeting visit to Joan next day to collect any mail. This could well be our last visit before we came by train in November.

Two locks and thirteen miles saw us moored once more at Fradley. Heather was unable to visit that evening but as we intended to be in Burton on Trent for about a week that should leave us time enough to see her.

The final eight miles to Shobnall Basin dropped through ten locks but as they were narrow, relatively shallow, filled quickly and were reasonably maintained, they caused no difficulty. It was strange to find that, when visiting an area for the second or third time, so much had altered in the interim. B.W. had a canal house on Bass Brewery land, it was still there but looking decidedly worst for wear.

At the Marina we were warmly welcomed by Jeanette who showed us our mooring and arranged for the services to be connected. As we were not taking up our winter mooring, the location could alter but the reassurance was there. We still intended to put in one last cruise, to the Stourbridge Rally, which virtually ended the Rally season. We organised to have "Athene" dry-docked so that we could re-black the hull and have our anodes checked. At the previous inspection all had been well but it did not pay to take chances with anything like that.

Heather visited with the children. We had serious concerns for Harry's well-being. Since August he had been suffering from mild convulsions and was not progressing as he should. Medical opinion was divided and the jury was still out on the seriousness of the prognosis and the identifying of a cure.

All in all, it was something of a worrisome time!

We had made the booking for the Stourbridge Rally in the Spring and paid our fee. There was little that we could do that would be seen as constructive. That being the case, we prepared the boat and set off!

We would travel to the Black Country and the year's final Rally!

21.
Pleasure and Pain!

Although Stourbridge only appeared to be a short distance away, possibly an hour by car, it was in fact a substantial cruise. Certainly not a couple of Sunday afternoon hops. As we had decided to go via the area where "Athene" was born and show off her new livery to Ken, her builder, before it became too travel stained, the route would be a long one. It would actually cover, 85 miles and 90 locks. Included would be three large flights, the Wolverhampton 21, the Stourbridge 14 and the Black Delph 8. Our return trip, although shorter would cover 59 miles and 60 locks. Definitely not Sunday afternoon dawdles!

For the benefit of folk faced with figures like these, the method of calculating an estimated cruising time is quite simple.

The maximum speed of travel on a canal is 4 mph., that equates to one mile every fifteen minutes. A ball park average for the time taken to complete a single lock operation is also fifteen minutes. This means that one lock operation can be taken to equal one mile, in terms of time.

This gives the simple equation;M (miles) + L (locks) ÷ 4 = H (hours)

The time calculation for our outward trip would be 85+90÷4 =44 hours. If we aimed for six hours or twenty-four lockmiles per day, the trip would take seven days. Lockmile is the term used for the combination of locks and miles.

We had planned our route along the Trent and Mersey, the Staffs and Worcester and a section of the B.C.N., areas so well known to us, that we were unlikely to meet with any untoward experiences. There is something very comfortable about the loved and familiar.

One thing had often struck us about the stretch of canal between Burton and Fradley Top lock, many of the bridges and lock entrances were very narrow. When the horse drawn working boats operated on this length it must have be somewhat frustrating. On the Stratford Canal where the bridges and locks are also narrow, the bridge arch is split to allow the towing rope to pass through, and the horse carried on its way. Here there was no provision for that. The rope must have been slipped at each obstruction and the boat allowed to glide through before being re-connected.

This must have been somewhat irritating!

It would seem strange to the old boatmen of the horse drawn era, if they could come back now to see their towing paths crowded with fishermen, cyclists, hikers, children and dogs. The only thing barred by statute from using the towing path, is the horse! In a small number of locations, horse drawn trip boats still operate. Occasionally permission has been granted for special celebrations to include horse drawn work boats but usually the difficulties posed in obtaining a license make the exercise unrealistic.

And all this has been done in the name of progress!

In those days canal banks had to be kept firm and shrubs that could create problems were removed. Now it is possible to find large lengths of canal where the integrity of the edges has been undermined by the unrestricted growth of reeds, willow and hawthorn. These roots do not bind and support the banks but actually add to its speed of destruction by displacing coping stones and breaking up aggregate. The roots begin to extend into the water to accelerate the silting process by trapping floating debris and forming new areas to be colonised by water plants.

We have cruised areas where the navigable channel has halved in width during the relatively few years that we have been making transits!

It is not all bad news, since the cruises recorded here , B.W., recognising the threat to navigation, have made heroic efforts with the inadequate funding available to them, to reverse some of worst effects of years of neglect.

We must pray that all is not, "Too little; too late!"

Now we were experiencing an Indian summer, the morning air was crisp and clean yet while the days remained bright and sunny, the temperature never became uncomfortable. After the prolonged dry, hot weather of the summer, the trees were preparing for the onset of winter. October was treating us to a stunning display of hues as the leaves turned colour prematurely, remaining on the trees in the still air.

The sight of mixed deciduous woodlands in their Autumn finery, riots of colour as each species showed different shades, was one to lift the saddest heart.

When the winds that heralded Winter began to blow through the land, it would be a different story. Where the canal was covered by arching branches forming leafy cathedrals, leaving the cool air smelling of a myriad different odours, the air would suddenly become filled with whirling, fluttering leaves. As these begin to settle on the water, a carpet will form, a mixture of browns and yellows, no longer bright, now sad and soggy. Our wake becomes a thick soup as dead leaves swirl through the water. So thick can they become, that the occasional burst of reverse thrust is needed to keep the propeller clear.

Even that is a small price to pay for our sight of the Autumnal kaleidoscope of colour, however transient their beauty!

We reached Great Haywood without making our usual stop at Rugeley then turned at the junction for our trip along the Staffs and Worcester. We crossed Tixall Wide and Tixall lock saw us begin the long, steady climb up to Gailey. Just beyond the first lock was a gorgeous canal-side house with immaculate, manicured lawns sweeping down to the waters edge. Kissed by the colours of the fading season it looked so peaceful and serene that, once more, we looked at each other and laid envious claim to it. Something we always did each time we passed.

In reality, neither of us harboured any burning desire to return to a life ashore, particularly into a property that would demand continual care and attention if it were to retain its beautifully groomed appearance. That never put us off our little game of admiring lovely houses.

And yes! Laying claim to them in our imaginings!

Crossing Milford aqueduct, we looked out over the flood plains and water meadows of the Sow valley. After the summer the water flow was down and the low-lying land, dryer than we had ever seen it. Soon our route became overhung with interlaced branches and we found a couple of trees that had succumbed to the dry weather and fallen into the water. With the channel partially blocked, we needed to travel in tick-over as we threaded our way through the clogged water. Once safely past, we continued to cruise towards our evening mooring at Penkridge, near to Midland Chandlers.

Once moored we wandered over and made a quick tour of the shop. I had never been fully satisfied with the tiny brass knobs on our front door but had never found a suitable replacement. At last, I found a set of small, solid brass, lever handles in an odds and sods box. They were just the job and going cheap.

We left well satisfied with our purchase!

Next day dawn saw us ready to cast off! We had planned a cruise that was set to be really extensive, if we were going to reach secure moorings by the end of the day. Our intention was to proceed to Aldersley Junction, enter the B.C.N. and climb the Wolverhampton 21, finally cruising the Wyrely and Essington to reach secure mooring at Sneyd Junction. Although lock free from Horsley Fields to Sneyd the condition of the canal would be an unknown quantity, as was the case with most areas of the B.C.N.

The route covered 21 miles and 29 locks which worked out to 12 hours travel but we knew that if the Wolverhampton flight was in good shape ,we could reduce that time considerably with a speedy ascent.

It took four and three-quarter hours to reach the start of the flight. Jean went ashore and began lock-wheeling. Conditions were perfect, most of the locks were in our favour and there were no other boats on the flight. As each lock reached full, I would exit, close the gates and paddles then head for the next lock. Meanwhile Jean would have prepared it. We climbed like clockwork with scarcely a pause. The water condition was good and two hours fifty minutes later we cleared the top lock. An average of 7 locks per hour, good going in anyone's book. Yet, it had all been done at a even pace, no rushing, no running between locks!

The 6 miles to Sneyd took a steady two and a half hours as the water was shallow and rubbish strewn. At least we had no problem with weeding and by keeping the revs, low we made uninterrupted progress towards our destination. When the M6 motorway bridge loomed up we knew that our journey's end was near. We had to negotiate an area where the foundations of another bridge were being laid, then, past the Tinker encampment, we reached the sharp turn into Sneyd Junction. The turn is executed in a large, but shallow, heavily silted basin. We had reached journey's end for that day.

50 lockmiles in 10 hours, not bad going!

When boaters have become experienced, it is rarely the case that lock operations take fifteen minutes. Flights, particularly when locks are close together, offer the opportunity to cut that time considerably, without over-exertion. For a two man crew 7 or 8 locks per hour is not extraordinary and with a larger crew times can be reduced even more.

With the horse drawn Fly boats carrying passengers on long distance routes, the lock times could be as little as three minutes per lock.

Now that is what I call getting a move on!

Sneyd was once a thriving depot with extensive wharfage. Now B.W. had a small base there but it was virtually derelict. Plans were afoot to reinstate the area and provide some longterm mooring.

The following day we completed our journey home, to Aldridge and "Athene's" birthplace. It truly felt like a homecoming! First however, Bandit Country; the Goscote Badlands would have to be negotiated. This was term-time and we would be passing through quite early, we shouldn't hit any trouble. In the event all we met were a few adults walking their dogs. It was appalling to see the devastation; even more council houses had been torched and were boarded up. the waste ground was strewn with rubbish and burnt out vehicles.

This must be as close to "Hell on Earth" as living gets in our "peaceful" country!

Now familiar landmarks were appearing thick and fast and we experienced flashes of immense pleasure and the occasional stab of pain as we noted the changes, improvements and deteriorations .Areas of housing had sprung into being and were now occupied, where we remembered green fields from two short years ago. The rate at which development, both of housing and light industry, devoured large tracts of land, was frightening.

I pleased myself, by negotiating the final, very tricky bridge before the boatyard with consummate ease, without threatening the concrete, something which I could never guarantee doing in the days when we cruised these waters as tyros.

Throttling back as we approached Northywood Bridge I brought "Athene" to a stop at the entrance to the dock arm. I sounded the klaxon and who should appear but old Tom. He was still there from the old days. Ken had cleared his bankruptcy and was now beginning to re-establish the yard. Tom waved a greeting then disappeared into the office, presumably to alert Ken to his visitation.

In no time we had been allocated a berth and were connected up to the mains electricity via our shore-line. Although impressed by the overall condition of the boat and her livery, Ken expressed some slight disapproval of our choice of colours for the lettering of her name. He considered it, rather garish! He did however approve of the addition of "Pallas" to the launch name and felt as we did, that it enhanced Athene's status.

Meeting with Sarah and the boys after such a long time was a happy experience and it was wonderful to see the yard slowly coming back to life. Ken and his workers will always occupy a warm spot in our hearts after the excellent job they had done, in building the shell for us and for their support during the sometimes fraught exercise of fitting-out.

The building that had once housed the Chandlery had been converted into a boaters club and it was now possible to share convivial company and a pint ,without leaving the yard. We stayed a few days, that gave Jean an opportunity to recover from her exertions and for us to get in some essential supplies and met old friends. We were in our element!

One thing had surprised us, the small number of Ken's boats we had met on our travels. He had kept in touch with most and it seemed that many had not left the B.C.N. but were tucked away on permanent moorings. A shame in some ways, for Ken's work was worthy of the publicity of being identified around the nation's waterways.

A couple of days rest prepared us for the trauma of tackling the Rushall and Riders Green flights. These would return us to the New Birmingham Main Line and the turn off for the Netherton Tunnel and Windmill End. This had been a regular stop for us but now we intended to proceed along the Dudley No.1 and No.2 Canals to overnight at the Merryhill Centre, known, irreverently, as Merry HelL This had been another heavy day and we had covered some 17 miles and 18 locks, taking just over eight hours. Time was running short and the next day would also be a long one, in numbers of locks if not distance.

The new Merryhill basin was partially open and it was possible to moor in reasonably deep water unlike the previous times when mooring on the embankment meant sitting on the bottom from time to time.

Next day we would descend the Delph Nine (actually only eight!) and then the Stourbridge Sixteen. Descending a flight always took longer than the ascent, even when the locks were in your favour. As the boat will be exiting an empty lock, it is much more difficult for the boater to open and close the gates and paddles. Jean invariably returned to help me out of the lock and we would share the task of closing the gates.

A much more complicated procedure, and more work for Jean!

The Delph locks were an interesting flight particularly when water levels were high, the overflow filled the side ponds and cascaded over the weirs near each set of bottom gates. This set up allowed the excess water to be absorbed without flooding the nearby land. The old stables part way down the flight had been converted into classrooms and all manner of canal crafts were taught. Colin Jones, who had instructed me in Fender making , was again teaching a group and we said a quick Hi! to him and his class as we cruised past.

The locks here were well used and in good general condition, something that we did not always find during our travels.

This area had been built on Heavy Industry and although this had now been discontinued, it was still possible to find poignant reminders of the glorious past, when the narrowboat was king and reigned supreme as the safest, most reliable means of transporting goods and materials.

A question we are often asked is, Which is your favourite Canal? The questioners think it is a cop-out when I reply that I can't nail my colours to the mast for any particular canal as we are not comparing, "Like with like."

When considering Industrial Canals, the B.C.N. comes high on my list, not because it is particularly attractive or well maintained, but because it has so much character. I compare it to a man who has worked hard and grown old in labour. He has become a bit crotchety and irascible, but if you catch him on a good day, he has a wealth of stories to tell and experiences to relate. This makes for real character.

Anyone interested in Industrial Archaeology, can glean a wealth of stories from the wharfs, buildings and locks that abound in this area. Surely they are every bit as interesting as the rural canals which for all their natural beauty are often slipping into benign decay and disrepair through neglect masquerading as conservation.

The locks of the Stourbridge 16 lead into the basin from which the Stourbridge Arm exits on its short trip into the extensive complex of restored wharfs clustered around the Bonded Warehouse.

We moored well short of the basin against the remnants of a goods landing stage. It was quite a walk to the rally site but the launderette was nearer from here. Just down to the bridge, and up the hill to the shops. Now that we had returned to Stourbridge it was our intention to pay another visit to Jaylyne and buy some more crystal. One or two of our original pieces had been damaged or broken during our travels and we were anxious to replace them.

The clear skies were bringing with them plunging night-time temperatures and overnight frosts, something we had come to expect during this Rally. Walking back to the boat in the late evening, when every-where was still and the air clear and crisp, was a grand experience. Later, during the Rally, when each boat was lit bow and stern by a small hurricane lamp, the effect would become magical.

Like Lichfield, Stourbridge had an excellent Repertory Theatre, it was here we had seen their performance of "The Greatest Little Whorehouse in Texas" which we had thoroughly enjoyed. This time however we were between performances.

One thing that could always be relied on was the standard of entertainment that would be provided for the boaters, so we were not unduly downcast. The main drawback here was a dearth of places to eat, outside of "normal" hours and arriving in the afternoon we found it difficult to get a meal. MacDonalds was open but this was not our favourite type of venue, even for a snack meal.

We managed the walk to Amblecote where Jaylyne was situated and replaced our crystal ware from their range of high quality seconds. That made the trip worthwhile!

The Rally lived up to our expectations and we had a grand time. Now we needed to return to Burton before the programme of Winter stoppages began. Our trip would take us back down the Town Arm to the Stourbridge canal, down four locks to Stourton Junction, then 35 miles and 30 locks to Great Haywood along the Staffs. & Worcester. The final stage to Burton was along the Trent and Mersey Canal.

The first night of our return trip was spent at the Bratch Locks, the second at Otherton and the third at Fradley. With a little time in hand, we took it into our heads to pay Mum a last flying visit before we settled down for the winter. We spent three days in Polesworth helping Mum to get the house back in shape, called at Joan's to pick up the mail, then had two days in Alrewas to see Heather and the Grandchildren. Harry was still improving but progress was slow. When we saw him again there was a recognisable change for the better and we prayed that things would continue to improve.

We travelled to Shobnall on Guy Fawkes night very concerned about the way in which young people seemed to ignore all the safety rules when it came to fireworks. Jean had never liked fireworks and was pleased when "Pallas Athene" was safely tucked into her berth in the Marina, and she could go below away from at least some of the noise.

It was a week later that the dry-dock became available and we could move our boat in to have her bottom painted. The dock here was unusual, it had been created from the lock chamber which formed the last remaining section of the Shobnall Arm. This had been a canal built by the Brewers to link up with the River Trent. The Arm along with the rest of the Trent and Mersey Canal had been purchased by the North Staffordshire Railway Company. Abandoned and filled in, it provided a route for a railway line. The 72 ft. lock chamber was all that remained of the Shobnall Arm. When Harry had taken over and restored the basin as a Marina the stub of the Arm had been converted into a dry-dock. Any boat using it was entitled to a plaque which allowed them to claim that they had negotiated the Shobnall Arm.

We decided not to buy one!

On a frosty Monday morning, our home was reversed into the dock and the water pumped out leaving her stranded on the keel stands. Due to a slight leakage from the basin, it was not the driest dock we had been in, but the steel mesh floor was a Godsend.

To save time and energy we had elected to have her hull pressure washed. This was very effective and we felt pleased that we had so little preparation to do. With the dock empty of water, I climbed in to check the anodes, once more it was clear that the would be O.K. for a few more years. A relief as it mean quite a saving on our overall costs. The Comastic paint had been purchased from the yard but we intended to do all the physical work ourselves.

The stern gear and shaft bearings were also in good condition and would be alright at least until the next docking. When the hull had dried out a very slight seepage showed on the rear swim base plate. It could be a flaw in the weld.

Our first priority was to get this re-welded! Harry ground the old metal back to reveal a tiny flaw which he sealed making an excellent job. Later we found a marked difference in the rate at which the bilges became damp.

With a number of 3" brushes left over from our re-paint the previous winter, we could begin the mammoth task immediately. When you stand at one end and look along a 65 ft. long by 4 ft. high wall that is awaiting your attention, the job takes on epic proportions. We had five days to complete the task, we would need to stick at it but there would be no pressure.

The hull would be completed with two good coats of gloss paint on the area above the top rubbing strake. Our stern bands were red and white, although one school of thought advocates, red and cream. We had no intention of changing from the colours used when we applied her original livery.

The propeller was starting to show the effects of the heavily rubbish strewn waters we had cruised. The blade edges were distinctly frilled. I worked on these with two hammers, a 4 lb. lump to act as an anvil and a 2 lb. ball pein as the beater. I managed to make an improvement but eventually it would require expert attention. The prop. had fulfilled all the requirements that made for excellence and we wished to retain it, not for us the 'Mickey Mouse Ear' blades of the traditional canal propeller!

The frosts were heavy and the temperatures in the shed rarely rose above 3 or 4 degrees C. in spite of the doors which were closed each night.

Living in a dry-dock, unable to light a fire, was daunting and our tiny electric fire did little to alleviate the problem. The cold water in the bow tanks kept the steel in that area very cold and subject to heavy condensation. This turned the Comastic brown there, still the whole hull had received two coats and we were happy!

Five days later we sailed back to our berth, coupled up the services and lit a fire; Sheer Heaven!

Our grandson Harry's progress had slowed again and the convulsions were worsening. Heather was getting really concerned. If things did not improve soon he would have to be hospitalised for a time while tests were carried out. This was a very worrying time!

With our boat looking great, we were happy to receive visitors. This was good as, out of the blue, Jean's brother Jeremy arrived for a flying visit. He was sitting in the local sessions and the Court proceedings had closed early. Unheralded though the visit was, it was welcome. Jeremy seemed to enjoy his short stay and regaled us with news about his grandsons like any other doting grandparent.

Just over a week after his visit we received some sad, if not unexpected news. Theo had died in the Pimlico Nursing Home where she had lived. Timothy Thomas, her solicitor and distant relative, contacted Jean to inform her that she was an executor to the will. When we attended the funeral in London he would take time to explain her duties. Effectively, his Law firm would do all the work, she would just be a signatory and a rubber stamp!

With the funeral set for Friday we decided to take a train down on Thursday and return on Saturday. We would stay in a hotel near the Crematorium at Putney, where the service was to be held. This proved to be an ill-fated decision, in order to obtain satisfactory accommodation we ended up committing ourselves to paying out much more than we had intended.

Dressed in Blazer and black slacks, I hoped to make a reasonable impression on the assembled mourners who seemed to represent many professions and not a few districts of the City. The service was set for eleven o' clock. Having walked the half mile to the crematorium in my seldom worn, polished black shoes, my deformed toes had been crushed. Walking and standing was now very uncomfortable and I was in considerable pain. By midday the service had been concluded. It had been muted and solemn, the eulogy had been delivered by Ann Mills with restrained emotion. As we gathered outside the building the small talk was of a woman, much admired, whose physical presence was no longer with us.

Jeremy, Stuart, Shirley and Ian had all driven to London. Jeremy from Derby, Stuart and his wife Shirley from Devon and Ian from Newcastle on Tyne. Drawing on his experience, Jeremy gave Jean some advice about her role as an executor. She had yet to speak at length with Timothy. A short while later they said their goodbyes and set off to their respective destinations.

Ann Mills was organising lunch and we found ourselves transported to her house along with a number of other mourners. Over the buffet meal, many anecdotes about Theo's life and times were related and Jean spoke of her life with Theo in India. When the guests had departed, Ann drove us over to the Nursing Home to clear out the remainder of Theo's effects.

In the small, cluttered room we felt a little like Dickensian ragpickers sorting through the meagre belongings for the errant gleam of gold, lest it should end up being discarded with the junk. It was a strange feeling, sifting through the detritus of a person's life and recognising how little dignity one is left with in death! Like many old people she had become secretive in her latter days and we discovered numerous caches of money hidden away in odd places. We collected them up and, together with an unopened Christmas present from the previous year that was addressed to her, we handed the items over to

Mavis, a large West Indian care assistant, who had been allocated to tend Theo and with whom she had developed a love/hate relationship. This had lasted for five years and she evidently missed Theo and mourned her passing.

Our task completed, we were driven back to our hotel with a suitcase full of odds and ends that still needed sorting. These were mainly manuscript pages belonging to the many books and articles Theo had written. Unfortunately they were badly creased and folded, not forming any discernable pattern being simply scraps rather than complete sections.

Sadly, we had to dump them along with much of the other material. They weren't worth storing.

Jean's conversation with Timothy had revealed that the will was simple just some small bequests and the rest of the estate divided equally between Jean, her two sons and Steven McCool , Jean's almost step-brother from Perth in Australia. Not that there was much to argue about, six years of paying the fees for a Private Nursing Home would have seen to that. Probate would not take long!

Next day we boarded a train to return to Burton after settling our bill, and paying what seemed like a substantial portion of the National Debt, for our accommodation.

We arrived at the yard to find the boat safe and secure if a little chilly, in the house a bundle of mail was awaiting our return. First priority was to get the stove lit and the boat warm. We had left a tiny electric fire burning while we were away but it had been fighting a losing battle against plunging temperatures.

Harry had rallied briefly and was showing progress once more but the constant worry was draining Heather and creating pressures within the family.

With most of the work on the boat completed we settled down to a steady life. Jean worked hard on her tapestry, while I continued to write and type, preparing copy against the day when a publisher would say; Yes! to my book.

Towards the end of November, the shops began to don their Christmas finery, the lights and decorations went up around the town. We realised that the large number of wheelchairs we saw around town were supplied by Shopmobility, a charity charged with providing help to disabled and elderly people, enabling them to shop with the minimum of support and inconvenience. We had not heard of it but the service turned out to be provided free to those who could prove a need and was not restricted to local people. Our immediate thought was ,Mum. What a wonderful opportunity! This would enable us to offer her a day out to do her Christmas shopping, in a large town but without hassle..

Then disappointment, this was the season when day-centres, care homes and institutions liked to give their people a break. Add the seasonal increase in demand and the organisation was at full stretch, It would be almost impossible to arrange matters.

With our thinking turned to that course of action we looked around for alternatives. The answer was close to hand. Harry, Jeanette's Dad; had a fold up wheel chair in the workshop. It had been bought when he was temporarily disabled. Could we borrow it? of course!

Arrangements were made for the first Friday in December. We phoned the Taxi firm that always drove Mum and arranged to have her delivered and collected. The fare they quoted was a great deal lower than the Burton Taxi firms. With Heather bringing Harry to meet Great Grandma for the first time, we could offer Mum a few hours shopping and a lunch.

Quite enough for her first day out in a long time!

Murphy kept his head down and all our arrangements went off without a hitch!

Mum's face was a picture as she was pushed around the shops and she saw the Christmas lights of a large town for the first time in years. It gave us real pleasure to watch her buying up the bits and pieces she needed to make up her gift parcels. To select Christmas cards after years of relying on other peoples choice seemed to offer especial joy.

We ascended to the balcony Cafeteria in the glass lift. Here we met up with Heather and Harry. Mum was obviously thrilled to see him for the first time, but her eyes showed the pain she felt when she saw the obvious retardation. Now she would pray for his recovery with renewed strength!

It was a magical day and after seeing Heather to the bus stop we pushed Mum to the car park where her taxi was waiting to return her home!

It was an experience that left us feeling richer and happier!

We had decorated the boat on December 1st. and the steady trickle of cards had been strung on the walls. The presents were wrapped and stashed beneath the tree. "Pallas Athene" was ready to celebrate Christmas and we were planning our Christmas cruise.

For now though; We could sit back and relax!

22.
Christmas Cruising.

A week before Christmas we checked with B.W. and received their assurances that the area we intended to cruise over the following ten days was not affected by stoppages and would remain that way; all things being equal!

Until this year it had been our practice to select and buy Christmas gifts throughout the year, whenever we saw suitable ones, usually at bargain prices. We tried to get quality goods and we had discovered that it was rarely necessary to pay the recommended price for items if you shopped carefully. At least that way we were able to give reasonable presents, targeted at individual recipients, without breaking the bank.

Very important for pensioners!

We would gift wrap each present and stow them in boxes in the "study". Then, during the course of our cruising, if we found ourselves within visiting distance of relatives or children, it was a simple matter to hand over the appropriate box. By November most of our presents had normally been distributed. It did mean that we missed out on the pre-Christmas excitement in some ways.

This year would be different!

The "study" was piled with boxes of gifts ready for delivery, now we were about to set out to do our duty by everyone and, in the process to share much more of the joy of giving and receiving gifts at this special time of the year.

The weather had been frosty and Mother Nature had provided some wonderful photo opportunities for us earlier in December when she had buried the boat yard in two or three inches of snow.

Now, it seemed to be set fair!

Our first port of call was to be Alrewas, where we could welcome aboard our son in law, Nick and our two grand-daughters, Emily and Rebecca. Our grandson Harry was in hospital and Heather was staying with him. This would offer Nick and the girls a break.

Geoff, Maureen and Ben their dog, our friends from N/b. 'Maelstrom' usually moored at Alrewas but now they had begun living on board so they might well be wintering elsewhere. That proved to be the case!

We phoned ahead and arranged for Nick to meet us just below the Navigation lock in Alrewas, that way we would be able to give the girls a short cruise of five locks up to Fradley Junction. "The Swan" was a nicely appointed pub serving excellent food. We intended to give them a festive meal as part of our Christmas largess.

As we were busy re-painting the boat at Market Harborough the previous year, it had been impossible to make personal contact at Christmas as the public transport links between there and Alrewas were abysmal. The journey would have taken longer than the time we could have spent visiting!

Once on board the girls soon settled down and we were able to cast off and set sail. The locks on this stretch are not daunting having an average depth of around six feet. Some folk can get "freaked out" by the experience of being in the chamber of a deep, narrow lock.

Although they enjoyed seeing Gran. Jean and Grandad again the girls were not terribly impressed with the boat. (They were not allowed to race around and play with our things.) A trip with us would never quite be the adventure that it may have been for other young people.

Once underway, the trip followed its usual pattern, Nick aided Jean with the operation of the locks; the girls stayed below and played with the toys they had brought with them while they ate some of the sweets we had provided. ("Not too many, they will spoil your lunch!")

It appeared that Christmas cruising was on the cards for a number of people as there was quite a lot of traffic up and down the flight, at least we rarely had to re-set a lock. Anticipating this, we had taken the precaution of phoning ahead to reserve a table for our party.

The lunch was most enjoyable, the girls had not over indulged on their sweets and ate well. After an exchange of gifts, hugs and kisses all round, (in spite of Grandad's whiskers.) Nick and the girls set out to walk off their meal with a gentle stroll back down the flight to Alrewas. We cast off and sallied into the gathering gloom, finally mooring up at Huddlesford Junction after giving Ray and the gang at Streethay Wharf a blast on the airhorns as we passed.

It was here that the Lichfield branch of the 'Curly Wyrely' had intersected the Coventry Canal. Although that branch had been abandoned in 1954 and had now virtually disappeared much of the route was traceable and structures like lock chambers still reasonably intact.

Plans were being advanced to restore and re-instate both this and the Hatherton branch.

These would be excellent schemes as they fulfilled the criteria of adding to the system by being incorporated into cruising rings that would help to open up sections of the B.C.N. which were currently in trouble because they attracted little regular boat traffic.

The remains of the arm at Huddlesford, which is still in water, was being used by a local Boat Club as long term and residential moorings.

In spite of the proximity of the railway, we spent a peaceful night and next morning set off to complete our cruise to Polesworth and Mum!

As Fazeley was so convenient for shopping while taking on water, we stayed awhile to top up our fresh water tank while I went into the village to buy a newspaper and some flowers for my mother.

The Glascote locks were also busy and along the moorings a number of members of the Tamworth Cruising Club were busy stocking up their boats for a Club outing. It looked like the waterways were going to be busier than we had expected for the time of the year.

With the area free from stoppages, a number of Hire boat companies were taking advantage of the situation and promoting short cruises which would help them to spread their cash flow over a longer period of time and continue to bring in revenue at a time when trade would be somewhat flat.

With time slipping away as we approached the shortest day, it made sense to make the most of the daylight and to cruise through Amington and Polesworth, down to the winding hole at Grendon, just below the Atherstone flight. Once winded we could return to Polesworth, moor ready to visit Mum and we would be pointing in the correct direction for an immediate start next day.

The hill into Dordon seemed to be getting steeper and now I was experiencing more regular stabs of chest pain when involved in any form of exertion. I still wrote them off as indigestion and started buying tubes of Extra Strong Mints to suck.

I was managing to hide my discomfort from Jean and carried on as usual, conscious only of a vague feeling of unease at the gradual increase in the incident of the spasms.

Mum was thrilled to see us and we were able to give her the flowers, her presents and a box of gifts for Keith, Margaret and their son. We also left Christmas cards for the extended family of Uncles, Aunts and Cousins who would be in contact over the coming days.

Next day Mum was scheduled to pay her weekly visit to Joan's house and we managed to persuade her that this would be a wonderful chance to enjoy a ride on the boat. We would book a taxi to take her to Polesworth, she could board and enjoy a pleasant cruise to Amington.

A one hour cruise with no locks; should be O.K. even for a hydrophobic!

In spite of the slight misgivings she had, Mum eventually consented to undertaking her ordeal by water. Actually, it was quite a brave thing to agree to, she really was a martyr to the horrors of being too close to water. She obviously though enough of us to face almost her worst nightmare. Early next morning I climbed the hill once more to collect her in person. It was the least I could do. We would return to the boat by taxi!

The day had dawned bright, crisp and glorious, the cruise was uneventful! I was careful to keep the revs, down and make wide sweeping turns into the bends and corners to avoid rocking the boat. Her reaction to the ride could not truthfully be described as ecstatic but neither was she traumatised by the experience. Jean told me later that Mum had sat carefully ensconced in an armchair and had enjoyed tea and home-made cake. When on-board at the moorings on previous occasions she had been known to stand at the window and wave to passing boats. This time there had been no passing boats but I've an idea that my dear Mum neither knew nor cared.

At least now, her ordeal was virtually over!

The canal banks at Amington were overgrown with grass and liberally decorated with piles of dog s-t, not the best of areas to disembark a passenger who walked leaning on a stick. Fortunately, the guy who did the canal- ware painting in the village, had a good concrete wharf at which he had agreed to let us dis-embark Mum. It was situated, very conveniently, right opposite the end of the road in which Joan lived.

We could not moor there. Mum and Jean went ashore while I drove to our usual berth, tied the boat up securely then returned to the intrepid travellers who were looking at the artwork displayed at the wharf.

We walked slowly up the rise towards where Joan's house was situated. Mum, although leaning on her stick, was actually making excellent progress. Joan seeing us coming up the street came out to the front door to welcome us. My sister was not keen on boat travel and I had not been able to persuade her to take a cruise. She was amazed that our Mum had really gone through with it, I think she had been expecting a last minute refusal.

David was on his Christmas break from University and Amy was doing 'O' level mocks so everyone except Peter was at home.

I had carried the box of presents up with me and Joan had a stack of mail for us, most of it as a result of her being our contact letterbox. While the statutory cuppa was being brewed I sat on the settee in the lounge and opened the envelopes. A large number of cards had been sent to Joan's address, marked for us. The strings of cards in the boat would need extending!

Although living a nomadic lifestyle, the fact we had a registered address, albeit "collect", seemed to ensure that we accumulated an amazing amount of "junk mail". We had made several mail order purchases, belonged to a number of organisations such as English Heritage and The National Trust plus we made bank account and insurance payment orders, so, our details appeared on enough computers to have triggered off this veritable avalanche of mall. Writing, "Not known at this address" on the envelopes of unwanted and unsolicited mall and posting it back had, apparently, done little to stem the output.

In line with our philosophy that, "Life is too short to take seriously", we invariably filed the majority of it, W.P.B.!

At least with Joan acting as a filter, little of this kind of mail survived to reach us at the boat. Envelopes claiming that we have won £10,000 if the reply is received within seven days were sometimes sent as Joan was loathe to risk our displeasure, should the claim turn out to be true. And pigs might fly!

Mail dealt with, we settled down for a cuppa and a chin wag, in the time honoured way that close families have developed. After lunch, much of the afternoon was spent catching up on the gossip, a quick run-through the "hatched, matched and despatched" list, as it related to ex school friends and acquaintances, then a session of "putting the World to rights ". With such long intervals between visits, there were always plenty of juicy tid-bits to pick over and none of the long, embarrassing, awkward silences.

Everyone was pleased that, for this year at least, we had been able to share with them, one small part of the Christmas celebrations. Once arrived at our destination we would definitely be inaccessible to all but the most intrepid visitors. Eventually we returned to the boat after having said our goodbyes to Mum and promising Joan that we would pay them a short visit before we set sail the following morning. All in all it had been a pleasant, if brief, stay.

Next day saw us, duty calls completed, goodbyes and Christmas greetings exchanged, ready to indulge ourselves in an orgy of selfishness, free to spend this festive season with no-one but ourselves to please.

When folk first heard that we intended to give up our land-based existence and live afloat aboard a narrowboat their first reaction was usually along the lines of; "How on earth will you two cope with living in each others pockets twenty- four hours a day in such a small space?"

The provision of a "study", to which one or the other of us could retreat, should we be overtaken by an overwhelming urge for privacy or a place to work, uninterrupted, was our "sop" to this idea. Over the years it has simply become the boat's main storage area. We have been so contented with each other's company, so fulfilled by our self appointed tasks and leisure pursuits, that it has never been needed in its designated capacity.

It retained the title "study" to remind us to follow our hearts and not to be influenced by other people's advice, however well meant.

We were intending to retrace our steps through Glascote, Fazeley and Hopwas to Fradley Junction, from there we would head North-West along the Trent and Mersey Canal. There was a water point about one mile short of our final destination, we could replenish our fresh water there. That should see us safely through the festivities.

The other outstanding task would be to lay in the usual stock of seasonal fare. Comestibles that could be stored easily had already been bought, now we needed to stock up with fresh vegetables, bread, a large chicken, pork pies and cold cuts for sandwiches. A short stop in Rugeley was indicated!

As we cruised slowly towards Fradley, the sky began to cloud over and the temperature dropped. We climbed the top three locks of the Fradley flight as daylight ebbed away. Considering that we had covered sufficient distance to make tomorrow's final leg reasonable, even allowing for the stop-off at Rugeley, we moored up just beyond Woodend lock, erected the T.V. aerial and went below to get warm.

The interior was cosy, with the heat from our solid fuel stove permeating right through it. Although happy with the stove's ability to heat the boat, it had two major drawbacks; Firstly, the heat it generated was often too fierce and could not easily be controlled; Secondly, combustion of solid fuel and logs created condensation and dust.

The condensation was well under control, the dust created was a different story. I normally rose early, cleared out the stove and re-lit it, before Jean was able to get out of bed, not because she was lazy but because the dust did her asthma no favours at all. Use of inhalers kept the problem under control and Jean could avoid the worst effects but we were rapidly coming to the conclusion that the only lasting cure for the difficulty lay in a change of heating appliance and fuel. The following summer we intended to instal a Kubola Old Dutch diesel fired stove and to build a pair of auxiliary fuel tanks, under the gunwales on each side of the foredeck.

As the light faded it began to snow. I went outside and stood on the bank. "Pallas Athene" lay before me light spilling out from the cabin windows and our Christmas tree complete with lights could be seen through the front windows glittering in the encroaching dusk. In the life ring on the cabin roof, Henry was perched with his red and white pointy hat complete with pom-pom, already heavily speckled with large, damp snowflakes.

Carried away by the quiet beauty of the scene, I collected my camera from in the cabin and took a couple of snapshots, using the flash as a fill in. I was hoping against hope that I would get acceptable pics., in spite of the poor lighting.

The next day dawned bright, crisp and COLD. It had snow heavily during the night and although it had stopped, everywhere was buried under a 25 cm. deep coating. The trees were sheathed in white and the branches drooped under the weight of the snow.

This was what winter cruising was all about!

In the boat, we had a number of Christmas tapes; A selection of Favourite Carols; Canto Noel, Christmas Plain Chant and our latest acquisition, A Cajun Christmas. Our in-boat stereo system fitted into the headboard of the bed. (A car radio/cassette player with stereo speakers) had an extra pair of speakers wired in and placed on the roof near the stern. With no-one to annoy we cruised for miles, the countryside around us echoing to the joyful sound of Christmas music. Even when confronted by the first signs of civilisation, houses lining the canal, we were met with beaming smiles and cheery waves from people startled out of their kitchens by our happy music. We cruised on with seasonal greeting drifting on the air above our settling wake.

In our element; we were loving every minute of it! This could go on forever!

All too soon Rugeley hove into view and when we had secured the boat, common sense told us that the speakers would have to come below while we completed our shopping. Goodwill is not really contagious, much as we would like it to be!

N/b. "Penguin" was on her moorings as we entered the town so there was a vague possibility that we might meet Sue and Godfrey while we were shopping.

As with many towns, in Rugeley we had established a pattern of shops which supplied us with items we required. In the Market Hall was the butchers stall from which, we always bought our meat. They were very good and supplied a large range of fresh and ready cooked meat. It was wonderful to be greeted like old friends in so many places, even though my elder daughter could never understand how we achieved such a measure of familiarity with so many people in so many locations.

The old maxim; "Laugh and the World laughs with you, cry and you cry alone." seemed to work for us!

As we headed into Boots the Chemist, who should we bump into as they emerged through the doors but our friends accompanied by their Staffordshire Bull Terrier, Samson. The chance booking of identical Maltese holidays had triggered off a lasting friendship. We spent a few minutes blocking the pavement while we petted Samson and exchanged gossip with Sue and Godfrey then, we parted, after exchanging warmest seasonal greetings. They were returning to their boat for a Christmas Cruise. In the opposite direction!

Well satisfied with our purchases we returned to our boat anxious to complete the cruise before the daylight faded. One thing was certain, we were not alone in our desire to spend a quiet, carefree Christmas, what did concern us a little was how many of the boats seemed to be heading in the same direction as us.

Five miles and two locks. Colwich and Haywood, would take us to Great Haywood Junction where we could refill our water tank. One mile along the Staffs and Worcester Canal, entered at the junction, would bring us to the Tixall Wide, one of the most beautiful stretches of water. It was a location that we loved and had always vowed would be our first choice as a destination for a Christmas cruise and the opportunity to spend a few days moored in these idyllic surroundings.

The Wide was famed for its population of kingfishers but as we had never stopped her for any length of time, we had never made a sighting. At this season of the year, we were unlikely to make good that deficit.

As the generator would play an essential role in keeping our batteries charged over the holiday period as well as supplying 230v. power for our appliances, we felt that it was important that we moored clear of other boats so that we did not create difficulties for anyone.

The walk into Great Haywood village each morning, to collect a newspaper, would serve to give us some of the exercise we needed to avoid adding to our already over ample figures.

Deciding at the last moment to delay our arrival at the Wide until the following day, we moored up below Haywood lock. That meant a short walk to the shops, a chance to complete any last minute shopping and the opportunity to cross the River Trent on the ancient Pack Horse Bridge to explore the wonderful winter play-ground that the snowfall had sculpted for us in Shugborough House Park.

With skies clearing and temperatures dropping we hoped that we could avoid a severe overnight frost that would freeze up the taps at the boatyard and prevent us from taking on sufficient water to last us for at least one week.

By mid-morning next day, we were moored against the B.W. water point ready to fill our tank.

There had been a frost, but the water in the taps was flowing freely!

With the tank topped up, we reversed "Pallas Athene", back past the junction so that we could make the turn and finally, head for Tixall Wide!

With snow lying on the ground and frozen on to the trees and hedgerows, the scene transcended normal words, at the very least, this was the idyll we had sought! A few boats were huddled together close to the entrance to the lake, looking very snug and warm with plumes of smoke from their chimneys hanging in the crystal clear air. We entered the broad expanse of water and made a wide sweep to bring us into the bank, in splendid isolation about 150 yards back from the other boats. Looping our mooring chains through the Armco, we tied up securely and set the boat up for a few days stay.

Later, Russ, the Harbour Master from Ellesmere Port Boat Museum, who we knew quite well, arrived in his 72 ft. converted workboat. He moored 50 yds. beyond us, facing west.

Next day would be Christmas Eve, the temperatures were dropping steadily and it looked as if we would get the magical, White Christmas, if only thanks to frozen snow and frost. We awoke next morning to find filigree fingers of ice weaving delicate patterns across the surface of the water. So impressed was I by this display of beauty that I wrote a poem that was later to win me the Adult Poetry Award at the Middlewich Folk and Boat Festival.

I had written a considerable number of poems over the years, as it was always something of a passion with me. A number were published and eventually I completed my anthology, Idylls of an Unrepentant Romantic. This has now been published and the following poem appears in its pages.

Ice on the Canal.

1. Christmas cruising; Peace and quiet,
   Far from madding crowd.
   Love and laughter; serene beauty,
   Happiness once vowed.

2. Silent hedgerows; naked branches,
   Mirrored water's glow.
   Mallards preening; Moorhens keening,
   Nature's Winter show.

3. Leaden skyscapes; pewter water,
   What's Creation done.
   Where her jewels, precious metals,
   Sparkling in the sun.

4. True, upon the velvet nightsky
   Stars, like di'monds shine,
   And, a gleaming crescent lighted,
   Speaks to me and mine.

5. Air like champagne, breathed out softly,
   Turns, to clouds of white.
   While across the distant landscape,
   Highways flash with light.

6. See, the water surface changing,
   Ice like lace, is born;
   Turning pewter into silver,
   Riches for the morn.

7. Gentle now, a silken curtain,
   Flutters to the ground.
   Snowflakes, soften twigs and branches,
   Wrap each surface round.

8. Now, the morning sky is cloudless,
   Poetry in blue.
   As the light, dawns on our vision,
   Memories renew.

9. While across a transformed landscape,
   Glitt'ring gems now show.
   Set, into a mount of silver,
   Cushioned by the snow.

10. Then, from nature's new paved highway,
    Hark! a mournful quack.
    No bread, no waterweed, no fishes,
    What more can they lack?

11. Slipping, sliding on the surface,
    Webbed feet do feel cold!
    Swans, ducks, waterfowl and sparrows,
    Hunting food, like gold.

12. Gone, the shrill, plump birds of summer,
    Winter's teeth are keen,
    Yes, the crumbs, the seeds, the forage,
    Life or Death can mean.

13. So, we share communal breakfast,
    With the noisy host.
    Life is good! here on the water,
    Let us drink a toast!

14. Here's to Nature and her mood-swings!
    Here's to teeming life!
    Here's to beauty, spread before us!
    Here's an end to strife!

    Here's to my sweet wife!

This poem was written to commemorate our first real Christmas cruise. Our children had all made other arrangements and we were free to please ourselves totally. It was fantastic, we enjoyed a WHITE Christmas! I make no apology for including the alternative final line.

Many of my poems are written for and dedicated to my wife. This is one and, for me, this is my chosen final line.

Although the skies were clear and the sun shone, temperatures did not rise above freezing. The skim of ice thickened, the waterfowl found themselves marooned in small lagoons in the ice field, kept clear by their constantly swimming in ever tightening circles. Eventually they would be forced to climb out onto the frozen surface or risk being trapped in the encroaching ice as they dozed during the night. Wrapped warm against the biting cold, we took a brisk walk down to the junction. Walking past the moorings we reached the lock, crossed over the bridge and entered the village. There would be no newspapers on Boxing Day as the small Supermarket that supplied them would remain closed

At the junction, we found a small group of craft from the Tamworth Cruising Club had moored and were intending to remain over the holiday period. The majority were G.R.P. cruisers and the prospect of being frozen in was exercising their minds. We chatted to one or two whose acquaintance we had made. They would not come down to the Wide but would stay put over Christmas.

It would be strange not to be attending Midnight Mass this Christmas Eve but, faced with the prospect of a long, cold walk at 1 a.m., we had decided to give the idea a miss. We could still celebrate the festival in our hearts.

Arriving back at the boat after our constitutional, we opened the front doors and staggered back from the billowing waves of trapped heat that met us. All the windows and hatches had been closed for security and the ventilators had bled out only a tiny proportion of the heat build-up. Closing down the stove almost completely, we opened windows and hatches wide in an effort to restore the internal temperature to comfortable levels in the shortest possible time. Our insulation was so effective that, with the exception of small areas around the vents., the whole roof of the boat was still thickly coated with frozen snow.

T. V. reception was poor, certainly not good enough to make it worth setting up to video programmes. We would spend a little time viewing, mainly films, but basically we were here for the peace and quiet, that's what we craved!

Santa had called early and the steps below the front doors were piled with brightly wrapped gifts. The piles grew as we added our last minute purchases, traditionally, "The sillies."

When darkness drew its sable cloak tightly around us, I felt that one thing was missing, the scene was one step short of perfection. The night sky glittered with a myriad chips of light but instead of being presided over by a magnificent full moon, bathing the landscape with soft light, we had to make do with a few days old crescent.

It lacked a tiny touch of magnificence!

With no young children to waken us, we slept late on Christmas morning, before rising, wrapping our naked bodies in dressing gowns and sitting down to breakfast. Much earlier, I had risen briefly. After cleaning out and re-lighting the stove, making a pot of tea, which we had drunk, in bed with a small plate of biscuits, we had settled back down for a final few minutes shuteye. (About 120 minutes!)

Not exactly Mr. and Mrs. Motivator!

Christmas dinner with all the trimmings would be served at 6 p.m., We would lunch on meat sandwiches and mince pies and, for me at least, breakfast would consist of a large slice of pork pie, bread and butter, all washed down with numerous cups of tea laced with whiskey.

Jean prepared the meals leaving everything ready to be cooked at the appropriate times!

With elevenses came the time to open our presents. As usual we had both been rather extravagant and the piles were extensive. We took turns in opening gifts, occasionally feigning surprise when their identity was obvious from the wrapping or we had prior knowledge of the contents. One mystery was solved. I now knew why Jean's handbag had sounded so heavy at Evesham. I opened one solid, weighty parcel to find myself the proud recipient of a beautiful Spanish Target Pistol, Jean had returned to the shop and bought it for me. I was over the Moon! There were enough genuine surprises to make the exercise great fun for both of us and any way, the immense joy we both got from exchanging gifts lifted the experience to almost spiritual heights.

Soon it would be time for "The Queen's Speech" and a hour with a box of tissues and "Noel Edmunds' Christmas Presents" We were unashamedly sentimental!

When we did eventually venture outside, it was to find that a severe overnight frost had seriously increased the thickness of the ice. Stepping on to the gunwale to go ashore we could hear the ice creaking as the movement of the hull created pressure waves. With the weather set to deliver more frosts, things would get worse before they got better.

We dived below into our snug, warm cocoon!

Dinner was cooked and eaten, crackers pulled, and once the washing- up was completed, we settled down to an evening of card games and television. Jean with her whiskey and dry ginger, me with vodka and lime.

Our idea of sybaritic decadence!

Dawn on Boxing Day revealed that another sharp frost had further thickened the ice, now it could support the weight of a child or small person.

After lazing our way through the previous day, we were resolved to get a little exercise. Wrapping ourselves in warm clothing we set out again to walk to the junction. Once out of the Wide, the canal proper was shielded by trees and hedgerows and the ice was a little thinner. A Fishing Competition was about to start. Each angler had come prepared. They had long lengths of rope with weights tied on the end. These had been used to smash channels through the ice, across the width of the canal. Much of the broken ice had slipped beneath the surface, immediately doubling its thickness. This would create some strange phenomena as the ice continued to thicken.

Before the day was out, a long narrowboat broke through, ice piling up at its bows and large sheets being thrust below the surface. It was an awesome sight and one which should have served as a warning to us. However, our complacency was such that we were confidently expecting an early thaw in spite of the dire warnings being issued by the Met. Office.

Days slipped by, no more boats appeared and the ice pack thickened!

After seven idyllic days, a slight sense of panic began to set in. Daytime temperatures were just above freezing but overnight frosts and short days meant that little was changing, although we convinced ourselves that the ice was thinning a little.

With our water supply running low, we made up our minds to leave during the morning of December 30th. Jean took up position in the bows armed with the short boat-shaft, I was in my usual place at the helm. Our first task was to clear a space around the boat. Using the 18 ft. shaft ,with its spiked metal tip, we were able to break up a considerable area

Eventually it was possible able to angle our bows towards the still visible track left by the passage of the boat on Boxing Day. It seemed to offer the most viable route out.

A number of people were walking along the towing path and soon Russ came along to offer moral support and advice. I was discussing with him the merits of heating stoves and explaining our wish to change ours for a diesel fired one, for Jean's sake. A man passing by with his dog called out to ask if I would consider selling him my old stove. Taken aback, I quoted £100 and offered a summer delivery. With some difficulty, we shook hands on the deal. He gave me a telephone number, and an address in Little Haywood, before carrying on his way.

At least something was going right!

The ice was horrendous, double thicknesses causing leads of clear water to open up, leading us in directions we did not wish to go and blocking our chosen route. Jean sweated, strained and cursed while I switched rapidly from forward to reverse in order to keep our momentum going. Using the weight of the boat and the power of the engine we gradually forced a passage but our freshly painted hull was rapidly developing a paint free zone around its waterline.

To draw a merciful veil over the rest of our suffering, suffice it to say that we took three and a half hours to cover a distance that normally took fifteen minutes. We arrived at the Junction, totally knackered, with an even shorter, short boat shaft and in awe of a covering of ice on the canal that had very nearly proved itself able to with-stand the assault of 20 metric tonnes of steel, thrust forward with the power of a 40 hp. Diesel engine.

At least we had avoided damaging any of the many G.R.P. cruisers that had been moored along our route, one of the major hazards connected with trying to smash a large, heavy boat through an icefield.

Once through the bridge into the Trent and Mersey, we breasted up to the wharf to take on water. Wonder of wonders, one water tap was still unfrozen. With a sigh of relief we were able to refill our fresh water tank.

Exhausted, we tied up for the night and spent New Year's Eve recuperating. The walk to collect a newspaper was shorter and we were able to check out Haywood lock to ensure that it was indeed, navigable.

New Year's Day found us willing, if not exactly ready to rejoin the fray. Temperatures were slightly higher and we had convinced ourselves that today, would be celebrated with major progress being made towards our final destination, Burton upon Trent.

After struggling past the moorings, we reached and successfully negotiated Haywood Lock. We found to our great joy that here the overhanging trees had sheltered the water and the covering of ice was much thinner. Our progress was fast and relatively painless until we reached open country then, once more, we had to fight for every metre of progress. Just before we reached Colwich lock we called it a day, tied up and went below to ease our aching limbs. We both suffered, for at the stern, fighting a bucking tiller bar and straining to steer a course with ice sheets steering the boat in all directions, was very tough on the shoulders.

At least my chest pains seemed to have eased a little!

We were so tired now that, although I walked into the village for a newspaper, we did not even bother to erect the Television aerial and hadn't done since we left our mooring on the Tixall Wide! After spending yet another day recovering, we set off on January 3rd., hopeful of reaching Fradley Junction at least.

The run down to Colwich lock created some problems but once through conditions improved again. With no G.R.P. craft moored along our route, we crashed happily along, ice screaming and crunching, left cracked and buckled as our wake thrust up beneath it breaking it into sheets.

All was fine, until we passed the boarding school at Bishton Hall. Here we reached open country once more and the ice gradually became, impassable. After a futile attempt to make further progress we fought our way in towards the towing path, moored up and went below for a hot drink.

Resigned to spending yet another night out in the boondocks, we supped tea, ate biscuits and mince pies, while we commiserated with each other!

Twenty minutes later, we heard the sound of ice moving against the sides of the boat and in the distance, the thud of diesel engines. Yes! two boats were approaching us from the direction of Rugeley. They turned out to be hire boats, abandoned by their crews at Fradley Junction and being collected by two members of staff from the boatyard at Great Haywood.

The lead boat was driving hard against the ice until bought to a standstill by the pressure, the second boat would then speed along its flank and into the ice. This seemed a very effective method as it continually changed the angle of attack.

They were making rapid progress!

As they reached us we were able to inform them that their path back to the Marina had been opened up. One of the pair we knew casually and were able to exchange a few comments before they continued on their way. Now in line astern!

Quickly we cleared our ropes, recovered our mooring pins and set off towards Fradley. Our route was clear and we made excellent progress to the Junction where we were able to fill our diesel tank before mooring for the night. The engine had been running under a heavy load and the generator for many hours, we were short on fuel.

Relieved to be there, we dined at The Swan, then retired for an early night.

With the last leg of our cruise in sight we were concerned to be told that the Coventry Canal was still blocked by ice and no-one had yet gone down towards Alrewas. We could always be first so we rose early and breakfasted well to prepare us for the fray.

We were drinking one final cup of tea when the working boat "Badger" passed us, bows high and engine thumping slowly. Seeing it turn into the Junction Lock our spirits rose, he would do the hard work for us. By the time we had filled the lock for our passage, the working boat was out of sight and the ice shattered.

That was the last we saw of it!

Passing through the village we arrived at Alrewas Lock to find that, below it, no trace of ice was to be seen. The River Trent adds its flow to the canal for two hundred yards here and the water movement had prevented the ice from forming. From here to Burton upon Trent, the canal had remained unfrozen.

After the traumas of the previous few days this was an anti-climax of epic proportions. Back at the Marina they would think we were shooting a line when we recounted our ordeal in lurid detail. In reality most Hire companies were fielding complaints from crews, who were blaming them for the weather and allowing them to be frozen in.

We turned into the Marina, eased into our berth and heaved a sigh of relief. We had enjoyed the cruise, had stored up some wonderful memories and seen some glorious sights.

Now we were glad to be "home!"

23.
Winter Layover.

Our 1995 cruise had proved to be the most intensive yet. We had covered 1,385 miles and negotiated 720 locks and all without subjecting ourselves to undue strain. The range of entries we kept in the log had gradually been extended until now I had a comprehensive record which enabled me to calculate a wide variety of statistics related to each cruise. As a trained engineer I have always been interested in data and being something of a control freak, I find it comforting to be able to ascertain how closely we are adhering to our projected timetable. It does not amount to an obsession, merely the reassurance of measurable performance!

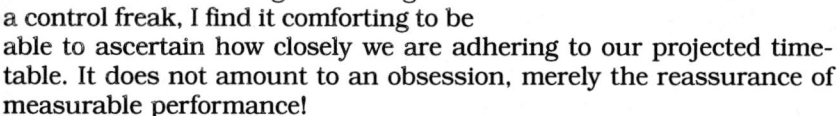

Keeping records has a positive side. By noting how much diesel is purchased, not only is it possible to compute the cost of cruising but also to check on consumption which, for a boat, is measured in hours/gallon or minutes/litre. Our figures are skewed by the fact that our diesel generator is supplied by the same tank as the engine, but its running times are also a matter of record. This means that we can at least get a ball park figure for consumption.

A sudden drop in performance figures prompts an urgent check of both engines although such drops may stem from a variety of reasons.

After the major stress placed on the boat, particularly the engine and transmission, by our exploits in the ice, I was anxious to have both checked over by an expert!

Time to call on the services of, Peter, the Boat Doctor!

With bad experiences behind us and not yet having established a system- wide circle of trusted and reliable engineers, we were only prepared to place "Athene" in the hands of someone coming to us on the highest personal recommendation. The boatyard sub-contracted Peter to service and maintain the engines of the boats in its Hire fleet and they were happy to make such a commitment.

Co-incidently, our grandson Henry, more often known as, Harry, was in a serious condition in the Burton General Hospital. Now we could spend some time each day offering our support to his mother and giving her the occasional break from her self imposed vigil. She had left husband Nick, in charge of the two girls and was living in the hospital. She assisted with Harry's care and slept in his room each night.

The general prognosis was not hopeful. The baby was suffering from a condition known as, "Infantile Spasms", whereby his small body was gripped by regular convulsions. During each one, his brain activity virtually stopped and returned slowly, only to be interrupted by the next spasm. This intermittent brain function was having the effect of seriously retarding the development of the motor and higher mental functions.

After batteries of tests had been completed it was decided that the effects could be controlled by a complicated drug regime. However the level of development on all but the physical side could well have suffered lasting impairment.

At nine months old he was a big lad!

Harry was discharged from hospital before Peter had got round to looking at our engine but not before Jean had managed to contract two of the viruses that were rampaging around the hospital. One was a vicious form of stomach upset, a mild form of dysentery, the other a respiratory infection which, given her asthma problem, knocked Jean sideways.

In spite of the area of stripped paint on our hull, we decided not to dry-dock the boat for a second time to repair the damage. The etching primer coat was still intact so the integrity of the hull was not in any real danger.

With the decision to change from solid fuel to diesel heating we had also resolved to discard the ALDE Central Heating unit. As a system it was excellent, given the correct location such as a large caravan, but taking into consideration the size of our boat I think I had been a little over-optimistic as to the level of efficiency I could demand from it. Boost pumps had been fitted to aid the circulation but the gas consumption was too high to make it's operation, cost effective. To all intents and purposes it had been redundant since just after its installation and had rarely been used. The multi-fuel stove had been wonderful, now that was being exchanged for the diesel one and both units would be coming out.

With advancing years I had developed an expanded waistline, thanks in part to our very good life on the boat and not enough regular, intensive exercise. Still troubled from time to time with chest pains, I was far more concerned over the deterioration of my arthritic knee joints, exacerbated by my weight, and problems with my feet, that dated back to childhood. The right foot was particularly bad. A short ligament had distorted my great toe until now it caused me intense pain to stand for extended periods of time.

Like steering a boat for five or six hours a day!

Through our G.P., I had arranged an appointment with a Consultant Orthopaedic Surgeon at the Burton General Hospital. Although it was to be National Health funded I was given excellent service and an early date for the consultation. The procedure would not delay the start of our cruising.

In spite of regular visits to the G.P. I had not broached the problem of the chest pains. I was not ready to think the unthinkable.

With the town easily accessible and the spectre of B.W.'s new Boat Safety Certificate looming large, I was able to check out how closely our boat came to compliance with the new regulations. Although we had taken great pains right the way along the line to ensure that our installations were up to standard, and B.W.'s assurance that boats with a full Certificate of Compliance would be okay, we identified a number of areas were the regulations were so complicated that to be sure of passing would cost us un-necessary money. Unrealistically generous ventilation requirements, electrical, gas and fire safety regulations which would instantly have taken a large percentage of caravans and not a few houses, out of legal use. With no local chandlery we were a little stuck but a van from a large Marine wholesaler visited the yard regularly and we were able to order most things.

Peter arrived to carry out the service and was quick to commend us on how well our engine had been fitted. It was so well mounted that engine and prop. shaft were in good condition and four years of intensive cruising had not damaged the mounting yokes. When running the engine under active load, he found that the drive plate between engine and gearbox was wearing and estimated that it could fail within twelve months. Rather than wait for that to happen, we elected to have it replaced during this service.

He costed the job, gave us what I felt was a very reasonable estimate and promised to return in two days after he had been to a supplier and assembled the required spares, oil filters and drive belts. True to his word, he returned as promised, the job was completed without fuss or undue mess and his estimate of costs proved to be amazingly accurate.

During the operation Jean supplied the obligatory cups of coffee and chocolate biscuits!

Round about that time we received a letter from the Discworld Fan Club that their first Convention would be held at the Britannia Sachs Hotel in Manchester in June. On top of the cost of attendance, the room prices at the hotel put the event out of our reach. However, the organisers had no problem with Conventioneers booking their own accommodation so we checked with the information bureau and booked ourselves into the aptly named Burton Arms pub on a B.and B. basis for three nights. We sent the deposit confirming the phone call, by return of post. Terry Pratchett the World famous fantasy writer, had written a series of books about the Disc-world and its characters. These books had reached cult status and were the only ones that had a permanent place on the boat, apart from our collection of reference books and the others that had sentimental value for us. My collection of over two thousand books had been destroyed by my ex-wife and so many of the books that Jean and I had exchanged had a very special place in our hearts. I adore Terry's work and find that our senses of humour and grasp of the ridiculous are frighteningly similar. His work is way out, you either love or hate it.

I absolutely Love it!

By that time, I was attempting to interest publishers in my first book, "Athene; Anatomy of a Dream" I had converted my manuscripts into double spaced typescripts as per recommendations and was preparing to post copies around. As I did not have a word processor, this meant lots of photo-copying as well as the buying of card- lined envelopes and postage stamps.

My typewriter was just about on its last legs and was creating serious problems. When I tried to get it serviced I was told that repairs would be likely to cost more than replacement and in those circumstances they would not take the job on. Obviously replacement was the best option so I went into Argos, who had a sale on, and purchased a Brother Electronic Typewriter. It was an upgrading, but still did not offer the versatility of a Word Processor.

January was preparing to go out in style. We woke to find the boat buried in four inches of snow which in some places had piled into impressive drifts. I climbed out onto the bows to be met with a world of white. Across the surface of the basin a thin skim of ice had been coated with snow. The boats were changed from hard, angular shapes into long forms softened by the white covering and the bright colours that normally dominated the Marina were muted, while large areas were totally obliterated. Enthralled I took many photographs, our only regret being that the boat was moored in a crowded Marina and not deep in the countryside, alone and surrounded by the magic of a snow- clad landscape. That was what we wanted, a photograph to use as a Christmas Card,

For the next few days the weather remained cold with persistent, if slight, additional snowfalls.

I took out the central heating boiler and many of the skirting radiators, 19mm. copper pipes with aluminium, heat distribution fins. As the radiators had been installed, before the final decorative cladding, I was left with a considerable restoration job to make good all the unfinished areas. The bathroom posed the largest problem. I had used a conventional radiator in there and its removal left a large segment of wall beneath the porthole looking sad and unfinished. Eventually I replaced the whole section and tiled both that and the surround to the shower unit with it's glass sliding door. Now most of the bathroom, including the shower cubicle was tiled and it looked really nice.

As I was not a joiner, when I had fitted out our boat much of the work was utilitarian, now we were beginning to notice this and I intended to do much more work on improvements

I just had to decide, where and how could make these modifications!

February began with a continuation of the snow falls and as we had planned to start this year's cruising on March 4th. we were keeping an eye on the sky and an ear glued to our radio each morning, hoping against hope for some promise of improvement.

B.W. were aiming to complete their round of maintenance in the area by March 1st. which was a little unusual. It meant that this year we could look to an early start to cruising but next year, an extended programme of work could well take the closures right up to the end of March.

We took our chances when we could! Harry had returned to hospital amid concerns over his progress and another round of tests were planned. An altered drug regime based on the findings could improve his rate of development. As least now we could see a marked improvement, both in his general alertness and increasing motor skills.

My appointment to see Mr. Green, the Consultant Surgeon, was set for March 1st., the day B.W. were due to complete their work, I had my fingers crossed that the appointment was not delayed. Still outpatient visits were rarely cancelled. Or so I hoped!

The snows ceased and melted, then February began to live up to it's folk-lore name, Fill-dyke. Day after day dawned cloudy, the rain poured down and as it fell, so did our spirits. Things were not looking too good for our proposed start date.

With a new drug programme prescribed, Harry's condition continued to improve. Heather would bring him into town with her each Friday and we would meet in the Octagon Centre for elevenses, before going shopping. The Centre was an excellent meeting place and had a wonderful balcony cafeteria where a number of outlets provided a wide choice of food. The seating area was dominated by a large clock, mounted in a building depicting a brewery storehouse. On the quarters the clock played snatches of tunes but each hour, the pièce-de-resistance, As the hours chimed, music would play and groups of figures would appear as doors and hatches opened, before our eyes was enacted a busy scene of off-loading grain and hops into the warehouse. This was a shopping day treat for children who watched as the scene was repeated each hour.

Harry was not yet aware enough to show great interest in things like that, even though he was eleven months old, but now he was able to smile, attempt to pull himself up and grasp objects in a much more positive way.

With the two girls at school, shopping on Friday was a much less fraught operation than the Saturday outings when they accompanied Mum in order to spend some time with Gran Jean and Grandad. By now Harry was taking up so much of Heather's time that the elder girl was becoming a surrogate Mum and taking on responsibilities beyond her age while the younger girl felt resentful at being out of the limelight. A middle child always seems to have similar problems but Harry's medical condition had increased the pressure immensely. It was difficult for us to please both parties without erring into over-indulgence. This, fortunately, was something we could not really afford to do!

Burton, like so many Midland towns, had a substantial Asian enclave and the launderette was situated in the heart of this area. Each trip with the laundry, took us past shops whose windows glittered with the rainbow hues of gorgeous ethnic fabrics. Marriage saris' decorated with tiny mirrors, flashed in the light, while rolls of material cascaded a riot of colour from the shelves.

Jean would become dewy eyed as the sight reminded her yet again of her experiences as a young girl brought up in a foreign land, albeit part of the great British Empire. These memories would re-awaken her long held desire to dress, for special occasions, in a beautiful Sari, so elegant and yet not out of place on women whose figures were somewhat on the generous side.

Visits to the Asian quarters in various cities, including Leicester, had resulted in our purchasing a number of sari lengths and from time to time Jean would wear these flowing, colourful dresses. I thought she looked really great, and told her so!

The secret of wearing a sari is knowing how to convert what is simply an eight yard long by four feet wide strip of filmy material into a simple but stunning gown in the most sublime colours. Jean had been taught the art by the Maharanees in the Zenana and could still remember the intricacies of the technique.

She was concerned enough to have asked a number of Indian women in various towns, if they felt that their culture was being insulted by western women choosing to wear their ethnic dress. Over and over again she had been reassured. Many considered the old adage, "Imitation is the sincerest form of flattery", was appropriate.

Towards the end of February the weather began to improve, much to our relief. I still had one task related to removing the Alde and that required a dry spell. The fume vent was still in place and needed to be removed. This left a 4" dia. hole in the roof which I had to plate. Not a particularly onerous task. Given a spell of good weather. Rather than put the equipment into store inside the boat until we could arrange to sell it, we did a deal with Jeanette and swapped it for two months moorings and electric.

Hopefully everyone was happy!

In the interim period I had been into the hospital X-ray department for my problem joints to be filmed for Mr. Green. March 1st. arrived and I kept my appointment.

After examining the X ray plates and looking at my "plates", his reaction was a little startling. He appeared unable to believe that I had been able to reach the age of 58 without someone, somewhere doing something about their state. I explained the reality of a childhood spent in a mining community during the early 40's and the difficulty faced by families, of obtaining medical treatment unless it was aimed at getting workers back onto the coal-face. Throughout my early life, including National Service, I had been refused the option of surgical intervention to repair, what was then, a relatively minor defect but one which could and did deteriorate dramatically in later life. He found the story unbelievable, but the proof was before his eyes, waggling two sets of crushed and distorted toes under his nose.

Apologising that nothing short of extended, major reconstruction of my feet could correct the situation anything like fully, he assured me that he could relieve the worst effects and get me walking properly again, with a relatively simple but messy operation on my right foot, the worst affected. Even that would see me incapacitated for at least six weeks.

Agreeing to this level of intervention, I was promised that the work would be carried out before Christmas 1996, preferably in early November. That suited me fine but it would mean a return to Shobnall Basin for the next winter lay-over.

Relieved that at last I was being offered the possibility of a measure of relief from my constant pain and walking difficulties, I was able to look forward to our yearly cruising with a measure of equanimity.

Jeanette could not guarantee me a berth for the following winter, but promised to do her best in view of the special circumstances. Next spring, (1997) would see our current C.of C. run out, that meant we would need to obtain a B.SC. for the boat. Jannel Cruisers had a resident Boat Examiner.

A phone call to B.W. confirmed that they had completed their programme on time and that the canals in the area would be fully open from Monday. We would not be cruising outside that area during March so were able to concentrate on stocking the boat, confident that our cruise could begin on time.

Saturday saw us engaged in a last minute flurry of shopping and a final visit from Heather and the children. On Sunday we filled up the fresh water tank, took on diesel and replaced the spare gas cylinder. Now all our tanks were full and the gas locker stocked with three 13Kg. cylinders of propane, one on line, one on auto switch-over and a spare in case of dire emergency. We had been on mains electric for the winter so our batteries had been kept fully charged by our Heart Interface, we were as ready as could be. Jean's recurring respiratory problems had been sorted and cured by antibiotics, the medicine cabinet was stocked with inhalers for her asthma.

Tomorrow! it would be all systems go, for 1996!

24
Animal Anecdotes!

One of the beauties of our life style is the close proximity it puts us into with wildlife. The putter of our engine and the gentle swish of water past the hull, seem to blend into the background as far as many animals and birds are concerned. Rarely do we appear to be creating any kind of consternation along our route.

On a warm, sunny day, the sight of a large, plump water-vole, lying on its back on a clump of crushed reeds, warming its belly fur, four short legs raised in supplication, is a comical vision. The passage of the boat, tilts the pad of reeds but apart from cocking a bright, black eye, inquisitively in our direction, our presence elicits no further response.

In terms of Animal Behavioural Science, our observations leave much to be desired. They are not empirical but based merely on tiny, isolated snapshots of individuals or small groups of creatures. Rarely can we observe for extended periods of time and so do not glean an in-depth picture of interaction. Our observation may be superficial but the joy and lasting pleasure we get from our contacts is immensely satisfying.

To some extent, Jean misses out on these pleasures. She is conscientious about the completion of her household chores and spends periods of time below, while we are cruising, engaged in the multifarious tasks needed to upkeep the boat to a standard that satisfies her.

When the weather is inclement, opportunities like these can provide the salve to a conscience concerned at being comfortably ensconced below while hubby is cold and wet, manning the helm. At times like that regular brews or warming mugs of "Cuppa Soup" serve as acceptable offerings. On the other hand, when the weather is warm and sunny, the surroundings lush and beautiful, the temptation to leave the work and join me at the stern can sometimes prove to be irresistible.

Because of this dichotomy, my list of kingfisher sightings, for instance, is much longer than Jean's and some of my close encounters of the fur and feather kind, were not shared.

Much to my regret!

Wildlife programmes on television are a source of great delight to us and form part of our small range of regular viewing habits. Although many are based on exotic locations and examine creatures that we are unlikely ever to observe "in the flesh" the occasional glimpses they provide of our own native species are spellbinding.

From time to time, the perceived wisdom of the chronicler can appear to be at odds with our own observations. Ours are based on very small samples, theirs on extended periods of watching, not one but many groups. There is however a selection process that takes place when deciding which behaviour patterns to highlight and even in the best regulated production the camera can still lie.

I simply report what I see!

One instance that struck us forcibly was part of a programme on British Water birds. The programme seemed to imply, that, from prolonged observation it could be concluded that coots and moorhens were not particularly good parents who were quick to leave their young to their own resources at a very early stage in their development. In contrast our own small sample of observations had shown us ducks and to a lesser extent swans, to be greedy and inclined to be careless of their young where supplies of food were plentiful. When mixed flocks had approached boats to be fed, adult ducks and swans would compete with ducklings and cygnets and usually devoured the lions share. Coots and moorhens on the other hand invariably tucked their broods away under the overhanging branches on the off-side, while they joined in the fray but transported scraps of food over to their young and shared the meal with them. However many times this took place, the situation was entirely artificial and we were the source of the food, nevertheless the greedy adult birds that we saw were not the coots and moorhens.

While we were on the Kennet and Avon, we were standing on the bank at Hungerford, feeding an assortment of waterfowl. In the flock was one single duckling shepherded by a multi- crossbred but basically Mallard duck. This was a regular feeding point and quite a ruck was developing. One lady, taking pity on the lone duckling threw a small crust which landed directly in front of it. In a trice the pack descended and from the centre, ejected like a cork from a shaken bottle of pop, shot a small back and yellow duckling. It splashed into the water outside the melee and paddled frantically away, squeaking pitifully.

Mum, with elbows sharpened, was happily fighting for scraps in the centre of the fray!

The obvious artificiality of the situation negates the validity of any observation as a behaviour pattern but it does nothing to detract from the immense enjoyment we get from watching the antics of the wildlife.

On the G. U. at Leamington Spa we saw a moorhen's nest on the steps of a pub. A bricked in doorway had once given access to the water now it served as the site of a cosy, des. res... This was a built up area and the usual collection of dead reeds etc. was not available, however soggy paper, twigs and polythene had been combined to provide a snug nest. The pièce de resistance was probably accidental and created by the wind, but Mama was safely tucked away on her eggs sheltered by a canopy of polythene which arched over the nest supported by some iron rods fastened into the brickwork.

It was an image that remained with me over the years!

Although canals are not subject to the currents and water level fluctuations that are evident on rivers the passage of boats does create some difficulties for nest builders. Nests built into the low branches of overhanging bushes are one answer as are nests constructed on floating pads of dead reeds at the edges of the beds. An adaptation to modern ideas can be witnessed in the regular use by some waterfowl of sheets of expanded polystyrene foam which can be found floating, trapped by debris, along the margins of many urban stretches of canal, to act as platforms for their nests. They can sometimes be seen put to use as mobile conference centres by small groups of ducks or drakes.

One ingenious use failed through not having been considered carefully!

Passing a small trading estate on the Staffs and Worcester, I noted that large numbers of polystyrene packaging sections had been dumped in the water. Wether by accident or design, a heron was standing on watch with his feet balanced in two of these forms. While he was standing still, the inherent instability of its perch must have seemed immaterial. As our boat approached it appeared to notice a fish and lunged down into the water. Oh! what a surprise!. What started out as a perfectly timed lunge turned into an ignominious belly flop as the two sections of floating waste, flipped backwards with the weight shift. The heron regained the bank looking very crestfallen, shook itself to settle its ruffled feathers then flung itself into the air and flapped away.

I swear it looked more like a flamingo as it disappeared into the haze!

Reported in isolation it is clearly nothing more than serendipity that places these odd happening within our purview but I never cease to thank the Creator of this wonderful diversity, that events like these are regular enough to be observed by diligent watchers.

Many people offer sanctuary to ducks etc. in their gardens by providing roosts and floating ramps so that the birds can reach land easily. Floating landing stages made of thick polystyrene sheets free to float up and down poles thrust into the canal bed, can also be seen quite regularly.

All the fun does not take place on the water and the antics of some of the wild animals on the bank are equally funny as readers of my first book will already have discovered.

We meet countless dogs. Often they are being exercised by their owners although, occasionally, it can appear to be the other way round. Many boaters own dogs, sometimes as much for security reasons as any other. In an uncertain world safety is of paramount importance. We see these dogs, racing towards us along the towing path, stopping every few yards to check on a new scent. Suddenly, they will skid to a halt, barking furiously, as they find themselves transfixed by the baleful stare of Henry's large, yellow glass eyes.

One thing really upsets us. The childish behaviour of some people, out with their dogs, enjoying the exercise, until a boat comes into sight. Then, sticks are thrown into the water in front of the boat and often, because they are taught to retrieve, the dogs will leap in and swim out towards the boat. We have no brakes; our vision of what is in the water ends twenty feet short of the bows and often, even if the dog does swim back to the bank, this can be sheer and quite a bit deeper when the water has receded due to the boat's passage. The animal can panic, owners struggle to haul them out, getting soaked in the process and the poor boater gets slagged off for behaving in a totally anti-social manner by cruising a boat along a waterway!

An acquaintance of ours had just spent a week on some private mooring, when he decided to refill his water tank. Down to the waterpoint, fill the tank, wind, then back to the mooring. Next day his wife rose early, stepped ashore ready to sort out her day; or that's what would have happened, if the bank had still been where she left it!

Think about that!

Dogs don't often make that mistake but we have seen them, in an over-enthusiastic effort to disembark from a moving boat, misjudge the distance to the bank and the purchase offered to clawed paws by a steel deck, and finish up in the canal.

The most usual scenario is one where, a dog who is not yet canal wise, decides it has spent enough time onboard and steps off for a run. A King Charles Spaniel, did just this as its owner was easing into a small space in front of us. Eyes fixed firmly on the bank, he stepped ashore, unfortunately some two feet short of the quay. The wash from the propeller swept him towards our boat, in danger of being crushed between hull and quay or worse being thrust under our boat. Immediate action was crucial!

I flung myself down across our bow, reached down and grabbed for his collar. Of course he wasn't wearing one! Only one course was left open. I grabbed a handful of sodden fur at the scruff of the neck, hauled the body up above the water, then manoeuvred it into my arms, grasping the wet, trembling bundle to my chest while Jean sat on my legs to stop me from joining him. With Jean's assistance, I managed to wriggle my way back into equilibrium, then to my feet. I stood on the foredeck, an expensive pedigree dog clasped tightly in my arms. Its eyes bulged even more than usual for the breed and its breath seemed frozen in its lungs. My shirt was saturated and streams of cold water eased past the belted waist of my jeans to soak my underpants.

I climbed ashore and handed their shivering pet to its distraught owners, I was dismissed with a perfunctory, "thanks ", while the poor dog was alternately fussed over and cursed for its stupid behaviour!.

I understood their reaction!

Fishing things out of the water is one of the things that we seemed, "to do". I have previously recounted our experiences with a baby rabbit and a group of moorhen chicks, so I won't review those episodes. On the Staffs and Worcester one summer we had another close encounter.

Jean was comfortable below, I was cruising steadily, when I saw an animal in the water, apparently swimming strongly. It was grey and quite large so I thought, water vole. Imagine my surprise when I reached it, without its diving below the surface, to realise that what we had was a very distressed, grey squirrel. I could see the once long, fluffy tail, trailing limp and scraggy in the water. Steering clear of the struggling body to avoid drawing into my propeller I put the engine into reverse and bought the boat to a stop before reversing towards the squirrel. Jean came out to see what was happening. The struggling animal was now in the centre of the canal so she bought our child's fishing net back to me. I leaned over and eventually scooped it up in the net where it lay, totally exhausted.

Its fur was completely water-logged, it was traumatised and shocked but it was alive. A tea-towel was warmed and the limp body cradled into it. Artificial resuscitation was out of the question so Jean spent thirty minutes applying gentle heat and massage. Eventually the soft, limpid eyes slid open and the breathing became less erratic. The heartbeat was strong if a touch rapid but it was making little movement, save for a convulsive swimming motion with its front paws,

We had a dilemma, squirrels are known to be destructive animals, it would not make a pet; With no way of knowing where the nearest Animal Shelter was, and no transport anyway, we couldn't place it, and if we took it out of its territory before release, the local squirrels would likely kill it.

In the end we placed it carefully back into the hedgerow, clinging to a forked branch, still shocked but warmer and dryer. We wished it well and consoled ourselves with the knowledge that life was still extant and it stood at least a chance of recovery.

If we hadn't happened along, it would now be one more soggy corpse in the muddy water!

Another encounter of the squirrel kind was much funnier!

Cruising along past a patch of concrete lined with tall trees, we saw a squirrel, sitting up in the open space, nibbling something. A second movement caught our eyes, a large black cat was stalking it. Belly brushing the concrete, tip of the tail swishing and flat eyes focused on the apparently unwary animal. The squirrel must have sensed the danger for, as the cat made its rush and pounce, the squirrel disappeared like a grey flash across the open space towards the nearest tree. Cat in hot pursuit, it didn't hesitate but climbed rapidly up ten feet of sheer tree trunk. The cat, totally engrossed in the chase, followed, finishing up six feet above the ground clinging desperately to a vertical surface, claws digging deeply into the bark. The squirrel, at home here, climbed back to cling, head downward, some two feet above the stranded cat. I could not help but imagine what took place, The squirrel, eyes firmly on its discomforted assailant would say, "Clever! now what are you going to do for an encore, sissy!" The cat stared for a few breathless moments then, flicking its body round, jumped to the ground landing safely on all four paws. It shook itself then stalked nonchalantly away, tail waving bravely in the air as if the cat were saying to itself, "Well! I really taught that silly creature a lesson!"

Our rate of travel is slow enough for us to make these observations, 70 m.p.h. on the M5. doesn't offer the same range of opportunities!

What never ceases to amaze us about many of the animals we observe is their obsession, often fatal, with obtaining, that blade of grass, nut or berry, which is out of reach but is so superior to all the others that it is worth any effort to reach.

Cows with a lush meadow to graze, will strain their necks between strands of barbed wire to reach a single tuft of scrubby grass in an other wise barren area as if it were the Holy Grail. Lambs on tippy toe, teeter on crumbling banks desperate to investigate that small lump of rock or a tree root protruding out of the water. For us each new Spring opens another catalogue of tragedy as we spy the bodies of young animals drowned in the canal, often as a result of nothing more sinister than, curiosity!

Some we can rescue, for the many help comes too late!

Mink are fascinating creatures to watch. Large enough to be easily spotted, they seem to have developed a tolerance towards humans in many areas. They do not always disappear from sight at the first sign of intruders. To watch mink dancing on a dew covered lawn in the dawn light is a wonderful sight. Their sinuous movements as they undulate across the grass in a wild chase, the early sun striking glints off their rich, deep chestnut fur.

Yet! we know them to be among natures most vicious killers with a blood lust that is legendary!

Our sightings of foxes have mainly been restricted to urban areas, where they appear to have colonised what would once have been, an alien environment.

Nature seems to have a way of modifying its needs to fit in with its surroundings. If we avoid contaminating habitats with toxic substances, cluttering areas with dangerous, discarded waste and litter and wanton, wholesale destruction of habitat by ripping out hedges and demolishing all the old buildings, simply to create larger fields etc., I am convinced that there would be far less talk of endangered species. We often concentrate on extending a specialist habitat where some odd creature or plant has established a toehold, ignoring the fact that this may upset an already delicate balance to the extent that other, well established groups could become threatened.

Contrary to popular belief, many stretches of canal have water in which it is possible to see the fish. On a sunny day with the light penetrating to the bottom, we can watch their antics as we cruise.

Enormous carp, sunning themselves in the shallows, heave their way into deeper water as the level recedes with our passage. We see shoals of fish swimming with the boat and darting into the disturbed water of our wake, feeding on the bounty dragged from the bottom by the suction of the propeller. Sometimes we gaze in awe at the sight of pike, slashing through the shoals in a feeding frenzy, then, as we cruise steadily by, we note with amusement how the fish seem to know the location of each fisherman and the big ones at least, seem to keep well clear.

From time to time we have cruised through the aftermath of a toxic waste spillage which had entered the water, either directly or through seepage. Countless fish of all sizes, floating belly up move in a slow dance of death as we thrust through the sickly miasma of corruption that overlies the scene.

Fortunately it is not a regular sight, but each one, is one too many!

Of greater concern is to see the havoc created during a long, hot summer, when rampant weed growth, low water levels and lack of dredging, combine to deprive the remaining water of oxygen and we are left watching fish choking to death in water that is little more than de-oxygenated, liquid mud.

I will stop here before I wear out my welcome and stand accused of continually banging on about a theme on which I hold passionate beliefs!

Anyone who turns away from the sight of nature's cruelty, would surely be disturbed by the sight of a cormorant feeding. A relatively common bird, the cormorant is a regular on canals and rivers near to the coasts and often way inland. Excellent fishermen, they have a superb ability to surface dive, stay under water for long periods and to hunt fish, swimming long distances beneath the surface.

Just outside the galley window of our boat, which was moored at the time, a cormorant surfaced grasping an eel in its beak. The fish was as long as the bird and as thick as a child's arm, it writhed and thrashed, attempting to coil itself around its attacker. The bird was making desperate efforts to turn the fish in order to grasp its head. Twice the eel fought free and twice the cormorant dived after it, resurfacing almost immediately still grasping the thrashing body.

Eventually, the eel was turned, the head gripped firmly in the hooked beak and slowly, in a frenzy of movement, the eel gradually disappeared into the cormorant's gullet. That it was still active was evident from the way the cormorant's neck and upper body were bulging and flexing as the eel wriggled desperately. At last, the final portion of the tail, disappeared into the gaping throat. How this seemingly impossible feat had been accomplished, I do not understand, but the bird swam away, body almost submerged by the weight of the meal and its neck still twitching spasmodically from side to side.

Nature is red in tooth and claw but when you are as close as we get sometimes, its hard to ignore!

Cats play with their prey, most dogs and hounds kill quickly, breaking their prey's neck with a twitch of powerful muscles. Stag hunting comes into a different category. When the prey is too large to kill cleanly it can be badly maimed by the pack before being dispatched. That aspect of hunting sickens me!

We are keen owl lovers, indeed one of my first poems was inspired by the graceful beauty of a Barn Owl on its nightly hunt.

We had just cleared Chirk cutting in the early morning mist, having moored overnight near the tunnel. Approaching the Marina we saw a wonderful model of a Little Owl, mounted on the corner of their notice board and were commenting on how lifelike it was, when it proved the point, by flying away!

Life on the canal is never boring, not while we have our wild friends to entertain us!

Amusement and entertainment are not the sole prerogative of wildlife, domesticated animals can always be relied on for moments of high comedy.

Many of the accommodation bridges that serve farms divided by the building of the canal, act as grandstands. If cattle are grazing on both sides of a bridge, we can be faced with a row of serious stares above sets of gently moving jaws, as our bovine gongoozlers study our passage. It can be disconcerting!

Moored at Wheelock one afternoon, dressed in blue denim, I went to the hedge to admire the view. The herd of cows grazing below, saw me and in unison, stopped feeding and raced over to the fence. I was bemused by this performance, as they jostled for a place close to me. Then, the farmer arrived, clad in blue denim but, carrying the vitamins and oil-cake he fed them with each day. One human may look very much like another, to a cow, but they can certainly recognise a blue denim suit when they see one!

Both sheep and cows have a well developed node of curiosity. Flocks and herds watch us with slightly bemused expressions as we cruise by, clearly wondering where these cans of humans have appeared from and where they disappear to. To them, one thing is certain, we hold a mysterious power that takes away their water as we approach but we always return it when we leave! Even if it is in a startling rush!

Due to the quantity and variety of waterfowl that frequent our routes, it is not surprising that they supply a large proportion of our "in cruise entertainment!"

They are natural born comedians!

We see the same situations happen over and over again but the experience never gets stale. There are endless variations and we never get bored or blasé about things. Springtime is wonderful, with new life arising in all direction. We see the trees slowly coming into leaf, blossom appearing and everywhere the silver grey of pussy willow. Birch and Hazel dangle Lambs tail Catkins in the breeze and in the fields the ubiquitous bright yellow of the Oil-seed Rape flowers spread across acres of green.

Everywhere birds are going through the age old mating rituals and we watch Crested Grebes performing their intricate dance. Coots and Moorhens display and challenges are made by males anxious to secure a mate. Rituals over, pairings achieved, nest building begins. These range from insecure little scrapes scattered with twigs to the large, untidy castles built by the swans. A mature pair will usually nest on the same site.

Mallards are amongst the most adventurous. The exploits of one pair when it came to ingenuity and choice of site inspired me to commit their efforts to verse.

The Adventure

1. The ways of Nature, stretch the mind,
   We all around, fresh wonders find.
   Yet none could more uplift the heart,
   Than mother love, at life's new start.

2. At Boston on the Wash, I'd moored,
   The eastmost limit we had toured.
   It's famous Sluice, the Boston Dock,
   A railway bridge, that spanned the lock.

3. Twelve feet above the waters dark,
   The girders, against the sky loomed stark.
   I passed beneath, to reach the shop,
   Then, movement brought me to a stop.

4. A flicker of a downward flash,
   And, far below, a tiny splash.
   Twice more the movement, ere I spied,
   Three ducklings, riding on the tide.

5. My startled eyes took in the sight,
   As others made the one-way flight.
   Beneath the tracks, their mother stood,
   And marshalled, at the brink, her brood.

6. As one by one they made the lunge,
   My heart stilled, as each took the plunge.
   While Mrs. Mallard, stood and swayed,
   Watching, as this new game they played.

7. At thirteen, Mother called a pause,
   "Wait here" she said, "this turn's not yours"
   Then down she flew, to put things right,
   And check, that none had taken fright.

8. As thirteen ducklings settled down,
   She raised her head, without a frown;
   Then called, to the remaining few,
   To show her, what each one could do.

9. Three more, with valour, made the leap,
   "Look lively now, don't fall asleep."
   Just Tail-end Charlie, left alone,
   To worry, and his fate bemoan.

10. His irate parent, called out loud,
    For him to jump, and join the crowd.
    But solitude doth cowards make,
    He's reticent that step to take.

11. At length, he overcomes his fear,
    And leaps into the abyss sheer.
    Two feet he falls, the bridge support,
    Is in his path, so now he's caught.

12. Another leap, another check,
    By now, he' thinking, "What the heck!"
    He tries again, makes the descent,
    Then, wonders where his siblings went.

13. A game of tag, around the support,
    Pure comedy, that stops for nought.
    Until assembled, Ma. and brood,
    Swim off, to look for Dad, and food.

Anthony H. Lewis.
Spring. 1995.

I witnessed these events and this poem is dedicated to that Mallard and her intrepid brood. We like to believe that some, at least, of her little ones, survived the danger strewn path to adulthood!

One final tale, to outline the inter-relationships that can be built up between man and his wild brethren. We had moored at Norbury Junction on the Shropshire Union, for the usual exercise of topping up the fresh water supply. As there was a considerable amount of stale bread in the boat, we sat on the bows breaking it into portions and tossing it to the assorted waterfowl who were clamouring to be fed. On the edge of the group was one particularly crazy hybrid. It obviously had a large helping of Muscovy somewhere in its gene pool. This duck appeared to be having serious difficulty with feeding. We tried throwing bread outside the compass of the feeding group in the hope that it would feed, all to no avail.

Then, it disappeared. We hadn't noticed her departure but there she was, gone!

When we had used up all the spare bread, it was time to consider our inner men. We walked towards the bridge where we could cross the canal to the hire boat centre where they had a tea-room. Another boat was moored some way behind ours and when we reached it, we could see a young boy sitting hunched on the cratch frame. Alongside of him, on the bow, was the duck helping him to demolish a large sandwich. From this range we could see that the duck's bill was deformed and she could not eat quickly.

The young boy was in his element, obviously thrilled with this close contact and quite happy to share his lunch. On the other hand, the bird was so well nourished, in spite of the handicap, that it appeared to have discovered a method of getting food which enabled her to feed at her own rate and kept her out of competition with the other waterfowl. It was by now a regularly employed ploy!

They may be comedians but they are surely not stupid!

Afterword

I have grown to thoroughly enjoy writing these accounts of our lifestyle. It is difficult to be aware at all times of the different needs people have when reading for pleasure and the wide variety of reasons which prompt a particular choice.

When you identify with your subject as closely as I do, it is easy to become verbose and risk boring one's readers by too close an examination of various facets of the subject. I trust that I have not fallen into that trap. I write in colloquial English and in, what I hope is an accessible style. I also write poetry and perform Prose and Poetry readings to interested audiences. What better practice than to perform your own work, I have no excuse if I fail to get the work over as the author intended.

This is my second volume about our narrowboat, "Pallas Athene", and our way of life. How it is received will determine wether there will be a third volume in due time.

In a letter to B.W. about the steadily increasing cost of all aspects of boating and the multiplicity of rules, regulations and restrictions that are being applied, often with no apparent thought to the consequences, I suggested to the then Chairman that an appropriate title for my third book might be, "Athene; The Dream dies!"

I hope most sincerely, that if a third book does eventually appear, that will not be the title!

May I wish all my readers past, present and hopefully future, "Good cruising" and peaceful hours.

Summer 1999.

Glossary of terms used in the book.

Aquadrive: A fluid drive which improves power transmission and changes from forward to reverse drive.

Aqueduct: Structure built to carry a canal, over a road, railway, river or valley.

Balance Beam: The large beam across the top of each lock gate to assist opening and closing by increasing leverage.

Barge: Working boat, of any length, (often less than 60 ft.) by 12 to 14 ft. wide. i.e. Liverpool Short Boats.

Boatmans cabin: Living area on a working boat. Modern boats reproduce this as an additional room / bedroom.

Boat-pole: 18 ft. shaft for pushing the boat off mud or obstructions. NOT for fending off

Bow Haul: Pull boat by hand using forward mooring rope.

Breasted pair: A motor boat and Butty, tied side by side, working a broad canal.

Bridge 'ole: The narrow section beneath bridges, usually solid edged.

Broad lock: Sometimes called a barge lock. As short as 58 ft. on the Leeds and Liverpool canal. Takes boats up to 15 ft. wide.

Buckby Can: Decorated water carrier, holding 2/3 gallons of fresh water.

Butty: Engine-less boat towed by the Motor boat.

B.W. British Waterways. Controlling body for canals.

By or Bye Wash: Water channelled past a lock when the pound is full

Cants: Raised plates on bow and stern, at deck level.

Centre Stud: Anchor point on roof, approx. in centre of boat. Used to secure a mooring line, particularly on long craft.

Counter: Flat plate under the stern. Propeller is beneath accessed via the weed hatch.

Cratch Board: Triangular board on bows. To support foredeck cover

Cruiser: Wood or G.R.P. boat with a cabin and an outboard engine.

Cruiser stern: Narrow boat stern, with extended deck covering the engine. Guard rails, fixed seating and control console.

Dollies: Waisted studs, anchor points for stern mooring ropes.

Double lock: On narrow canals, locks were sometimes built in pairs to ease congestion. Good examples on T & M north of the Harecastle tunnel.

Draft: The amount of the boats hull below the water line. It is measured from waterline to skeg. Usually the lowest point.

Drawing the paddle: Using the windlass to lift gate or ground paddles to allow the lock to fill or empty.

Engine 'ole: The space between cabin and cargo hold. Housed engine, tools, provided extra storage. Ventilated by the Pigeon Box, access was via double doors on either side.

Fenders: Side fenders are rope buffers protecting the sides when moored. Bow and stern fenders protect the boat when it is moving.

Flash: Flooded area created by subsidence.

Flight: Group of locks, fairly close together, taking the canal up or down an extended slope.

Freeboard: The distance between gunwale and waterline.

Gas locker: Gas tight, ventilated box for storage of gas cylinders.

Gate paddles: Paddles built into the top gate of a lock that allow water to enter from the pound.

Gauging Station: Narrow section of canal where freeboard could be measured to assess weight of load.

Guillotine Locks: Instead of normal gates, this lock has its top gate mounted in slides. It can be raised and lowered to allow boats in or out of the lock.

Gongoozlers: Boat watchers, to be found at interesting lock flights, most weekends and bank holidays.

Ground paddles: Control the flow of water into and out of the lock chambers, via sluices built into the structure.

Gunwale: On a narrowboat, the step around the hull where the cabin walls are welded on.

Heart Interface: Electrical power management system controls battery charging and power distribution.

Leggers: Men paid to propel boats through tunnels where engines cannot be used.

Legging: Propelling a boat through a tunnel by lying on a plank fastened to the foredeck and "walking " along the walls. Only the Dudley tunnel still requires legging.

Lined out: A hull fitted with insulation, floors, bulkheads, gas and electricity.

Lock up or down: The procedure of passing through a lock.

Lock Wheeling: One or more persons working in front of the boat preparing locks for use.

Keel Plate: The 10mm. base plate for a flat keel.

Keel Cooler: Box built into the engine room swim. Cools engine by dissipating heat from water jacket using the steel side of the swim as a heat sink.

Motor boat: Boat with an engine. Other half of a working pair. (see Butty.)

Mouses Ears: Two definitions

One. The shape of the traditional propeller blades.

Two. The shapes painted across the stern doors, which identified the carrying company the boat was with.

Mushroom vents: Brass roof vents. Named for their shape.

Narrowboat: Craft up to 72 ft. long but no wider than 6 ft. 10 ins.

Narrow lock: Built to take boats up to 72 ft. by 7 ft.

N.R.A.: National Rivers Authority

Pigeon Box: Ventilator over the engine room. Lift up flaps often pierced with small glass portholes.

Porta Pottie: Portable, cassette toilet. Needs regular emptying.

Paddles: The plates which control the flow of water in or out of the locks.

Pound: Stretch of water between two locks